THE FIRE IN MOONLIGHT

STORIES FROM THE RADICAL FAERIES

1975–2010

• THE WHITE CRANE WISDOM SERIES •

White Crane Institute's guiding principle: "fostering the gathering and dissemination of information about the critical role sexuality and gender plays in the development of cultural and spiritual traditions and to provide a nurturing environment for the continuation and expansion of those explorations for the greater good of all society."

As Gay people we bear wisdom. As Gay people we create culture. White Crane is proud to present these valuable treasures through our Gay Wisdom Series. Our aim is to provide you with fine books of insight, discernment and spiritual journey.

White Crane Institute is a 501(c)(3) educational corporation, committed to the certainty that gay consciousness plays a special and important role in the evolution of life on Earth. White Crane Institute publishes *White Crane, the Journal of Gay Wisdom & Culture.* Your contributions and support are tax-deductible to the fullest extent of the law.

White Crane Institute
22 County Route 27 • Granville NY 12832
www.gaywisdom.org • editor@gaywisdom.org

THE FIRE IN MOONLIGHT

STORIES FROM THE RADICAL FAERIES

1975–2010

Edited by Mark Thompson and
Richard Neely (Osiris) and Bo Young, Associate Editors

Foreword by Will Roscoe, Ph.D.

WHITE CRANE BOOKS
Granville, New York

Published as a White Crane Book, March 2011
White Crane Institute, 22 County Route 27 • Granville NY 12832
www.whitecranebooks.org • www.gaywisdom.org • editor@gaywisdom.org

ISBN-13: 978-1-938246-04-3
ISBN-10: 1-938246-04-7

Library of Congress Cataloging-in-Publication Data

The Fire in moonlight : stories from the Radical Faeries : 1975-2010 / edited by Mark Thompson ; Richard Neely (Osiris) and Bo Young, associate editors ; foreword by Will Roscoe
      p. cm.
Includes bibliographical references.
ISBN-13: 978-1-938246-04-3
ISBN-10: 1-938246-04-7
   1. Gay men--Religious life. 2. Radical Faeries (New Age movement)   I. Thompson, Mark, 1952- II. Neely, Richard. III. Young, Bo.
   BL65.H64D36 2010
   299'.93--dc22

                 2010039292

Dedicated to Harry Hay and John Burnside

A Circle of Acknowledgments

From the Editorial Collective:

We thank Don Kilhefner, Ph.D., for first suggesting this collection and his support of it, especially during the beginning stages of the project. His dedicated efforts on behalf of the Los Angeles gay and lesbian community during the past four decades is likewise deeply appreciated.

We wish to thank the wonderful and trusting contributors to this volume. Thanks also to Joel Singer for his inspired cover image, Will Roscoe for his magnificent Foreword and William Stewart for compiling and writing the Radical Faerie Resource section. And, of course, thanks to the late, great gay poet James Broughton for his poem, "Call to Devotions," used here as an Epigraph.

Finally, our gratitude to the late Bradley Rose for his original illustration, "Faerie Tongues," used here as the book's Frontispiece.

From Mark Thompson:

Bows to my colleagues for their unwavering belief and hard work in bringing this timely book to fruition. Blessings to my life partner, Malcolm Boyd, who knows well what it means to have wings.

From Osiris:

I wish to recognize a love that knows no end. To my husband, Tim, thank you for always being there to support me—no matter how far out on a limb I've gone.

From Bo Young:

I want to thank Harry n'John for summers under the walnut tree and the Faeries for sanctuary. I want to acknowledge my life partner, my love, William J. Foote, for unquestioning support, a gentle, skeptical eye and for being there to spoon up when all the late nights of reading, fine tuning and editing were done and the lights were turned off.

Table of Contents

THE FIRE IN MOONLIGHT

STORIES FROM THE RADICAL FAERIES

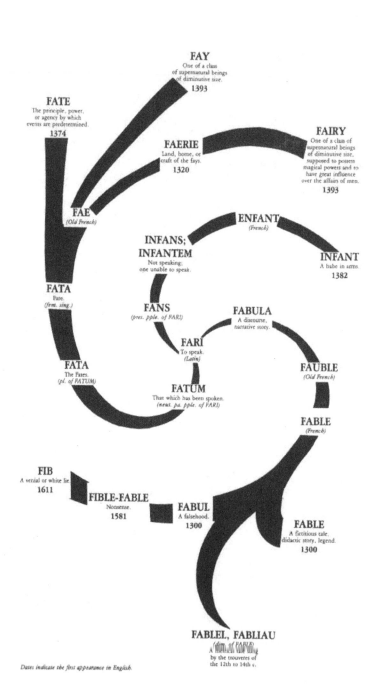

FAY
One of a class
of supernatural beings
of diminutive size.
1393

FATE
The principle, power,
or agency by which
events are predetermined.
1374

FAERIE
Land, home, or
craft of the fays.
1320

FAIRY
One of a class of
supernatural beings
of diminutive size,
supposed to possess
magical powers and to
have great influence
over the affairs of men.
1393

FAE
(Old French)

ENFANT
(French)

INFANS;
INFANTEM
Not speaking;
one unable to speak.

INFANT
A babe in arms.
1382

FATA
Fate.
(fem. sing.)

FANS
(pres. pple. of FARI)

FABULA
A discourse,
narrative story.

FARI
To speak.
(Latin)

FATA
The Fates.
(pl. of FATUM)

FAUBLE
(Old French)

FATUM
That which has been spoken.
(neut. pa. pple. of FARI)

FABLE
(French)

FIB
A venial or white lie.
1611

FIBLE-FABLE
Nonsense.
1581

FABUL
A falsehood.
1300

FABLE
A fictitious tale,
didactic story, legend.
1300

FABLEL, FABLIAU
A *metrical fables*
by the trouvères of
the 12th to 14th c.

Dates indicate the first appearance in English.

Faerie Tongues
by Bradley Rose

Introduction

THIRTY IS A DELICATE AND decisive turning point in a life. Adolescent flings are in the past and unknowable questions remain ahead. One can as easily fall back into sleepy denial or charge ahead to meet future challenges. And so too it is with the Radical Faeries, the gay community's last authentic global grassroots movement.

Since their sudden inception on a remote site in the American Southwest in 1979, the Faeries have grown like some exotic species of flora around the world. That seminal first Gathering—a three-day flash point of profound revelation and personal reclamation—resulted in a kind of gay tribal diaspora, with each of the two hundred participants returning to home roots in every corner of the United States, Canada and Europe.

What happened next is the story of this book. Like fertile seeds scattered to the winds, the Faeries began to grow and cultivate new gardens for being. A new way of living for gay men flowered—an identity and a mythos still largely ignored or not comprehended by more mainstream cultures, no matter what color of the rainbow they may be. To large populations of culturally assimilated gay men the Radical Faeries remain an enigma, something akin to a shimmering mirage once glimpsed or heard about. To non-gay people, the Faeries seem like a ridiculous fiction or, at best, a bizarre aberration on the lowest end of the gender totem pole.

But we Faerie-identified men (and now some women) live among you as the realest of Planet Earth's real people: contrary and complex guardians for the best of the old ways, zealous and righteous advocates for new possibilities in a world of diminishing returns. We are the last of the original tribes to spring out of that heady brew concocted by late 1960s gay liberation, sexual revolution, civil rights, environmental concern and feminism. Much has changed during the forty years since that big bang, but the questions regarding authentic self and essential goodness remain— at least in our hearts and minds.

So what exactly is a Radical Faerie? The phrase itself sounds more than a bit preposterous, if not a tad *louche*. One way to explain would be to claim there have always been Faeries, and we don't mean those fictional characters found in children's books or a garden dell. The word *fairy* has long been a slang term (often pejorative) used to define homosexual men, usually those with an effeminate bent. This was the spelling used on the "call," or broadsheet, that was circulated announcing the first National Conference for Radical Fairies in the desert outside Benson, Arizona. (Perceptive readers will note that spelling is retained when referring to that historic event.)

But once the Faerie idea—indeed, *ideal*—began to carry itself across the land in multiple regional Gatherings, weekend retreats and even households and permanent sanctuaries in the decades to follow, the more generic and sanctified usage of the word quickly took hold. A true *fae* spirit is one who is fanciful, to be sure, but also gay-centered, engaged and revolutionary. And so like the actual faeries of yore, we gay folk today, who carry the word as a living tradition and cloak of honor, strive to uphold those qualities.

Too cute for words, or utterly serious with a divine mission and purpose? Perhaps a bit of both, which makes being a Faerie at once a questionable act and a highly principled one. The real truth of the matter, as exasperating it may seem, lies in a mixture of both. That paradox, enhanced by our own unique style, is what being a Radical Faerie is all about. There are dark Faeries, silly Faeries, ponderous Faeries, fabulous Faeries and Faeries with no fashion sense. There are Faeries adrift and way too many Faeries permanently gone.

But at the core of this jumble of identities and intents, we, the editors of this book, assert that there now exists a Faerie Nation—albeit one made of invisible borders and defined as much by a state of mind. It is an actual living world with great significance and potential created wholly from the lives of queer folk soulfully led. As Harry Hay, that grandest of Radical Faeries said: "It is time to pull off the ugly green frog skin of heterosexual conformity." And so we did. And continue to do.

A story has to start somewhere, so this one does three decades and a year ago. But there have been many antecedents and many ancestors for what follows in these pages. Self-aware gay men have always existed on society's borders and margins. But after the Stonewall Rebellion in 1969—a three-day uprising in New York City that set off alarm bells around the world—the liminal territories we had traditionally occupied were suddenly enlarged. We jumped from being a half-caste people to full-bodied ones and all sorts of political and cultural experiments in redefinition took strength.

Hard-boiled rage was bottled in many forms of political activism, especially on the East Coast. The Western United States, with its vast undeveloped lands and more permissive cultural influences—from Hollywood dreams to Beat poetry to postwar Zen Buddhism—yielded a more laid-back approach, open to a wider synthesis of cultural forms. Things here were not so much reformed as reinformed and in many cases outright birthed. There was a palpable pioneer spirit in the air, no less so for gay people.

Hay, one of the creators of the Radical Faeries, first came to prominence in 1950 as the galvanizing force behind the creation of the Mattachine Society, the nation's first ongoing gay organizing group. The political machinations following his bold moves have been well documented elsewhere. But out of this gutsy seedbed arose two decades of steady achievement, no matter how burdened by inside winnowing and outside fear mongering.

The nation's first gay publications, educational and religious groups and other cultural infrastructure were largely coined here. Similar activities were being posted up and down the West Coast during this time as well. It was time for the credo of a manifest destiny to really come home and roost. These forward steps were inevitably betrayed by homophobia-fueled retaliation. Yet slow but steady gains were made. The progress noted was all within the dominating system of patriarchal control, however. It took the deep rumblings of balls-out gay lib—in which Faerie co-creator Don Kilhefner played a pioneering role—to make any sort of viable alternative culture happen.

By the early 1970s, avowed gay liberation activists from all over the country were setting up new home camps in Los Angeles, San Francisco, Seattle and other sister cities. The more deferential and conservative methods favored by a previous generation of gay leaders were suddenly out of style. It was no longer enough to cautiously reform society, but to make society vividly anew. The old tropes about what constitutes a religion, the state, one's gender and sexuality, were all fodder for the blender of fast-changing times.

By mid-decade, Bay Area proto-Faerie leaders Arthur Evans and Murray Edelman were inviting intimate circles of gay men to explore their spirituality by "drawing down the moon" and to evoke ancient gods and goddess, such as Cernunnos (the Horned One) and Gaia.

A landmark 1976 conference titled "Faggots and Class Struggle" was held on queer-owned land in Wolf Creek, Oregon. Its cultural reverberations were widely noted. Two years later, Mikel Wilson hosted the first of three Gatherings exploring the frontiers of gay identity on Running Water Farm, nestled in the mountains of North Carolina. Among those attending from around the Southeast was a liberated group of young gay men from New Orleans, Louisiana Sissies in Struggle, who were already defining themselves as Faeries.

Visionary writers like Carl Wittman (author of the seminal 1969 essay "Refugees from Amerika: A Gay Manifesto") were advancing new paradigms through which gay men could see themselves differently, in upstart publications like *RFD*[1], San Francisco's *Gay Sunshine* and Boston's *Fag Rag*[2]. Such fresh and daring explorations into radical forms of gay consciousness were emerging everywhere.

But these brave soundings into the deep unknown didn't find a national unity until the First Conference for Radical Fairies was called on Labor Day weekend in 1979. Where before there had been sparks, now there was a fire—a fire mirrored in the hearts and souls of nearly every man who attended. Now there was a wide scale and abiding faith in being *fae*—that is, a Faerie. At long last, the joke was no longer on us.

That fire quickly spread. It burned bright in some places, then dimmed or jumped elsewhere. But the concept of being a Faerie was carried person to person, like runners with a torch, continent to continent, until it was known around the world. This book of many voices continues that early call—a call for freedom of mind, body and spirit from the petty, awful tyrannies of those who have tried every means to destroy us. It is about how being a Radical Faerie has changed a life. May these stories inspire you to action, putting wind beneath your wings.

— Mark Thompson, Los Angeles, 2010

---

[1] Originally *RFD: A Country Journal for Gay Men Everywhere.* Founded in October 1974 in a drafty farmhouse in Grinnell, Iowa. *RFD* continues today, celebrating thirty-five years of publishing.

[2] *Gay Sunshine* was founded August 1970 by a collective of gay men living in Berkeley, California. In its first editorial *Gay Sunshine* vowed to unite all people oppressed by the white, straight, middle class. In 1971, the Boston Gay Liberation Front established *Fag Rag*. In the early days of Gay Liberation, numerous small newspapers and magazines popped up all over the country; in addition to those mentioned above: *The Gay Liberator* (Detroit), *The Gay Alternative* (Philadelphia) and *The Body Politic* (Toronto). They were small, with irregular publication schedules and financed out of pocket.

Prelude: Welcome to Planet Faerie

by Will Roscoe, Ph. D.

A FLASH OF LIGHTNING LIT UP the canvas walls of the Big Tent and thunder rumbled in the mountaintops. Inside, the heavy air vibrated. A hundred Faeries, knees touching, leaned forward in anticipation as the old man took a deep breath.

"I am saying to everybody who will hear that now we must begin to *maximize the differences between us and them.*"

Squalls of thunder and lightning appeared several times over the second Radical Faerie Gathering, held in Colorado in the summer of 1980. But it was the bolt of Harry Hay's words that struck closest to me. Their implications made me shudder even as I found myself whispering, "Yes!" under my breath.

Looking back now, I realize that day marked my point of no return, when I committed myself to a radical way of being with little idea where it was going to take me—and it was too late to turn back.

It is hard to convey the fervor of those first Gatherings or the times in which they occurred. Three months before I stepped into my first Radical Faerie circle in Arizona I had been throwing bricks at City Hall in the riots that erupted in San Francisco following the trial of Harvey Milk's assassin. The double assassination of Milk and Mayor George Moscone; the horrific Jonestown suicides (a community that was to have been a progressive utopia); the steady unraveling of a decade's progress as Anita Bryant triumphed in Miami and gay-rights ordinances were repealed across the country; the rise of an energized Right proposing increasingly repressive measures to deny the fundamental human rights of lesbians, gay men, bisexuals and transgender people; the spread of anti-gay violence; and, in our own community, determined assimilationists squelching the last vestiges of gay liberation's radical, noisy origins. We arrived in Arizona part of a generation of queers who had rushed out of the closet, emboldened by the sight of the burning bridges behind us. It was 1979. It was time for the other shoe to drop.

Something was about to happen.

For those of us who made our way to the first Spiritual Conference for Radical Fairies, as it was officially called, this feeling of anticipation was palpable. But
whether what was to come would be the dying gasp of patriarchy, with a New Age
to rise from its ashes or the darkening clouds of a new, American fascism taking gays
as the object of its genocidal fantasies, we didn't know.

Harry Hay's writings in those years, a series of inspired essays widely circu-
lated among the early Faeries (if not always widely understood) are riven with this
ambivalence. Under such titles as "Gay Liberation: Chapter Two, Serving Social/
Political Change Through Our Gay Window," "A Contribution to the Principles
of Gay Liberation," "New Breakthroughs in How We Perceive the Nature of Gay
Consciousness" (a workshop co-facilitated with Don Kilhefner), "Towards the New
Frontiers of Fairy Vision...subject-SUBJECT Consciousness," "Some Beginnings to a
Sacred Quest...the Search for ANCESTORS," Harry interspersed ecstatic visions
of a political and spiritual New Age, Faeries in the vanguard, with grim forebodings
of repressive political regimes and dire economic crises. These seemingly opposite
impulses were perfectly balanced in the project that Harry considered the calling of
his life. Indeed, for Harry, those early Gatherings were not to be ends in themselves,
but springboards for this vision, what came to be known as the Faerie Land Trust.

This was the subject of the meeting that summer in 1980 when Harry first ut-
tered his "maximize the differences" maxim. This was the royal road to "shedding
the ugly green frog-skin of hetero imitation," an ungainly slogan he first used at the
Arizona Gathering and which, in the months and years that followed, became our
mantra. But to do it right, to truly escape the heterosexual hegemony, we needed a
sanctuary. In Harry's words:

> To even begin to prepare ourselves for a fuller participation in our
> Gay subject-SUBJECT inheritance, we must, both daily and hourly, practice
> throwing off all those Hetero-imitating habits, compulsions and ways of
> misperceiving, which we constantly breathe in from our environmental
> surround. For this practice we need the constant company of our Fairy
> Families. We need the spiritual and emotional support of that non-verbal
> empathy which Sociologists assure us comprises almost seven-eighths of
> communication in any culture, that empathy we now refer to as Body
> Language. We need the marvelous input of each other's minute-by-minute
> new discoveries, as each of us begins to explore this vast new universe,
> this subject-SUBJECT frontier of human consciousness. As ours are the first
> deliberate feet upon this pristine shore, there are no guide-posts as yet

erected, nor maps to be found in bottles, nor even the prospectuses of ancient visionary seers.

The sanctuary would be located on land to be held in trust and preserved in a natural state, in perpetuity. It would not merely serve as a site for Gatherings, although that would certainly happen. Its main purpose was to provide a home for a collective of Radical Faeries—a Faerie Family of Conscious Choice—pursuing queer spiritual studies and practices day in and day out. The breakthroughs that awaited us at the frontiers of subject-SUBJECT consciousness—Harry's term for the unique way of perceiving and interacting with the world he believed the Faeries bore witness to—could only be achieved through intense practice and deep interpersonal commitments. What lay ahead of us was nothing less than the re-examination of "every system of thought heretofore developed, every Hetero-male-evolved subject-OBJECT philosophy, science, religion, mythology, political system, language...."

These breakthroughs would take the form not only of ideas and insights, but, in Harry's words, "visions and visitations." When the Faeries at the first Gathering embraced the hidden dimensions of their inner selves, Harry wrote, "The explosive energies released by the jubilations of those reunions were ecstatic beyond belief."

Membership in the on-site collective—the Circle of Loving Companions, a name Harry had first used in the 1960s—was not open. Those who would join had to demonstrate commitment and be accepted by consensus of the existing community. Behind Harry's back we often called the project the "Faerie monastery." But I signed up for the duration and in early 1981 became a member of the Faerie Land Trust collective, along with Mark Thompson and my partner Bradley Rose. In Harry's master plan, laid out that afternoon in Colorado, a network of Faerie land trusts and sanctuaries would one day dot the land, growing soybeans and quinoa, building rammed-earth huts and yurts and generating electricity for their computers from falling water and windmills. (Actually, we didn't have personal computers yet in 1980—Harry added that later.)

"Do you realize," Harry wrote in March 1979, with his effusive punctuation, "that—with all our hard work over the last three years and our gratifying breakthroughs in Gay-conscious thinking—we may actually be on our way to learning... AS FAIRIES...TO LEVITATE!" When the car I was riding in back to the airport following the Arizona Gathering broke down on a dirt road miles from the freeway, we formed a Faerie circle around it, closed our eyes and chanted. The car started on the next try and we were on our way again. Faeries were reporting collective visions at Gatherings and Gatherings were transforming lives. Suddenly, everyone had a new name and an amazing story to tell.

Back in San Francisco, I began having dreams of levitating.
Something was about to happen.

And lo, much has happened!

In the three decades since that circle in the desert, the Faeries have been busy. Without any form of institutionalization above the local level, Faeries and their friends have created sanctuaries and retreats in Oregon, Tennessee, New Mexico, Canada, Australia and, I'm told, France! Various websites and informal events in nearly every major city provide an entrée for those ready to spread their wings and discover, as one Faerie put it, that there's more we can do with our sexuality than just accept it. Many creative and busy souls have found inspiration dancing with the Faeries. The spirit of the Gatherings has been captured and shared widely by writers and artists such as James Broughton, Mark Thompson, Andrew Ramer, Toby Johnson, Randy Conner, Franklin Abbott, Agnes De Garron, Dan Nicoletta, Richard Feather Anderson, Charlie Murphy and teachers and mentors such as Clyde Hall and Joseph Kramer. (Goddess forgive me for all those I've forgotten to mention!) Cross-fertilizations connect the Faeries with the Sisters of Perpetual Indulgence, the Black Leather Wings and Billy community, the Comfort and Joy camp at Burning Man and publications such as *White Crane, RFD* and the *Faerie Dish Rag.* Indeed, thanks to Eric Slades' documentary film of Harry's life, *Hope Along the Wind,* and occasional vignettes in the popular media (a *Queer As Folk* episode featured a character based on Harry), the Faeries have gained a toehold in the American popular consciousness.

But above all, the Faeries have held Gatherings, faithfully following the magical spell that the organizers of those first events taught us. Tap your heels three times. Find a safe, natural space, away from urban centers, free from prying heterosexual eyes and ears. Put out the call. And when the tribe has gathered, close the gate behind you. Begin to function, for a few days, as a community of equals. Decide by consensus; feed, shelter and care for each other; listen to stories without judgment; create rituals and get nonlinear; strip off "the ugly green frog skin," "slip the ego"— and when you do all these things you will surely soar!

At Faerie Gatherings, gay and queer men find out who they might be, how they might talk and walk and adorn their bodies, what might be the feelings they could share if, for one moment, judgment, rejection, condescension, or the ever-present threat of violence did not hang over their heads.

But the Faeries have an importance that reaches far beyond these all too brief interludes, for they are the bearers of an alternative version of queer history, one that mainstream GLBT historians have neglected. This genealogy addresses one of the fundamental questions facing modern homosexuals. Given the institutionalized homophobia of Western culture, the absence of gays from its stories of the past, how do we find insight into the meaning of our difference? How do we answer the questions that Harry proposed to the Mattachine founders in 1950 (America's first grassroots gay organization) and again to the Faeries in 1979:

Who are we? Where did we come from? What are we for?

Many mainstream GLBT scholars today, for reasons of "theory," say we have no proper history and cannot claim one; that what we are is a socially constructed identity, a kind of fiction, with no essence beyond a label. This is the logic of assimilationism: the only difference between ourselves and heterosexuals is what we do in bed.

But Faeries have answers to these questions. Faced with Western history's blank pages, we look beyond and find ample evidence of queer social roles in which sexual and gender differences are not only expressed but integral. Many times these roles encompass religious and creative activities. And some of those who bore these identities contributed to all our histories.

The most well known examples are the Native North American two-spirits. Referred to as "berdaches" in the anthropological literature, two-spirits were males and females (and no doubt inter-sexed individuals as well) who occupied an alternative gender role that was neither male nor female. Often, they served as religious leaders and shamans. For Harry, two-spirits were the premier example of how being queer could be the basis for a distinct social contribution. He devoted many years to learning whatever he could about these traditions.

Now we know of many other alternative gender roles and identities, in Oceania, Asia and Africa and in cultures that preceded or survived the rise of the patriarchy in the Old World. A fruitful field awaits Faerie researchers who will uncover more about these remarkable people and their stories.

The other important historical lineage of the Faeries is represented by the writings that were so avidly photocopied and passed around at the early events. Some of these authors, like Harry Hay and Edward Carpenter—are acknowledged pioneers of gay rights, but without the interest of the Faeries their contributions to gay spirituality and psychology might be forgotten. Other key writers in the Faerie canon include John Addington Symonds, Gerald Heard, Arthur Evans and Judy Grahn. In the 1970s, Don Kilhefner gathered together many of these texts for his "Voices and

Visions" workshop; several appear in Mark Thompson's *Gay Spirit: Myth and Meaning* and Harry's collection *Radically Gay*.

Standing at the head of this lineage is the mercurial figure of Walt Whitman. In Whitman's poetry, same-sex love and desire give rise to an exalted, universal form of consciousness, which is described with the imagery of a shamanic trance. For Harry, Whitman was always our most important teacher. Without role models or traditions, Whitman found spiritual expression for his homosexuality through reflection on his own nature and on the deepest yearnings of the American experiment. Same-sex love, he believed, was distinguished from heterosexual love by the sameness and equality of those it united. Whitman called this adhesive love. Harry, drawing on twentieth-century advances in psychology and sociology, took these insights one step further, giving a name to the distinct mode of awareness this love of sames and equals fosters—subject-SUBJECT consciousness.

I'm not sure many heard Harry's call to "maximize the differences" that rainy day in Colorado. Perhaps the thunder drowned out his words. I suspect many Faeries simply found it too separatist, too in-your-face. I did not hear Harry repeat it often, whereas "shedding the ugly green frog skin of hetero-imitation" remained among his favorite catchphrases.

The Faerie Land Trust had a similar fate. The self-governing collective of Faerie adepts it envisioned struck many as elitist. Since the project needed the material support of Faerie brothers in the urban centers, this made it impractical. By 1982 the project crashed and burned, the collective in disarray. From its ashes arose Nomenus, the organization that has successfully operated the Faerie Sanctuary at Wolf Creek for the past twenty-five years.

I played a role in transforming the Faerie Land Trust into Nomenus. In retrospect, I find myself wondering what we gave up as well as what we gained. The "gay monastery" of Harry's vision was to have been a place of study and introspection, an exploration of collective living, where Faeries, each with distinct interests and talents, would be in heart-circle mode 24/7. Brad and I got some small glimpse of what this would be like by living with Harry and John for six months in 1982. It was a heady experience of nonstop conversation, reading, cooking, Harry taping music from the radio into the wee hours of the night, John building his kaleidoscopes in the workshop, while Brad and I practiced applied meditation in the camper parked in the driveway.

Could it be that after all these years there are still dimensions of Faerie experience and insight yet to be discovered? "Let us enter this brave new world of subject-SUBJECT consciousness, this new planet of Fairy-vision and find out," Harry wrote in 1970.

For those seeking a road map for the next thirty years, I humbly suggest that we start with a re-engagement with our dual lineages: the heritage of alternative gender roles and the writings that inspired the early Gatherings.

Here I must begin with a complaint. Too often at Gatherings of Faeries (and others!) one hears Native two-spirit roles spoken of in the most sweeping generalities, as if the tradition existed everywhere, in every tribe, in precisely the same form and that it was universally accepted. In fact, two-spirit roles have been documented in only 150 of the estimated 400 tribes that occupied North America at the time Columbus arrived. Each tribe had its own word for the role—*lhamana* at Zuni, *winkte* among Dakota speakers, *he'eman* in Cheyenne, *bote* in Crow and so forth. From tribe to tribe the characteristics of these roles varied a great deal. We are fortunate knowing the life stories of such traditional two-spirits as We'wha, Hastiin Klah and Osh-Tisch. These were remarkable individuals with abilities our Western mindset cannot fully explain. But not all two-spirits were remarkable and not all tribes had such gender roles or tolerated homosexuality. That's why, when I speak of two-spirits, I try to refer to the traditions of specific tribes that I have taken the time to study and to use tribal terms for them (even at the risk of mispronouncing them).

As the film *Two Spirits* powerfully reveals, Native American LGBT people often face virulent homophobia within their communities, where two-spirit traditions have been broken or forgotten. If the Faeries truly wish to affirm the Native two-spirit tradition, they need to find concrete ways to support contemporary Natives seeking to restore this tradition and provide essential services to their brothers and sisters.

Harry himself never advocated imitation of two-spirits or any other Native American tradition or ceremony. In his view, two-spirit people were embedded within specific cultural contexts. Their magic, which could be powerful in that context, simply would not work in ours. And so he would say and I can hear his words now, "If we can't rediscover…*reinvent.*"

This is the real lesson Harry learned from his years working with Native people. In an oral culture, tradition is reinvented in each generation and he observed many instances of Native people seeking to restore broken traditions by doing just that. But ultimately, Harry believed we had to turn to ourselves and each other and draw out of our own experience, using the language of our own time and place, the meaning and purpose of our sexuality.

To my thinking, Harry's concept of subject-SUBJECT consciousness remains his most important and beautiful gift. Many Faeries may not realize that when they pass a talisman in Heart Circles, allowing each person time to speak without interruption or competition, when they listen intently to each others' stories for hours on end, when they make decisions, painstakingly, following the principles of consensus, they are observing practices that were inspired by the idea of subject-SUBJECT consciousness. For Harry, these customs were merely the etiquette that served to create, in the short span of the Gathering, space for the truly mystical dimensions of subject-SUBJECT consciousness to unfold.

Now I see that Harry's call to maximize the differences was not misfired but merely premature. Back then we hardly knew what we were for and what our differences were, let alone have the means for maximizing them in the face of the dominant culture. Now we have the words and the exemplars we need to describe our differences. The challenge is to fully actualize them and this requires that we focus our attention on them intently, discuss them, share them and act them out in safe settings. I can think of no better maxim to guide this exploration than the one Harry offered in 1980.

Maximizing the differences is the touchstone to a hero's journey—a journey we are called to, not only by our own inner voice, but by the times we live in. It begins with a separation from a culture that has denied and repressed us and a turning inward to find within our psyches that which precedes patriarchal socialization—what has escaped it and survived. We must relinquish lingering, residual attachments to the approval of others—take the risk of rejection, of being incomprehensible—and move forward believing that there is still something more to know about being gay. Maximize the differences leads us on a quest into unfamiliar inner spaces and far-away times and places. But in due course, the separation realized, we return to the larger community empowered fully to contribute what we distinctly have to share.

Welcome to Planet Faerie! The preface is over; now the story begins.

Call to Devotions

Come forth   brother souls
claim your liberty
Time for devotion
time to fraternize

Bring your orbits
into harmony
Time to plant starseed
in one another's eyes

Cavort together
in singular twos
firm in your footloose
crazy in your wise

Comrades   come forth
hurdle the taboos
Joy will be the wonder
love the surprise

— *James Broughton*

FAERIE ROOTS

The Making of a Tribe

by Stuart Timmons

Remember, the serpent is still living in the Garden of Eden—only the heterosexual couple was expelled.

— Edward Carpenter, *Civilization: Its Cause and Cure*

IN THE FAERIE CIRCLE, EACH man's story matched down to the subtlest details. The green meadow, the blue sky, and their very bodies seemed to glow as each shared early memories of feeling different. They had always been called sissies, but they always knew that they were somehow strong. And however many years they had been out of the closet—succeeding in business, in organizing or in the bars—they felt that until they found the Faeries, something had been missing.

A carved talisman was passed around the circle, and where it stopped the group's undivided attention focused. A delicate black man wearing only a sparkling scarf and hiking boots took the talisman into the circle and while walking slowly, addressed the ring of two hundred. "We Faeries need to stop saying, 'My consciousness is better than your consciousness.' That's heterosexist. No one person, no one group, no one ideology has the answer. You need a spirit."

It was the search for such a spirit that had led them all there, including Harry Hay. A short time after he had gone into retirement, he was out again, and was part of the circle—in fact he had worked hard to call it into being. Privately, he regarded the Radical Faeries, as this new phenomenon of gay identity came to be known, to be a flowering of the Circle of Loving Companions, a joint quest for an adhesive gay comradeship. The Radical Faeries responded to the emptiness of both the straight establishment and assimilated gay society. Those who flocked to the Faerie gatherings had found little distinction between the two—to them, both were oppressive, shallow, and mired in such macho value as male competitiveness and dominance. Don Kilhefner, who with Harry helped create the Faeries, wrote that "gay activism has given us a little breathing space" from the stifling decades of oppression. It was the aim of the Faeries to find out what could grow in that new atmosphere.

The spirit seemed to flow through the circle. A heavy-set, gray-haired man wearing a floppy hat stepped into its midst and told of his career as a lawyer. "I deal every day with people who fight with each other—and they're all he-men. Policemen who abuse power. Judges. And because I am a Faerie, I feel great pain in that world." He struggled momentarily with his emotion, then continued. "All of those people are he-men. I come to my fellow Faeries because I need the love that I get here. And so many times in the gay world I do not get that. I get the same kind of alienation that I get in the world of he-men."

A young, hardened street person from San Diego spoke. A long strand of bells stretching from his neck to his left sandal strap tinkled in the still mountain air when he walked. He offered the Circle a verse from Jean Genet: "Faeries are a pale and motley race that flowers in the minds of decent folk. Never will they be entitled to broad daylight, to real sun. But remote in these limbos, they cause curious disasters which are harbingers of new beauty."

The crowd whooped and applauded. A voice called out, "Right on, Madame Genet!"

When the Circle closed, the men came together, arm-in-arm, body-to-body, and a deep *om* began to sound, vibrating through the huddle of men, each more completely a living part of the Circle. Male voices rose in humming harmony and the sound gained momentum, like dozens of fingers on wineglasses. As they dispersed, flute music played as if from a sylvan sound track. Voices accompanying it sang: *Dear friends, queer friends, let me tell you how I'm feeling / You have given me such pleasure, I love you so.*

The Radical Faeries, like their mythological antecedents, cannot be easily defined or pinned down. A mixture of a political alternative, a counter-culture and a spirituality movement, the Faeries became Harry's "second wind" as a major figure in gay culture and found him enmeshed in a new kind of organizing—a networking of gentle men devoted to the principles of ecology, spiritual truth, and, in New Age terms, "gay-centeredness."

The term "movement" could not contain what the Faeries were all about; in fact Harry carefully avoided that term at first. He saw the Faeries rather as a process or way of life. Just as he took to describing gays as "not-men," the Radical Faeries could be called a "not-movement." One early participant, David Liner, attempted to explain the phenomenon thus: "What Harry Hay did was give thousands of gay men the space to get over the most painful wounds that this society could possibly inflict on them."

It was Harry's idea to couple the words *Radical* and *Faerie*, and the combination was carefully chosen. "Radical," in this case, meant "root" or "essence" as well as "politically extreme." The term "faerie" also had two meanings, one modern and one ancient. In recent times "fairy" was a scornful epithet, but one that many gay men were now re-evaluating. (Parallels of this in other minorities include "Chicano" and "black," which both began as pejorative terms.) The ancient fairy, on the other hand, was an immortal, luminous nature spirit who danced in circles in the moonlight and did good deeds at whim. By combining these meanings, the Radical Faeries expressed one of their basic tenets, the oft-bandied notion that gays are a spiritual tribe.[1]

Harry always used the antique spelling in what seemed an effective visual reminder that this was a new—or at least resurrected—meaning of the word. The potency of the image came partly from its mythic heritage. In selecting fairies as a role model for gays, he combined logic with inspiration to surpass the medieval Mattachines—to a pre-Christian time and beyond human limits.

Harry's thinking on this had evolved over several years and reflected an obsession with homosexual semantics that had concerned him since the Mattachine days. In 1969, in a speech commemorating the 150th birthday of Walt Whitman, he had wrestled with the old problem of a lack of language to describe who gays *were* instead of who they were not. He wrote, "What had bedeviled Gays and Lesbians in particular was that, from the very first days of the re-invention of 'Gay Identity,' we kept trying to explain in STRAIGHT language…and it kept coming out all wrong…which is the Butch and which is the Femme? Which one does the dishes? Our explanations seemed to raise more questions than they answered." Over many years he considered a basic question: Since gays had always organized in reaction to the brutish forces of oppression, could not a newer, greater wave of the movement base itself on an essential nature of gay people?[2]

The following year, in his keynote address to the Western Homophile Conference on February 14, 1970, Harry coined a new phrase to explain gay people in new terms. "We are a minority of a common spirituality," he said, "[and] this shared commonality of outlook is a world-view totally unfamiliar to the accrued experience of our parent society. It is a view of the life experience *through a DIFFERENT WINDOW!*" The term he soon settled on—and with which he liberally sprinkled his discourse—was "Gay Window." At the end of that address, he slipped in the word "faerie" as a positive description of gay people. "Let the Spirit be betrayed, let coercion or opportunism bind us against our will, and PRESTO, like the Faeries of Folk-lore, suddenly we are no longer there." He sensed that this quality of quicksilver elusiveness explained why a gay movement had gone unorganized for so long, noting, "Our Faerie characteristic is our Homosexual Minority's central weakness." But, he added, "paradoxically, [It is] also the keystone to our enduring strength…We Homosexuals are moved to act ONLY when the call—as heard in our hearts—is a spirit call to freedom."

By the time he moved to New Mexico from his life-long, Los Angeles home in May 1970 Harry freely promoted the term "Faerie" as well as "Gay Window" and "Gay Consciousness," all with related theories. He pondered, researched and started paper after paper about these ideas; often he was unable to get beyond the first page.

Meanwhile, the gay public, from which Harry had retreated, was evolving. The counterculture wave of the 1960s, with its open-minded spirit, hit gay people in the 1970s and the emerging gay community became a bubbling laboratory of names and identities. Long-familiar words such as "queer" and "queen" were tried out, along with newer ones like "groovy guy." The most enduring proved to be "gay," although in some regions, the militant "faggot" was a close second.

Sometimes there was an air of competition; in San Francisco, gays known as the Sissies professed disdain for those they called STIFs—straight-identified faggots. Genderfuck, an outrageous form of costume combining exaggerated signals from male and female—such as a beard, bouffant hairdo, and glittering Kabuki eye makeup, all on one person—was employed as a cultural guerilla attack on rigid sex roles. As the decade turned, gender-fuck groups like The Cockettes and the Angels of Light spoofed political events with camp, consciousness-raising spectaculars in both San Francisco and New York.

At the same time, popular interest in non-Western spirituality was growing, as epitomized by the Beatles' pilgrimage to the Maharishi. This cultural drift affected gays too. In 1976 writer Arthur Evans mingled radical politics and pagan models to begin "the faery circle" in his Haight Street apartment in San Francisco, where a dozen men explored the Dionysian tradition of "the magic of nature and the creative sexuality of gay men." The faery circle was part of Evans' research into the spiritual history of gay men which he published as several articles in the gay journals *Out* and *Fag Rag* and in the book *Witchcraft and the Gay Counterculture* (1978).[3]

As the 1970s wore on "gay ghettos" sprouted in cities across America. These rapidly expanding gay neighborhoods were quickly seized upon by an army of entrepreneurs; both gay-owned and straight-owned ventures sought to exploit the new territory. The gay community became the gay market. So many gay businesses eventually formed that gay business councils formed around them.

The new-style resident of the gay ghetto was the "clone," a close descendant of the straight-identified faggot. In the sexually active age-bracket, the clone was athletic, square-jawed and swinging. His trumpeted masculinity was almost caricature: muscles, mustache, mirrored "cop" sunglasses, bomber jacket and boots became a veritable uniform for the scores of gay men so identified. (The gay painter Buddha John Parker christened this rampant new breed as "male impersonators.")

Fashions, urban hot-spots, and in that pre-AIDS decade, sex itself were steadily packaged by ever-creative marketers. Because their gay identities had been delayed, clones were perfect consumers, ever living out long-suppressed fantasies. This emphasized such a restless, materialist outlook that many gay men complained that the chase from object to object tainted their ability to achieve intimacy in relationships. The dubious ideal of the clone was, in reality, only a high-profile minority of homosexuals. Nevertheless it was widely emulated.

Some clone-weary gays retreated from ghetto life. Big cities, the traditional "end of the rainbow" for gay men, had for years offered anonymity and opportunity to those fleeing small towns and stifling straight society. But as the 1970s progressed, a few began to leave the cities, some carried by the hippie back-to-the-land movement, some just burned out from urban excess. Though they hardly constituted an organized group, rural gays had established several collectives by the mid-1970s.

One of the most long-lasting was the RFD collective, founded in Iowa in 1974. When the countercultural *Mother Earth News* refused to run an ad with a gay reference, this seven-member group began a home-spun publication that sold for fifty cents: *RFD: A Magazine for Country Faggots*. While protesting the "adamant heterosexuality" of existing rural magazines, *RFD* also provided recipes, poetry, farming information, and pictures for isolated gay people living on the land. *RFD* took its name from the postal designation Rural Free Delivery, but extended it every issue to "Really Feeling Divine," "Raving Flamer's Diary," "Rabbits, Faggots and Dragonflies" and further amusing titles. The contributors and readers of *RFD* overlapped substantially with those gays who would soon call themselves Faeries; gatherings of rural gay men were already advertised in its pages during the 1970s. However, the favored term at *RFD* was "faggot."

The piece Hay sent to *RFD* in 1975, which he dedicated to his mother, was the first of many of his writings that *RFD* would publish. Poetically written, it discussed gayness as a genetic mutation difficult for the individual but ultimately beneficial to the group. "To be a true homosexual," he proposed, "is to be…put at odds with home, school, and society…We are so *other* that we have to learn early how to protect our very survival." He finally called for "Gay love, Gay life, Gay vision, and Gay creative self-fulfillment." His conclusion that gayness lay in "our stubbornly perverse genes" elicited a lively commentary from the publishing collective.

One member, Carl Wittman, provided the most supportive response. Revealing the depth of Harry's challenge, he wrote, "I yearn for such words. I am embarrassed to use them. Who talks of vision, light, splendor and strength? It certainly would not do, not on Castro Street or in the pages of *Fag Rag* … The notion of foundling, growing up a foreigner in family and culture, and returning to the larger whole—this notion I put on gently, like a new robe, wondering if it becomes me." He found that the concepts in Harry's essay "fit," though Wittman still expressed some doubts. "But politically, is it misleading? Where are my hard-won ideas about separatism, confrontation, group consciousness? Isn't it a bit spiritual, ignoring the real needs to unite politically? I reread it and decide not… Yes. Brothers from New Mexico, thank you."

Harry held the affirmation from Wittman especially dear. Carl Wittman was a Red Diaper baby who had grown up to be national secretary of Students for a Democratic Society in the 1960s and was highly visible and effective in the anti-Vietnam War and civil rights movements. Wittman became a Gay Liberation celebrity for his *Gay Manifesto* which he wrote a year before the Stonewall riot and which was widely published and read. Hay and Wittman's interest in a political analysis of the gay movement were close and they later developed a friendship and correspondence.

The following year, 1976, Harry refined these ideas even further in a position paper called "Gay Liberation: Chapter Two," which he regarded as his most important piece of writing and as a central catalyst of the Radical Faerie movement. This self-described "position paper" was inspired by a bitter exchange of letters he read in the alternative press between a young gay Leftist and his straight comrades in the Pacific Northwest. Distressed that struggles between gays and the Left continued twenty-five years after his own separation from the Communist Party, Harry wrote a letter to Faygele Singer, the embattled gay Leftist, hoping to comfort him with "newer levels of Marxist perceptions which were emerging in me as gay values."

Harry used personal experiences to illustrate his points and halfway through recalled his peers in high school manipulating their opposite-sex dates like objects to "score." This he contrasted to his secret fantasy of finding a lover who was "a wondrous being with whom I would always share as I shared with myself, not subject to object, but subject to subject." As he wrote this, he realized he had made a breakthrough. "I was just beside myself with excitement," he recalled. "I ripped the letter out of the typewriter and began to write the position paper."

"Chapter Two" presents a new theory about gay people and politics. As background, Hay traced the development of models of modern thought from the Cartesian-Newtonian model of a limited universe that man could control to the Twentieth-century view, which, though modified, still survives in most social sciences and refuses to allow for the existence of gay people.

"Add or subtract, GO or NO-GO, (if you're not a man you're a substitute woman—what else is there?)" was Hay's characterization of the dominant mode of thinking, which he called binary or subject-OBJECT thinking. But the style Hay promoted, which he called "analog thinking," factors in relativity and other expansive dimensions of comprehending the universe. He proposed that it had an attendant "subject-SUBJECT relationship" that was similarly more dimensional. He also posited that this was inherent to all gay people, arising from the egalitarian bond of love and sex between two similar.

It went on to pervade all the relationships of a gay person—even relationships with things not human, such as nature, craftsmanship or ideals. "Humanity must expand its experience of thinking of another *not as object*—to be used, to be manipulated, to be mastered, to be CONSUMED—*but as subject*— as another like himher [sic] self, another self to be respected, to be appreciated, to be cherished."

With Einstein's famous warning in mind that "the unleashed power of the atom has changed everything save for our modes of thinking and we thus drift toward unparalleled catastrophes," Hay then called for mass change in thinking. He proposed that the qualities of non-competitiveness and creativity, characteristics often observed in gay people, made gays naturally suited to guide this change in thinking:

> Natural selection, early on in human evolution, set into the revolving whirl a small percentage of beings who appeared to counter-balance a number of prevalent characteristics of the emerging human conformity. Humanity, thus, would be wise to finally give consideration to these deviants in their ranks...to begin to grant the GAYS the peace and growing space they will need to display and to further develop in communicable words and in models of activity, the "gift"—the singular mutation we GAYS have been carrying so unfalteringly and preserving so passionately, even over the not infrequent centuries of despair and persecution.

To Harry this "GAY gift" was a difference in consciousness that could introduce new ideas necessary for human survival. In the 1950s he had argued that in the ancient world it was the gays who passed on certain craft skills with greater devotion than heterosexual family lineages, whose blood devotions surpassed all other. This sort of role in favor of cultural evolution always shifting with changing social needs, was, he suggested, the biosocial reason for gays—and could be used as their political justification. Hay concluded his essay by calling on "Gay Liberation Faeries" to "reassemble" and help society at large "learn to respect us precisely for our behavioral and perceptual differences… [then] the laws and customs favoring us with Space and Freedom…will take care of themselves."

This paper served as more than one milestone for Hay. Aside from achieving a theory for gay identity—a goal toward which he had long worked—it showed a rare distancing from his past political ideas. By moving beyond the "binary" basis of Marxist dialectical thinking (where opposites of thesis and antithesis produce a new truth), Harry was able to release some of his loyalties to Marxist formulas. His paper bemoaned that Marx and Engels, who he said were of "exemplar integrity," had been born too soon to reorient their theories in the light of the Twentieth-century discoveries—an oblique and polite bow away from his idols who, like so much of the rest of the world, had shut out gays.[4]

Harry Hay's ideas caught the imagination of many who found in the concept of subject-SUBJECT consciousness a deeply felt yet unspoken truth. The argument that there existed a gay reservoir of untapped potential was refreshing to those for whom ghetto liberation had grown hollow. Continuing his tendency to take up the baton of such thinkers as Walt Whitman and Edward Carpenter, Harry posed that homosexuals carried an intermediary consciousness and that once this was made clear, a new era would begin.

Hay submitted his paper for publication to *RFD*. "They rejected it as gobbledygook," he shrugged to a friend in a letter, and indeed, his eccentric use of mixed typefaces with italics and capital letters could be visually wearying, as was his insistence on writing "subject-SUBJECT" to emphasize his new idea. Harry continued to send copies to friends and colleagues and promoted its ideas at every opportunity.

Hay's most receptive listeners were two Californians, Don Kilhefner of Los Angeles and Mitch Walker of Berkeley. By 1978, along with Harry, they formed the cabal that would catalyze the Radical Faerie movement. Since Hay was then sixty-six,

Kilhefner thirty-nine and Walker twenty-five, they spanned the generations. Their personalities held strong parallels but also striking differences.

Kilhefner was known for shouting down anti-gay bigots at public events but when it came to friends, he mildly addressed everyone as "Toots." He had grown up in an Amish-Mennonite community in Pennsylvania, left at seventeen and went to Howard University, where he studied cultural history. He came out at Howard and became active in anti-Vietnam War campaigns and in the Student Nonviolent Coordinating Committee of the civil rights movement. Following graduation came a stint in Ethiopia with the Peace Corps, then a move west to U.C.L.A. By the late-1960s he was involved in the Peace and Freedom Party and carried Mao Tse-tung's *Little Red Book*. With Morris Kight (also in the Peace and Freedom Party), Don led the main activities of the Gay Liberation Front, which lasted from late 1969 to 1971.

Dedicated, righteous and introverted, Kilhefner preferred to work behind the scenes and leave the spotlight on Kight. In time, GLF's anti-establishment, anarchical tenets gave way to the practical concerns of nonprofit organizational service for the disenfranchised, and GLF evolved into the Los Angeles Gay Community Services Center which became a prototype for such institutions. Kilhefner was its first executive director. He also founded Van Ness House, an alcohol recovery facility for gay men and lesbians. His earthy persona and hippie apparel of jeans, bushy beard and wire-framed glasses masked his managerial prowess. But within a few years, Kilhefner was administering millions in dollars in grants when the Center moved from its ramshackle Victorian residence of 1614 Wilshire Boulevard to a building it owned on Highland Avenue in Hollywood.

As it matured the Center (renamed after a contentious struggle, the Gay and Lesbian Community Services Center), sought the support and involvement of rich gays; many felt it had abandoned activism for a slick hybrid of social work, public relations and bureaucracy. Disheartened by this rapid assimilation, Kilhefner took a leave of absence from his post as executive director in 1976. A connoisseur of various human-potential movements, he spent a year in retreat with Baba Ram Dass (author of *Be Here Now*), the psychedelic guru incarnation of American psychologist Richard Alpert.

Kilhefner wanted time to reassess the movement. "I was concerned that the gay movement had become all about assimilation into the mainstream culture," he told *The Advocate* in 1987. The idea was: you come out and the journey ends. Growth stops. For me that just didn't make sense. I didn't know what it meant to be gay. Something that was missing from this gay identity was a consciousness, a sense of spirit."

The third of the Radical Faerie triad was Mitch Walker. From a middle-class Jewish family in Hawthorne, a suburb of Los Angeles, Walker studied psychology at U.C.L.A. in the late-1960s, but did not integrate his studies with his coming out until a 1971 transfer to U.C. Berkeley. There he focused on Jungian psychology as well as academia. The turned-on-and-tuned-in gay scene in the Bay area influenced Walker and his persona became long-haired, leftist and quintessentially Berkeley.

Walker's proposed Master's thesis at Lone Mountain College was a gay sex guide balanced with historical anecdotes and psychological reassurance. This was approved, then rejected by his faculty committee[5] but was published by Gay Sunshine Press in 1977 as *Men Loving Men: A Gay Sex Guide and Consciousness Book*. In his book he expressed frustrations similar to Harry's regarding the Gay Liberation movement. "Anybody who feels they're gay," he wrote, "has a hell of a time…with little encouragement and much resistance—even active hostility—within our so-called gay community."

If Harry Hay was the homophile Father and Don Kilhefner the Stonewall Son of the Faerie trinity, Mitch Walker was inescapably the New Age Holy Ghost. Following his studies he applied himself to become a shaman, a modern embodiment of the traditional role about which Edward Carpenter had written. Walker described the initiation into shamanism as landing him in "a bizarre psychotic realm…a shadow, a gleam of light, the kitchen, might all suddenly…become evil."[6] He also regarded himself as being "forced into my vision" and he persevered with his protracted ordeal, but it rendered him barely able to sustain himself—he worked in a factory gluing the eyes on beanbag frogs and rarely socialized.

A regimen of Humboldt brownies and meditations at the underground pool of the Ritch Street Baths intensified Walker's already intense personality. What was left was a stern gay version of Carlos Castaneda who blended magic, psychology and Gay Liberation. Often silent for hours at a time in group settings Walker was ceremonious and keen in private conversation. He could be witty and insightful and some of his readers and friends regarded him as the new gay messiah, a post-Stonewall seer. Others, however, considered him a mind-tripper with an air of psychological supersophistication and mystical superiority.

Walker learned of Harry through a mutual friend named Matthew Rush who had lived in New Mexico. Rush and Walker met at a slide and lecture series in 1976 by Arthur Evans. There Rush asked Walker what he did. "I work in the spirit and I'm a gay spirit worker and I'm a gay shaman and that's what I do," Walker answered. To this, Rush replied, "You sound just as kooky as someone else I know. You should meet him. He talks just like you and he's really old. He lives in New Mexico."

For Walker, hearing those words was "like a light going on." He immediately got Hay's address and began a correspondence that lasted almost a year. To his delight he found that they were both "working on pretty much the same stuff. When I wrote him and he wrote back, we were already so much in harmony that it was like meeting a brother, a twin." This temperamental compatibility finally compelled Walker to buy a plane ticket to New Mexico. He flew out and stayed for most of February, 1978.

The beauty of the place charmed him. Harry served as tour guide, taking him, among other places, to the part of Tsankwe Pueblo where Enki told him the queer people had lived. "He took me to this mound of pottery shards that he said was the queer mound and shoveled around with his hands and pulled out a few little shards and gave them to me. He said I had to promise to bring someone else to this place and give them a little piece of one of these pots, too…It was wonderful."

Walker understood Harry's rarefied language of Marxist historical theory as applied to gays and encouraged him to expound. They recorded twelve hours of their discussions on history, mythology and the meaning of gay consciousness which Walker proposed to transcribe and edit, possibly for a pamphlet. Harry had heard of women calling retreat conferences in the mountains of New Mexico and suggested they call a gay male conference based on the ideas they'd been discussing. Hay's life partner, John Burnside, observed a "tremendous excitement and great affection" developing between Harry and Mitch.

Meeting Walker was a critical link in Harry's development of a new kind of gay movement. In some respects Walker's position was analogous to that of Rudi Gernreich in the Mattachine: Walker and Hay formed the "society of two" that grew into the Radical Faeries. The mythic, hidden aspects of gay identity that they had studied separately suddenly converged with a greatly increased current. Personal passions may have blended with the political ideals that united them—particularly on Harry's side. Walker commented in 1989, "I wouldn't have put it in those terms, but that's probably the truth. Historically, love is often involved in these things. Certain passions cross and with us gay people they are intertwined with our politics." When he boarded the plane back to California, Walker felt a solid connection had been made and that "we were well on the way to starting the Faerie movement."

Don Kilhefner had met Harry twice, once in Los Angeles and once while passing through New Mexico when they had a long talk. In December of 1973 he wrote to Harry, "The visit was so important to my thinking that I have had an idea buzzing in my head ever since. I would like to do an extensive taped interview with you concerning the Homophile Movement (second priority) and the development of Gay Consciousness (first priority) … Our gay brothers and sisters need to hear your ideas and share in your observations."

They did not begin a sustained relationship, however, until after a third meeting in May of 1978 at Lama, Ram Dass's retreat just north of Taos where John Burnside had been invited to show his Symmetricon (a kaleidoscopic projection device he invented and manufactured). At that encounter Hay gave Kilhefner a copy of his subject-SUBJECT position paper.

Once Kilhefner returned to Los Angeles, where he lived in a yoga commune, he exchanged a steady flow of letters and phone calls with Harry and John, often addressing them "Beloved Brothers" and surrounding his signature with fluttering hearts. Kilhefner valued "the talking connection" with Harry more than what he got from Harry's writings, but he felt that Hay was the first fellow traveler he had met in a long search for a new perspective on Gay Liberation. He was deeply excited. He even inquired into the job market in Santa Fe, suggesting that he might move there if Harry and John could not bring themselves to move west again.

In the fall of 1978 Kilhefner was asked by therapist Betty Berzon to participate in the annual conference of the national Gay Academic Union. Berzon, then chair of G.A.U., arranged for Kilhefner, Walker and Hay to lead a workshop titled "New Breakthroughs in the Nature of How We Perceive Gay Consciousness." Harry and John traveled to Los Angeles for the conference, held at the University of Southern California that November. An overflow of more than fifty gay and lesbian academics from around the country sat in a circle, passed a talisman, and, instead of discussing any academic theory, were invited to drop the academic mask and share personal, subjective concerns. (Mitch Walker, flaunting his rebelliousness and his personal tastes in enlightenment, scandalized Kilhefner by lighting and passing a joint.) Their debut in the G.A.U. forum was a success, and afterward Hay told Walker that with "this magnificent organizer," Don Kilhefner, they were now a society of three. Their dreamed-of conference could now proceed.

Walker wrote several letters to Harry complaining that the financial demands of the straight world were cramping his gay spirit work and pleaded with Hay to hurry up with his plans for a retreat where they could all live together. Harry reassured Mitch that he would not have much longer to wait. Indeed, the Circle of Loving Companions, including John Ciddio and Pat Gutierrez, was growing restless in New Mexico and the promising work with Kilhefner sweetened the prospect of moving. Once Kilhefner joined the Circle they sealed the decision to leave their paradise by the Rio Grande and move back to Los Angeles.

Though Walker was in Berkeley, Kilhefner was in L.A. and Harry and John were in San Juan, a group identity congealed via continued calls and letters. The three radicals made a "three-sided square," according to Walker, with John Burnside "hovering around the edges" helping out as needed.

Kilhefner, again working at the Gay and Lesbian Community Services Center as education director, developed a course called "Gay Voices and Visions." A sort of primer on gay consciousness and spirituality, the class was a combination of a traditional seminar (with Walt Whitman, Edward Carpenter, Walker, Hay and other authors on the syllabus) and a touchie-feelie encounter group with massage, personal sharing and exercises for retrieval of childhood memory. The phone wires between L.A. and New Mexico buzzed with descriptions of the breakthroughs and excitement the course elicited from its students. This was like gasoline to the flickering hopes of Harry, Don and Mitch that this new gay consciousness could be organized, that Gay Liberation was indeed approaching a new chapter.

In the early spring while investigating a site for the conference, Kilhefner came across a prospect in *The Advocate* when he found an ad inviting gays to meditate at the Sri Ram Ashram, a spiritual retreat in the 5,000-foot-high desert near Benson, Arizona. It seemed perfect for their needs, so he contacted the owner, an American who went by the name of Swami Bill. Swami Bill sent Don a plane ticket, so Don flew east and Harry and John drove west from San Juan.

When they converged there, forty miles off the main highway, Sri Ram Ashram greeted them like an oasis. The entrance led through a landscaped garden with a fountain, to a complex of buildings surrounded by shade trees, beds of flowers and statuary. By the pool (spring fed and Olympic-sized), scenes from the Buddha's life were painted on a low stucco wall. There was a meditation tent carpeted in orange-and-salmon parachute silk. Ponds of carp nestled in beautifully kept emerald lawns.

Harry took a quick distaste for the owner and discouraged the others from using the place. Kilhefner, however, persevered and by the end of the following day he was arranging for Sri Ram Ashram to serve as the site of the conference. Harry finally decided he too felt that this was the perfect place and momentum for the conference increased.

He and John continued west to Los Angeles to look for a house and to visit as guest lecturers during the "Voices and Visions" class. Walker joined them and the four incipient Faeries stayed in Kilhefner's one-bedroom apartment in Hollywood. These quarters were small. And in the cramped space, friction between Walker and

Hay which had briefly surfaced during Walker's visit to San Juan, was aggravated. Much of the tension stemmed from personality differences. Walker had grown up fatherless and Harry's physical and psychic embodiment of a gay patriarch had a strong effect on him. He regarded Harry as a man of intellectual and spiritual power and sometimes spoke of himself as the heir to that power.

Walker identified their differences as ideological—based on their differing stance regarding psychological theory. Jungian analytic psychology was central to Walker's worldview. Harry had a long-standing disdain for the entire subject and had never factored it into his thinking. But to Walker it provided crucial explanations. He viewed psychological awareness as vital to the political process and applied it to the gay movement. The younger man also worried that Harry's tendency to dominate decision-making threatened the nascent Faerie movement with its ideal of collective process. In Walker's view, the solution was that Harry should convert to psychoanalytical thinking—and change parts of his personality.

The psychologist-shaman attempted to convey this one afternoon when he and Hay strolled to Wattles Park, a quiet garden at the base of the Hollywood Hills, not far from Kilhefner's apartment. Taking the offensive, Walker hammered at Hay for his refusal to make such a conversion and accused him of being incapable of ethical leadership because he "projected his shadow." (In Jungian parlance this refers to seeing in others the qualities suppressed in the conscious self.) Walker saw in Jungianism "a new moral imperative" that everyone must adopt. "Once psychology was invented," he explained later, "you could no longer be neutral. It's ethically true for everyone. You must not project your shadow unconscious anymore, the way humans always have."

From Harry's perspective, the encounter was less a holistic counseling session than an ambush. "He wanted to talk to me about my 'leadership complex,'" Hay recalled. "And I didn't understand, because as far as I know I don't have one. He was rather rough and he insisted for about half an hour. He said, 'You have it and you've got to face it.' I felt threatened and frightened."

Indeed, Harry's self-image was of a person who "walked with others," and he made a point of correcting anyone who called him a leader. According to Walker, Hay lashed back with dramatic curses and threatened to leave Los Angeles and their work. Harry ran from the park and called Kilhefner, who immediately left his desk at the center to attend to the situation. Only his soothing intervention prevented Harry and John from leaving the new movement right then. But the conflict between psychology and politics was to be a continuing tension.

During that visit, Hay and Kilhefner secured a home that could fit the entire Circle of Loving Companions. It was a 1920s house with three bedrooms located on the fraying eastern edge of Hollywood, on a quiet street called La Cresta Court. There was even a workshop and a garden. After considering it, Walker decided not to move in. Harry and John returned to New Mexico to spend several months packing. Kilhefner moved in and so did John Ciddio and Pat Gutierrez. Kilhefner and Ciddio took such a strong dislike to one another that the Chicano couple soon moved to a separate residence.

By July, Kilhefner joined Harry and John at their New Mexico compound where they packed a rented moving truck so full that it sank into the soft dirt road. When that truck, driven by Kilhefner, and their own small truck hit the road, they parodied the citizens band radio craze by calling themselves Big Faerie and Li'l Faerie. Barely had they set their boxes onto the porch of the La Cresta Court house when the dizzying demands of producing the Radical Faerie conference overtook them. The boxes stayed there, untouched until that winter.

Each member of the group took on a specialized role: Hay handled the political duties; Burnside was concerned with logistics and mechanics (though in matters of decision he usually backed Hay); and Walker was the spiritual leader. The manager, Kilhefner, was prized for his budgetary and administrative genius. He poured his efforts into the Circle with gusto and compared the new movement to the high-spirited early days of GLF work.

The organizers were uncertain that the undertaking could even break even financially, and their hopes (they needed at least twenty-five enrollees) depended on spreading the word through an effective flyer. It was at this point that Harry coined the term "Radical Faerie" and he always referred to this as "the Call" that started the Radical Faerie movement much as he credited his 1948 and 1950 prospectuses with starting the homophile movement. (A biographical fact sheet he wrote later said that he "invented the concept and called into being" the first Gathering and the ensuing movement. Though others would argue that he was one link in a chain, he saw himself as the blacksmith.)

The flyer was stunning. Bruce Reifel, who had created flyers for GLF's Gay-ins and gay dances a decade earlier, created an image of a nude Adonis watching a huge sun rising over a desert rock. "A Call to Gay Brothers" breathed across the masthead in cursive script and below that bold type announced "A SPIRITUAL CONFERENCE FOR RADICAL FAIRIES." [sic]

Slated for Labor Day weekend the conference promised a blend of the spiritual, the radical and the "fairie"—and to further the tease, the reverse side quoted New

Age politician Mark Satin, Aleister Crowley and Harry himself. It suggested a synthesis of spirituality and politics "beyond Left and Right" and assured gays that they had a place in the "paradigm shift" to the New Age. All that was said of the secret location was that it was "Don Juan country near Tucson." The flyer was sent to gay and leftist bookstores, schools, gay community centers and health food stores. The three-sided square waited anxiously.

Some 200 men recognized themselves in the flyer and showed up at Sri Ram Ashram which could accommodate at most seventy-five. That space was found for everyone symbolizes the freewheeling magic of that weekend. The gay men who trickled in from all directions had no idea what to expect. As they registered, they were warned of the dangers of midday sun and scorpions. Many were progressives, most were feminists, and, at least for the weekend, all were Radical Faeries.

The definition of what "fairie/Faerie" meant seeped in through bits of jargon; no "workshops" were scheduled, for example, only "Fairie [sic] circles." Fairies joining in a ring was, after all, a known magic formula. People chatted about the times the word "fairy" had been hurled pejoratively at them, or about the secret fascination they'd had with fairies. New friends would huddle excitedly, staring at one another in wonder, as if their eyes had opened for the first time, and repeating the word as the appropriateness of the identity sunk in. "Faeries." When one urbanite searched for an electric outlet to plug in his travel iron—to keep his trouser pleats sharp there amid the sleeping bags and desert—someone cracked, "Now *that's* a Faerie!"

That evening, at the first Radical Faerie Circle, a spontaneous theme of paganism emerged. Invocations were offered to spirits; blessings and chants rose and fell. Some people shook rattles or clusters of tiny bells. Harry, whom many recognized from the film *Word is Out*, gave a short welcome and presented his remarks about subject-SUBJECT consciousness. He called on the crowd to "throw off the ugly green frogskin of hetero-imitation to find the shining Faerie prince beneath."

For listeners who had felt a lifelong proscription against being truly themselves, this message was profoundly moving. Will Roscoe, who first met Hay that night, recalled, "The scene was dramatic. Harry wore a caftan and appeared statuesque in the twilight. When he made his call, many of us cried." Stu Szidak, who recognized Hay from the GLF days in Los Angeles, agreed. "Harry Hay worked his magic that night."

After a slide presentation called "Erotic Consciousness" by Christopher Larkin,[7] the strangers in the desert night found places to sleep, mostly on the lawn. Of that first night, one person wrote that "there was much giggling and some lovemaking and hardly anyone slept because we were excited about the prospect of being together."

The following morning more people arrived to find a new Faerie aesthetic blooming: cosmetic rainbows trailed from the eyelids, past mustaches and around nipples; feathers, beads and bells dangled everywhere; any clothing was worn for shade or to pad a seat. Modesty was quietly banished. Everyone felt a deeper transformation. To Fritz Frurip, "It was lovely to see so many people shedding clothes as they shed anxieties and fears and found themselves among friends who thought as they did. There was no one around except gay men. We were the society. We weren't meeting in a building outside of which were heteros. We were the society and we were beginning to experience what it was like to be the majority and make the rules." Stories of growing up gay were told with such fervor that the Circle did not realize it had gone hours over schedule.

At a certain point, indefinably but undeniably, the conference "clicked." There are many descriptions of the change that occurred—from a spirit descending, to a veil being torn away by the moon. Time and physics had somehow altered and one participant noted, "I recognize the symptoms. I'm on a four-day acid trip—without the acid!"

Harry later described the phenomenon, which became a regular dynamic of Faerie Gatherings, as a "collective gear-shift of consciousness which galvanized us as a group. That consensus of shared subject-SUBJECT consciousness was the doorway we went through and once through it, you knew you had changed irrevocably."

Circles overlapped one another, finely tuned sensitivities harmonized at all levels of interaction and mealtimes were blissfully thrown off by hours. A blackboard served anyone who wanted to propose a topic for a Circle and invite others to join. The tremendous variety of topics soon scrawled on it included a native desert plant walk, politics of gay enspiritment, gay publications, massage, a guided orgy, rape and violence, ritual makeup, Celtic and English country dancing, healing-energy, autofellatio, silly sissies, myths of male bonding and nutrition.

The word "conference" was quickly rejected as "too hetero" and replaced with the word "Gathering." Impulsive dances frequently broke out and men confessed that the sullen, macho standards of the gay ghettos had inhibited their dancing impulses for years. Suddenly, they were able to dance their true dance.

The idea of fairy circles or fairy rings has mythical precedent, but Hay, Kilhefner and Walker quickly imbued it with a political ethic. A "Faerie Circle," they explained, had no head, no foot, no hierarchy. The form seemed to harness goodwill, candor and humor. For many, it proved to be the most egalitarian way that they had ever conducted business.

The event that everyone remembered most from that first Gathering was a spontaneous ritual involving mud. This came about the second morning when someone said, "I have this fantasy about taking water out there and making mud— and seeing what happens." About fifty naked Faeries carried gallons of water several hundred yards from the ashram and mixed it with the fine clay dust.

Situated in the womblike hollow of a dry river bed they seemed to become possessed by tribal instincts as they covered themselves and each other with the red mud. Neal Twyford, one of the participants, recalled, "It was centered around a guy who was lying down and had an erection—everyone built it up with mud until they'd created a huge earth-phallus on this earth-covered man and put laurel leaves around his head." The man was lifted above everyone's heads as an *om* rumbled out of the huddled, be-mudded circle. A harmony and ecstasy built and seemed to go on and on. Intense dancing broke out; and it too seemed endless. Near the ashram, as they hosed each other off in a prolonged sensual baptism, many murmured, "Scraping off the ugly green frogskins."

There was an uncanny feeling of power in the mud ritual. Twyford puzzled, "For years I've been asking myself, 'Why was that little event so powerful?' I remember looking around and saying, 'Holy shit, we're in another world. We're back in time…'" Similarly, John Kyper wrote in *RFD*, "It evoked a sense of timelessness that I sometimes feel during especially satisfying lovemaking, that I am in touch with something thousands and thousands of years old." Haunting photographs taken at the time seem to glimpse just that: a different tribe from another time. Harry, Mitch and Don were all at another circle, but John Burnside partook of the earthy rapture.

On the last night of the gathering a more planned ritual also had a powerful effect. Fritz Frurip, a participant who had studied theology at Notre Dame, recalled, "I learned more about ritual that [night] than I had in five years of study." A slowly building procession crescendoed to a cacophony. In the thick of the cathartic howling and drum beating some people reported that a black bull appeared near the group and stood with the evening star just over its shoulder.

Some saw this as a visitation, a vision straight from some ancient frieze. Others doubted that such an animal could have been in the area at all. Bull or not, everyone reported having undergone a transcendent high and, as the culmination of an extraordinary sequence, many found themselves deeply moved. As gay people, most had renounced spiritual beliefs because religion had renounced them, but the spiritual jolt of the Gathering caused them to undergo a complete re-evaluation.

On the last night there was a performance of John Burnside's Symmetricon. Its glowing mandalas flowered and tumbled like the rare blossoms of the ecstatic feeling and expanded consciousness that comprised this shared time. Harry made a few closing remarks as the new comrades spent a last night together. The following morning, Frurip saw "simple brothers, washed clean of the night's Faerie glamour, stronger and more serene." Still, no one wanted to return to the world, which demanded their relinquishing the magic they had found. One car loaded with Faeries overheated while still hours of desert highway from the Tucson airport. "We did a Faerie Circle standing around the open hood," one recalled. "The car started up perfectly and we all made our flights."

Twice as long as the first Gathering and almost twice as large, the second Spiritual Gathering for the Radical Faeries in August, 1980 became known as Faerie Woodstock. Whatever the first Gathering had produced, this one produced more of it. It was held in the alpine meadows above Boulder, Colorado, in Estes National Forest. Mountain streams and piney hills could only enhance the romantic otherworldliness in the hearts of the more than 300 who registered. Harry and John drove out a week early to help the Denver Faerie Circle plan, order and transport everything needed—including food for two dozen mass meals, a giant striped tent and 500 restaurant candles in jars.

To properly prepare the site, Mitch Walker insisted on going up before anyone arrived. In his shaman garb of skirt, vest, bangles, beads, and bells—and un-dissuaded by the presence of curious straight couples in campers—he communed with the spirits of the land and blessed the areas where the Faeries would gather. This was done with the encouragement of the others; he had done the same at the ashram, and seemed to be fulfilling his role as official mystic. Soon all the supplies, plus toilets, plumbing for hot showers, and the generators for power, were carted up the hill and assembled by Faerie hands.

On the first morning and at regular intervals thereafter 300 men linked up in a huge circle on a meadow rimmed with dark pines and dotted with small daisies. Just surveying the circle was a mind-altering revelation. There was no hesitation this time; these were Radical Faeries. They wore straw hats, sun bonnets, overalls, body paint, hostess pajamas, plaid flannel shirts, scarves, sneakers and their male bodies. The vividness of freedom rushed into them faster than in the previous year as they poured out stories of their travels toward being gay, their wonder at the rare occasion of togetherness, their great possibilities as a people who were finally coming together.

The Denver Faeries had compiled a collection of chants and songs. The Seven Goddess chant by Deena Metzger and Charlie Murphy was the most popular. The names Isis, Astarte, Diana, Hecate, Demeter, Kali, Inana—a super-invocation of goddesses of Egyptian, Assyrian, Roman, Greek, Hindu, and Babylonian cultures—reverberated into the air in thickly woven harmonies of male voices at morning Circles and again at late night campfires. The theme of neo-paganism—reflected by the popular books *Witchcraft and the Gay Counterculture* by Arthur Evans and *The Spiral Dance* by Starhawk—was becoming strongly integrated into the new Faerie culture. The Rainbow Family gatherings and womens' music festivals were also cited as inspirations.

That was something Hay had to battle for among the Mattachines—the creation of a culture. But here, a gay culture took off like a wild weed and flowered with numerous, often topsy-turvy innovations. At the first great Circle of the Denver Gathering it was proposed that since snakes were sacred to the ancient Earth goddess, the hiss should be a sign of approval. Thereafter, happy Faeries hissed.[8]

Faerie names were adopted with increasing frequency. Some came to the gathering with names they had already chosen, such as Crazy Owl (a homeopath) and Kevin Woven (a weaver), but most were acquired at Naming Circles. Favorite categories emerged, such as astronomical names (Star, Morning Star and Ultra Violet Nova); meteorological names (Neon Snowflake, Beautiful Day and Rosy-Fingered Don); and botanical names (Oak Leaf, Flower and Marvelous Persimmon). Some Faeries, like Toy, Judy Jetson and Gidget pilfered pop culture. Ideally, a name would come to a Faerie as a result of deep inner searching or during a moment of openness to the divine. The first Faerie Directory, littered with Faerie names, ultimately grew into the Holy Faerie Database, tended by a Faerie named Baba Ram Rom.

An important emblem of Faerie culture was presented at that Gathering by Dennis Melba'son, who belonged to a New Orleans collective called Louisiana Sissies in Struggle (LASIS). Inspired by a vision, he crocheted a triangular shawl with an eight-foot hypotenuse. Inside was a precise lace portrait of Cernunnos, the horned god of wildlife who was the Celtic version of the Greek god Pan. His horns and beard reach to the points of the triangle. Over the grinning, bearded face, a stout phallus spewed a garland of leafy vine.

For many the shawl became the favorite talisman of the Faeries, sent from Gathering to Gathering to be worn by each speaker at every large Circle. Over the years it embraced thousands of shoulders as Faeries shared, argued, wept and wondered with one another. In Colorado, as in Arizona the previous year, deep personal transformations took place. Friendships blossomed, lovers paired, souls healed—all in the ineffable Faerie cloud.

Two sweat lodges that Faeries had built stayed in constant use all week. Nightly circles turned into ecstatic dances. One of these was a ceremonial bonfire for Kali, the Hindu Mother Goddess, as well known for her aspect of destruction as for her life giving. The fire consumed objects imbued with unwanted qualities—oppression, self-hatred and envy. On the last night of the six days, a spontaneous circle began around a fire. "That ritual mushroomed into an intense, orgiastic connection with the spirit world," recalled a Faerie named Aro. "It was much like the mud ritual the year before. But because it was this Eastern death goddess, a few Baptists were freaked out." The hundreds of rejuvenated gay men conjured their purest energies; it seemed an ancient, profound communion with a glorious power of gay men that reached through millennia.

The next morning, convinced that their lives had been unalterably changed and that they had found the magic to change the world the Faeries scattered once again.

[1] The anthropologist and mythographer W.Y. Evans Wentz collected essential information on fairies in his *Fairy-faith in Celtic Countries*, published in 1911. Hay found the book in his thirties and was particularly interested in the author's discussion of the pygmy theory of fairies, which posited that a race of small people known as the Faerie tribe had inhabited the British Isles, where the fairy faith persisted.

[2] It was this concern with the "gay essence" that brought his work great popular interest as well as earning him no small antagonism as a leader of the so-called "California essentialists" in the period when academia largely favored the model known as social constructionism for the gay identity, which asserted that gayness was societally produced rather than inborn. This was unfortunate, since Hay himself favored the societal constructionist argument in many instances, especially his insistence that homosexual identity evolved in response to changing social conditions.

[3] Evans and Hay have never met, though both have acknowledged parallels and synchronicity in their independent work.

4 Hay claimed for the record that his only influences for this work were Konrad Lorenz's books dealing with ethology, particularly the development from individual consciousness to group consciousness, as well as various readings in archeology and anthropology. An early New Age book called *The Morning of the Magicians*, published in 1960 by French authors Louis Pauwels and Jacques Bergier also influenced his thinking. Hay insisted that despite similar terminology, his thinking was not related to that of Martin Buber or Simone de Beauvoir.

5 Walker's replacement thesis was a Jungian treatise called "Gay Depth Psychology."

6 For more on Walker's account, see his essay "Becoming Gay Shamanism" in *Visionary Love*.

7 Larkin was a wealthy gay man who produced the 1974 gay-themed feature film *A Very Natural Thing* and later, under the name Purusha, a coffee-table book on radical sexuality called *The Divine Androgyne*.

8 Not long after that Gathering, gay playwright and director Martin Worman was bewildered to hear half the audience hiss his San Francisco production of *Dear Love of Comrades*—until he was informed that Faeries were in the audience and that this was how they did things.

"After Long Ages Resuming the Broken Thread": Walt Whitman and Edward Carpenter Dream Up the Radical Faeries

by Joey Cain

FOREBEARS AND ANCESTORS ARE SOMETIMES prickly and always necessary for any group looking to see itself as more than a momentary and transitory phenomenon. "New" movements tend to imagine themselves as either creating something never seen before or else reviving some lost golden age or idea. No doubt the truth lies somewhere in between. For me the question of Radical Faerie progenitors is one of tricking out from our suppressed and stolen faggot history a continuity of certain unique ideas and conceptions that same-sex-loving men have had about themselves and their place in the world.

At the heart of the Radical Faeries is a recognition of and exploration into gay mens' souls: our unique way of viewing, experiencing and being in the world. It is the seed kernel from which everything else sprouts. It puts the radical in Radical Faerie. A corollary to this understanding is the belief that our unique "gay window," which informs our individual spirit and being, has a role to play in the larger human community: a social, spiritual and political role that must be played if there is to be a redress of the wacked-out, profit-driven destruction of the Earth. Proceeding from this understanding there come two same-sex-loving Faerie comrades from the past whose visions and spirits rise up and reach across the centuries to embrace our bodies and place kisses upon our lips: Walt Whitman and Edward Carpenter.

It would not be an understatement to say that Walt Whitman forged the language, words and self-consciousness that created the modern same-sex-loving man and, by extension, he is directly responsible for the way every gay man or Radical Faerie thinks of himself today. There is literature aplenty articulating this aspect of Whitman. What I want to explore here is how his vision of our love, sexuality and consciousness whispers across time into our receptive Faerie ears.

Sometime in 1859 Walt wrote a series of poems entitled *Live Oak With Moss*. It was a poetic cycle delineating the coming into self-consciousness of a faggot man through his falling in love with another man and the eventual breaking up of that affair. In and of itself this work was a breakthrough for its original articulation of a queer man's inner world. But *Live Oak With Moss* was never published. Instead, Whitman had a vision that the deep emotional and sexual love he felt for other men, his "fervid comradeship," was the basis for a political and spiritual movement that would be "the counter balance and offset of our materialist and vulgar American democracy and for the spiritualization thereof." He declared:

> I confidently expect a time when there will be seen, running like a half-hid warp through all the myriad audible and visible worldly interests of America, threads of manly friendship, fond and loving, pure and sweet, strong and life-long, carried to degrees hitherto unknown… I say democracy infers such loving comradeship, as its most inevitable twin or counterpart, without which it will be incomplete, in vain and incapable of perpetuating itself.

Under the influence of this vision Whitman transformed his *Live Oak With Moss* from a personal story of love gained and lost into a moving prophetic proclamation of the powers political, spiritual and creative that the love of comrades engenders. Grown to a sequence of forty-five poems, it was published in the 1860 edition of *Leaves of Grass* and given the title of *Calamus*. The title comes from the name of a large grass plant similar to a cat-tail that has a distinctly phallic shape. It grows in the marshy area between the liquid water of pond and solid earth of dry land. It is also known as *Sweet Flag*. In poem number four of the sequence he gives his reason for the title:

> *And here what I now draw from the water, wading in the pond-side,*
> *(O here I last saw him that tenderly loves me—and returns again, never to*
>   *separate from me,*
> *And this, O this shall henceforth be the token of comrades—this calamus-root*
>   *shall,*
> *Interchange it, youths, with each other! Let none render it back!)*

Since its 1860 publication, *Calamus* has spoken to the deepest selves of queer men all around the world in a way that nothing before it had. For the fifty years after its publication, just about every significant hero in the struggle for gay freedom and liberation—no matter what country they lived in—was in part awakened to their mission by Whitman and the *Calamus* poems. Yet, while coming from the soul of a gay man, its vision is universal and speaks to and inspires everyone. But it has a secret and special music, a unique resonance, for gay men—and Radical Faeries in particular.

Nothing can replace a complete reading of the poems' sequence in its entirety. I strongly recommend doing so in the original 1860 version. After its first publication Whitman continued to tinker with it for the rest of his life and the tinkering weakened it.[1] What I want to do is share some excerpts, a Whitman sampler so to speak, that tease out those elements of his vision which speak directly to some of our Radical Faerie purposes and visions.

Calamus begins with a poem that reads like a Call for a Radical Faerie Gathering:

In paths untrodden,
In the growth by margins of pond waters,
Escaped from the life that exhibits itself,
From all the standards hitherto published—from the pleasures, profits,
  conformities,
Which too long I was offering to feed my Soul;
Clear to me now, standards not yet published—clear to me that my Soul,
That the Soul of the man I speak for, feeds, rejoices only in comrades;
Here, by myself, away from the clank of the world,
Tallying and talked to here by tongues aromatic,
No longer abashed—for in this secluded spot I can respond as I would not dare
  elsewhere,
Strong upon me the life that does not exhibit itself, yet contains all the rest,
Resolved to sing no songs to-day but those of manly attachment,
Projecting them along that substantial life,
Bequeathing, hence, types of athletic love
Afternoon, this delicious Ninth Month, in my forty-first year,
I proceed, for all who are, or have been, young men,
To tell the secret of my nights and days,
To celebrate the need of comrades.

It's all pretty much there. The call to leave the everyday world in order to enter into a magical space where we can respond as we would or perhaps could not elsewhere so that we can explore the life, our hearts and souls, that does not exhibit itself yet contains all the rest; an exploration that is deeply personal but is achieved in the collective celebration of our shared needs.

In the fifth poem of the sequence Whitman declares his very Faerie-esque political agenda:

States!

> *Were you looking to be held together by the lawyers?*
> *By an agreement on a paper? Or by arms?*

Away!
I arrive, bringing these, beyond all the forces of courts and arms,

> *These! to hold you together as firmly as the earth itself is held together.*

And what is it that he was bringing?

There shall from me be a new friendship—It shall be called after my name,

> *It shall circulate through The States, indifferent of place,*
> *It shall twist and intertwist them through and around each other—Compact*
>   *shall they be, showing new signs,*
> *Affection shall solve every one of the problems of freedom,*
> *Those who love each other shall be invincible,*

  . . . .

It shall be customary in all directions, in the houses and streets, to see manly
    affection,
The departing brother or friend shall salute the remaining brother or friend with
    a kiss.

Whitman has taken his own same-sex-loving feelings and desires and used them to envision a new and radical social/political order, one not based on coercive laws and armies but on the affection of one person for another. Men will actually kiss in public and affection, not guns and police, will solve the problems of freedom.

Only I will establish in the Manahatta, and in every city of These States, inland
    and seaboard,
And in the fields and woods, and above every keel little or large, that dents the
    water,

Without edifices, or rules, or trustees, or any argument,
The institution of the dear love of comrades.

Walt's political vision is grounded in experiences and understandings that most Radical Faeries will recognize: imminence and direct action, decentralization, mutual aid, spontaneity and a basic belief in the solidarity of humanity and its interconnection with nature.

One of the most deeply loved poems of the sequence speaks to the power and force, the sheer exhilaration, of discovering the other, be it a single person or a community of lovers as often happens at a Gathering:

We two boys together clinging,
One the other never leaving,
Up and down the roads going—North and South excursions making,
Power enjoying—elbows stretching—fingers clutching,
Armed and fearless—eating, drinking, sleeping, loving,
No law less than ourselves owning—sailing, soldiering, thieving, threatening,
Misers, menials, priests, alarming—air breathing, water drinking, on the turn of
*   the sea-beach dancing,*
With birds singing—With fishes swimming—With trees branching and leafing,
Cities wrenching, ease scorning, statutes mocking, feebleness chasing,
*   Fulfilling our foray.*

A great achievement of the *Calamus* poems is that Whitman expresses not only the joy of the love of comrades but speaks just as deeply to our hurt and longing. When Radical Faeries come together in Circles and Gatherings we do so to celebrate our love and fabulous selves. We also seek to share our losses and pain and, by joining together, to heal ourselves in each other's presence. In poem number nine Whitman speaks to us as if in a Heart Circle about the loss of the one he loved. In doing so he takes us to a deeper level of bonding with each other.

Hours continuing long, sore and heavy-hearted,
Hours of the dusk, when I withdrew to a lonesome and unfrequented spot, seating
*   myself, leaning my face in my hands;*
Hours sleepless, deep in the night, when I go forth, speeding swiftly the country roads,
*   or through the city streets, or pacing miles and miles, stifling plaintive cries;*
Hours discouraged, distracted—for the one I cannot content myself without, soon I
*   saw him content himself without me;*

Hours when I am forgotten, (O weeks and months are passing, but I believe I am
*   never to forget!)*
Sullen and suffering hours! (I am ashamed—but it is useless—I am what I am;)
Hours of my torment—I wonder if other men ever have the like, out of the like
*   feelings?*
Is there even one other like me—distracted—his friend, his lover, lost to him?
Is he too as I am now? Does he still rise in the morning, dejected, thinking who is
*   lost to him? and at night, awaking, think who is lost?*

In these few lines he plunges into the deep pool of our soul and we see ourselves reflected, instinctively reaching out to hold and console. Were this to be said
in a Heart Circle we would spring from our seats on the ground to encircle him in
a group embrace.

Walt understood that same-sex-loving men have a different and unique experience of the world that sets them apart from the heteros. He knew we had different
ways of perceiving and being in the world and because of that we were, as Harry
Hay said, a separate people. Echoing across the century and a half since its creation
comes this poem that speaks directly to a deep element of our being:

Among the men and women, the multitude, I perceive one, picking me out by
*   secret and divine signs,*
Acknowledging none else—not parent, wife, husband, brother, child, any nearer
*   than I am;*
Some are baffled—But that one is not—that one knows me.
Lover and perfect equal!
I meant that you should discover me so, by my faint indirections,
And I, when I meet you, mean to discover you by the like in you.

And again:

That shadow, my likeness, that goes to and fro, seeking a livelihood,
*   chattering, chaffering,*
How often I find myself standing and looking at it where it fits,
How often I question and doubt whether that is really me;
But in these, and among my lovers, and caroling my songs,
O I never doubt whether that is really me.

As this is only a sampler there is much of the Radical Faerie Walt I have not
included. He left his faint clues and indirections scattered throughout all of his work.

But this is enough to get you started with him and, as he wrote in the closing poem of *Calamus*:

When you read these, I, that was visible, am become invisible;
Now it is you, compact, visible, realizing my poems, seeking me,
Fancying how happy you were, if I could be with you, and become your lover;
Be it as if I were with you. Be not too certain but I am now with you.

If Whitman gave us the soul language that enabled us to speak to one another, it was Edward Carpenter who took that language and used it to explore and articulate our natures and our places in the world. Echoing Whitman he stated:

> ...the Uranian [a term for *same-sex-loving men and women*] people may be destined to form the advance guard of that great movement which will one day transform the common life by substituting the bond of personal affection and compassion for the monetary, legal and other external ties which now control and confine society.[2]

Born in 1844 to an upper-middle-class family, Carpenter behaved as any privileged young man of his class was expected to. He attended Cambridge University and eventually took orders in the Church of England. But he could not bear the hypocrisy he was forced to swallow as a minister and quit the Church. He sought to alleviate some of the injustice he saw around him and break the barriers of class that so tightly controlled the English body and mind. He became a lecturer for the University Extension Movement, created to bring education to the poor who had been denied access to it. Carpenter's movement away from upper-middle-class privilege and towards resisting the social and class system was driven by something in his own soul that he had found when, in 1869, he read a collection of writings by Whitman.

> From that time forward a profound change set in within me. I remember ... feeling all the time that my life deep down was flowing out and away from the surroundings and traditions amid which I lived. ... What made me cling to the little blue book from the beginning was largely the poems which celebrate comradeship. That thought, so near and personal to me, I had never before seen or heard fairly expressed...[3]

In 1877 Carpenter set sail for the United States to visit the man who had given him "a ground for the love of men." During his stay with Whitman, the two made

love, a result of which was to intensify Carpenter's desire to create the loving band
of comrades that would change the world. As he wrote to Whitman during his visit:

> For a long time I have cherished the thought that if I came to know
> you and be known by you, I might be the beginning, or at least one, of a
> small band of followers who by force of personal intercourse and attach-
> ment might have the strength (which is so hard to have alone) to move the
> world, or rather to form the nucleus—you being at the heart of it all—for
> that great vitalized organization of human love and fellowship which must
> be—without which modern civilization will be merely nothing.[4]

Carpenter returned to England and became a leading writer and activist in the
visionary socialist/anarchist movements of the late nineteenth and early twentieth
centuries. He traveled in India and studied with a Gnani,[5] became a vegetarian and
active proponent of women's rights. He was an early critic of a purely mechanistic
science that abstracted itself from human concerns and he bitterly opposed the
profit-driven capitalism that was destroying millions of workers' lives and the very
earth itself.

In 1882 he bought a farm in the north of England and moved there to pursue
market gardening and live his evolving belief that in the simplification of life lay a
path toward redressing the social and spiritual imbalances at the root of modern life.
He started to explore the sexual and emotional longings in his soul. This led him
into a series of love relationships with men who were for the most part straight or
bisexual with wives. Then in 1892 he met a working-class man named George Mer-
rill who had cruised him on a train. The two would become loving companions and
live together in an open relationship for the next thirty years.

The emotional and spiritual energy released through his relationship with
George generated a deepening of Edward's exploration of his gay being. It also
caused him to look for evidence of us and to begin to write and publish what he
found. Through his study of anthropology, literature, history and his observation of
the society around him, Carpenter began to identify some of the roles and social
functions that same-sex-loving men and women performed. Between 1894 and
1914 he published pamphlets and books that contained his findings and argued for
the recognition and acceptance of same-sex-loving people in contemporary society.

He saw us in the arts, education and administration. In the history books he
found us filling the roles of priests, prophets and warriors. In his own life and the life
of the Uranians around him he saw us helping the straight world of men and women

explain themselves to each other. At the basis of all these roles he believed was the development of a new evolutionary phase of human consciousness.

> I say that I think perhaps of all the services the Uranian may render to society it will be found some day that in this direction of solving the problems of affection and of the heart he will do the greatest service. If the day is coming as we have suggested—when Love is at last to take its rightful place as the binding and directing force of society (instead of the Cash-nexus), and society is to be transmutated in consequence to a higher form, then undoubtedly…Uranians…will have an important part to play in the transformation. [6]

His farm in the north of England, called Millthorpe, became a refuge and nexus for a broad cross section of the most radical thinkers and activists of his day. It was there that manual workers, urban intellectuals and country people all came together to break bread and share their lives. At the center and heart of it was the unique energy—the unmistakable gay spirit—that infused the place, generated by the two Radical Faeries at its center, Ed and George.

Edward's poetry, pamphlets and books on the Dear Love of Comrades were passed knowingly, half hidden, from hand to hand, country to country. Because of that Millthorpe and the loving companions at its heart were sought out by same-sex-loving men from around the world as a place of sanctuary, healing and love. But the story does not stop there.

In 1922, the eleven-year-old Harry Hay managed to get the librarian of his local library to leave the library in his care while she went to get her hair done. The first thing he did was grab the keys to locked bookcase that held a book with the word "sex" on it, believing it held pictures of naked men. There were no naked pictures of men but what he did find was a book that gave him an "earth-shaking revelation" and forever changed the way he thought about himself. The book was Edward Carpenter's *The Intermediate Sex*. In the words of Harry's biographer Stuart Timmons:

> Carpenter's writing inspired a vision within him—a heartfelt awaken-ing to the knowledge that love was possible to him as a gay person, both in finding an "other" and in affirming his own value. With his discovery of Edward Carpenter, gay relationships would become for Harry more

than immediate physical stirrings, and he was set on his lifelong course of persistent detective work to find clues to gay history in obscure books.[7]

And, I would add, envision and call the Radical Faeries into being.

[1] You can find all the iterations of *Calamus,* as well as the original unpublished *Live Oak With Moss,* online at www.whitmanarchive.org.

[2] *The Intermediate Sex: A Study of Transitional Types of Men and Women.* London, Swan Sonnenschein & Co., Manchester, S. Clark, 1908.

[3] *My Days and Dreams: Being Autobiographical Notes.* London, George Allen and Unwin, 1916.

[4] 1877 letter from Edward Carpenter to Walt Whitman, Syracuse University.

[5] *"Gnani"* (alternately *Jnani, Gyani*) is a term in many Indian languages meaning "wise." The term is added to the names of various individuals, but does not denote a specific person.

[6] *The Intermediate Sex: A Study of Transitional Types of Men and Women.* London, Swan Sonnenschein & Co., Manchester, S. Clark, 1908.

[7] Stuart Timmons, *The Trouble With Harry Hay.* Boston, Alyson Publications, 1990.

Queer Spirit Memories Grown in the Midwest

by Donald L. Engstrom-Reese

THROUGH THE 1970S, 1980S AND 1990s I witnessed, from my Iowa front porch, a queerness slowly growing, which promised to fill the sacred queer-shaped emptiness echoing in the heart of our current overculture. I heard it singing on the winds. I tasted it in the fruits of our gardens. I felt its velvet flesh while in the arms of my lovers each night I dared to dream of this gestating promise.

By the time *RFD* was born (Autumn 1974) in the heart of the rich lands of the Tall Grass Prairie, the Mississippi Watershed was already nurturing nests of emerging Queer Spirit. Queer folks, who would later name themselves Witches, Heathens, Radical Faeries and yes, Queer Spirit Folks. They were slowly awakening to the powerful mysteries of sacred queerness.

Circles of gay men were beginning to gather to explore each other as sacred sexual beings and queer transformers of culture. These circles of Queer Spirit were beginning to deeply root themselves in places like Arkansas, Missouri, Illinois, Minnesota, Iowa, Wisconsin and Kansas. The earliest stirrings of the emerging Cultures of Beauty, Balance and Delight were making themselves known in gay collectives, consciousness raising groups, bars, classrooms and households throughout the region. The Three Queer Brothers and other Mysterious Ones were making Themselves at home in the hearths and hearts of faggots, fairies, sissies, hippies, fems and gay activists living up and down the Mississippi Valley.

I remember in the mid 1970s sitting in our back garden, as an intense thrill ran through my blood and bone, when suddenly ecstasy and inspiration filled us (a small collective of gay men) as we came to our first understandings around gay sexuality as a spiritual gift. This understanding seemed to spring, as if by magic, from deep within our own inquiring queer selves. We needed no one else to verify this self-evident reality. We simply knew that queer sex was a blessing, a gift given by Mystery to enrich the lives of all beings, human or otherwise.

The day that the Queer Gods first touched my heart, awakening me to glimmers of what amazing adventures of spirit and flesh were still yet to come to me and my people, my old paradigms shattered. That day I saw visions of possibility, some magnificent, some horrific. The most important gift to come from this experience, was the solid knowledge that the Divine was not limited to a heterosexual, bi-gendered, universalist worldview only, with no room for my own experiences springing from a newly formed understanding of the cosmos from multiversal view. The taste of this freedom touched me in all ways, transforming, once again, all previous possibilities of being queer in the world.

I remember the first time we welcomed queers of like mind, travelers all the way from Arkansas, to our Iowa Faggot Farm, bringing with them the clear understanding that Queer Spirit had truly reawakened across the whole of the Midgard.[1] Our conversations, our shared meals and dreams all told me that yes, Queers of Power were reawakening. It was not just my own small group. There were queer folks everywhere coming into their own.

I remember in the late 1970s, hearing the first rumors coming out of California about folks who had started to name folks like us, Radical Faeries. We wondered hopefully about this gossip. Some of us made our way to the Colorado Faerie Gathering and to our joy found many more who were clearly related to our own queer clans, tribes and households.

One hot Midwestern afternoon in the early 1980s I completely awoke to the shivers of deep sacred pleasure as groups of us lay naked stroking one another's newly-rediscovered holy flesh. Again, these pleasures and flesh knowledge seemed as if they were a recovered long lost treasure hidden in the very core of our beings. Cock-sucking became a sacred feast. Tongues slowly licking chest and thighs realized that they were tasting the Divine. Assholes were revealed as a multilayered gift of lust, love and sensible function given to us by the Mysterious Ones and the slow steady choices of ancient life some now call "evolution." We awoke to the realization that each kiss we offered and received was an expression of succulent sacred flesh, spirit and mind made one.

A few summers later, I remember beginning to understand that queerness was not merely about whom one had sex with or desire for. But rather, it was daring to truly live an authentic life, daring to be one's own authority, while yet remaining fully engaged in community.

Therefore, a Queer was simply someone who chose to embrace and openly celebrate their own life, willing to accept the consequences of their choices. From my home in the Upper Mississippi Valley, I continue to hear rumors and see signs in my own backyard and from around the world that tell tales of a Sacred Queerness returning, emerging as if from a deep sleep, to touch, inspire and restore a fractured human nightmare.

I see the sacred queer-shaped emptiness being filled with a vitally alive Queer Culture fed by a worldwide awakening essential to the continued growth and nurturance the Cultures of Beauty, Balance and Delight. Let the transformative knowledge of queer growth and rich harvest inspire us all to continue to tend our own regional expressions of this amazing opportunity to bring Midgard back into balance with the blessed Cycle of Life, Death and Rebirth.

May we all dare to live lives of wonder and majesty.

---

[1] *Midgard:* (an Anglicized form of Old Norse *Miðgarðr),* is one of the Nine Worlds and is an old Germanic name for our world and is the home of Humans, with the literal meaning "middle enclosure."

THE FIRST GATHERING

Army of Lovers:
An Evocation of the First Spiritual Conference
for Radical Faeries

by Allen Page

LABOR DAY WEEKEND. 1979. Two hundred of us gather in a circle in the hot Arizona desert.

A young man in glasses rises in our midst, offering to tell us a story.

Weeks ago, when he first got the Call, he agreed that the conference was a good idea but felt no urgency to attend. When another announcement later came to his attention, he asked the Goddess to show him whether he needed to be there. The Goddess was silent, but at the urging of friends he drove cross-country, thinking the trip would be a good vacation at least. The ride was long and hot. And on the floor of the ladies' room at a highway rest stop, he unexpectedly found a woman giving birth. The Goddess had finally spoken, and the young man knew why he had been called to the conference. It was his destiny to assist his brothers in the birth of a culture—the creation of a new and more meaningful mythology.

Bells tinkle. Witches among us go shrill. Shamans circle with their feathers. We are fathers, artists, athletes and sissies. We do not fear gentleness and have no need to compete. We believe in the power of contradictions and the magic of laughter. That the quality of energy exchanged in lovemaking is more important than the gender of bodies. We acknowledge the sacred desert around us. Invoke guides from the spirit world. Evoke our true selves. Free of heterosexist oppression, we have gathered in this space to explore and affirm who and why we are, provide a sense of community and nurture each other's growth.

The moon grows full. We dance in its light and review the lore of fairies. Elders remind us that fairies were mischievous, magical nature spirits originally—the oppressed remnants of the antecedent Goddess religion. A lithesome race with its own ethical code, and often misunderstood—even when it helped the unfortunate. In the west, a race variously associated with the Druids, Wicca and Pan.

In patriarchy, the history of the oppression of fairies parallels that of homosexu-als. Thus have homosexual males (in particular) been pejoratively called "fairies." In some cultures, however, homosexuals were openly respected as praise-singers, sha-mans and reminders of the psychically androgynous ideal. Only in patriarchy have they been condemned as evil—along with all things feminine—including magic.

The stars twinkle in the clear desert night. Around our great circle, various brothers stand and express what they would like to experience and contribute over the next two and a half days. It is clear that we all hunger for a fresh and supportive appreciation of ourselves; that we wish to retrieve what we have lost. Wish to discard the models we have inherited and establish new ones for how we seek to be. From this open-ended session is formulated a variety of events and experiences to be led by ourselves and undertaken in an unstructured way.

In the purifying heat, with the taste of our bodies' salt on our lips, we meditate, explore ancient myths, run healing energy on one another, practice yoga, stroke the horses, learn ancient Celtic dances, walk and identify desert herbs, discuss good nu-trition, prepare vegetarian meals, watch the rabbits, examine our dreams, exchange massage, share poetry, swim, discuss the spiritual significance of sexuality. We play. Make music. Make love. Make magic.

Nude, a group of us walks the cracked earth into the desert. Here we cover our bodies with burnt-orange mud, forming a circle, arms locked around each other.

> *Wearing our long-winged feathers as we fly,*
> *Wearing our long-winged feathers as we fly,*
> *We circle around,*
> *We circle around,*
> *The bound'ries of the Earth.*

On the ground in the center of the circle, one of us is stretched on his back. Mud is layered on him. Twigs, sprouts and flowers are planted on him. The chant's rhythm accelerates, sweeping us along with its momentum. We are soon screaming and shouting invocations—mud-covered sprites, dancing to the voice of a solo pipe; by some holy madness, bringing Earth to flower.

Spontaneously, our wailing subsides. The "living" man is lifted above our heads and presented to the sky. Lowered to a standing position, eyes closed, he becomes the silent, stable center around which we enclose and hold each other. In a long line, holding hands, we weave back towards the ashram, a heady desert snake. Brother to brother. Empowered and transformed.

We are one in the spirit.
We are one in our love.

It is difficult to leave such a place. But the richness of this singular retreat requires we return to our ordinary worlds to more fully digest what we have shared. The pain of imminent parting hangs heavily over the closing circle. While much remains to be done among us, our work in the world must also begin. Listening to my brothers express what these three days have meant to us, I recall an elder's words yesterday…

> We embody masculine and feminine energies in a unique way… the unconscious regenerative Earth Mother and the conscious constructive Sky Father. These seemingly opposite qualities often prove destructive when used in and for themselves. Our work as Faeries is to bring harmony between the two—to take the gifts of the Father back to the Mother.

A young man shakes a rattle and stands up in a speckled dress. Despite the feminine reserve suggested by his old print garment, he is shaking with emotion. He reads a letter he has just received, recounting how a girlfriend has been raped in a southern city. The account leaves him crying over the violation. Several brothers rise to comfort him. We who remain sitting sing softly. Our brother is soon calmed but his anger against the rapist goes unresolved. He asks for our energy to help dissipate the anger, sending it back to the universe.

Though most of us have had no direct experience with rape, we *are* able to relate to some form of psychological violation we have endured. We rise and circle our brother. Our chanting intensifies. Someone sobs. Others are openly crying. We invoke our sisters; scream in fury; shout in defiance, a righteous rage. The rape of one is the rape of us all; all things gentle; all things feminine. The Earth. Our Mother.

A cool breeze refreshes us…an elder breaks the mood with a witticism. A proud silly sissy reminding us of the healing power of laughter. But someone among us dissents against laughter, demanding justice to all rapists. Another among us rises awkwardly, refusing to hate anyone, even Patriarchy—unwilling to transmute his loving into aggression and violence. Stunned by his emotional eloquence, the rest of us are silent as we wonder what can be done about the rapists. Somewhere in the circle, someone tells us…

Love them to death.
Love them to death.

Thus, our work is set. Let us move into the world, an army of lovers.

Someone else gives birth to a new chant in our midst. It sweeps us along like a regenerative fire…

> *In the beginning, we flew!*
> *In The Beginning, We Flew!*
> *IN THE BEGINNING, WE FLEW!*

The clouds move. The quality of the light is changed. Our vision renewed, ourselves made whole, now freed of anger we make our farewell embraces.

We return among you, reminded of our gifts and our desire to help heal Earth. In gentleness.

With laughter.

Lovingly.

Bursting My Chrysalis

by Sequoia Thom Lundy

WHAT HAPPENED IN THE ARIZONA desert on Labor Day, 1979? I can only speak for myself: I began life anew.

The Spiritual Conference for Radical Fairies was the epicenter of a period of personal transformation. The few years just before were a time of letting go of the past and intense soul searching for my authentic self. Twelve years before, I came to the Arizona desert from my Brooklyn, Catholic, Republican family, to reluctantly train to be part of the war machine at Williams Air Force Base, east of Phoenix. I knew the pilot I became was not the real me. Yet it was essential to measure up to the cultural norms of masculinity before I could feel powerful enough to reject them. That young lieutenant would never have imagined what was in store in that same desert a dozen years later.

During the 1970s, I joined the critical mass coming out in San Francisco. I took the bold step of declaring my gayness to the otherwise straight men who were re-defining their masculinity at the Berkeley Men's Center. I was amazed to be warmly welcomed and respected, even loved, by those men, some of whom are still good friends thirty-five years later. I marched in gay Pride and anti-war parades, buried my parents, studied yoga, meditation and massage, met my guru and rejoiced that my spiritual side had found a truer expression.

I explored the bars and baths that were the obvious place to look for love and was saddened to see that so much of "gay life" was an alcohol and drug-driven meat market, devoid of heart and soul. I acutely felt the dichotomy between sex and spirit that I had been taught at home, in church and in the larger culture, was now being painfully played out in our emerging gay culture. I knew in my soul there was a deeper connection that I had not yet seen manifested.

As my thirty-fifth birthday approached in the summer of 1979, I was ripe for radical change. I had even toyed with the thought of taking a "spiritual" name to express who I yearned to become and was inspired by the redwood trees during a yoga retreat at Mount Madonna. I reflected on the beauty of the name: "Sequoia" has all the vowels and is kind of androgynous. It also seemed audacious, even gran-diose, to claim it for myself.

When I saw the call for "A Spiritual Conference for Radical Fairies" on a bul-letin board in San Francisco my soul said, "Yes! Go!"

I joined my housemate Hal, who was a newly-out father of two young boys, and off we went in my fourteen-year-old requisite hippie VW van, complete with rag top that would give us full access to the Arizona sun. Upon arrival, I was touched to meet Harry Hay and John Burnside, whom I had seen just months before in the movie *Word Is Out*. I felt welcomed by these elders into a new family and tribe. When I wrote "Sequoia" on my name-earring, I had no idea that many of us there would be taking on new names to symbolize the new selves we were embracing and celebrating together.

The name stuck. The next year I amalgamated this new "Faerie name" with my family name and legally became Sequoia Thom Lundy. A friend gave me a book on the life of Sequoyah, the Cherokee who created their alphabet, and I learned that in Cherokee, the name means "peacemaker," a role to which I aspire.

Life has never been the same since. Within six months of our time together at the desert sanctuary, I let go of my former occupation as an instructor pilot and began teaching yoga and doing holistic massage. This would later evolve into Sacred Intimate work helping other men discover and deepen the connection between the erotic and the spiritual. I was also inspired to begin offering men's retreats with the intention of replicating the heartfelt connection of Faerie Gatherings in a more grounded, focused and intentional format; and to also welcome men of all sexual orientations who resonate with the yearning to openly love other men.

When I look back thirty years to that fateful weekend in the desert, my memo-ries are a collage of impressions: the amazing sense of freedom that two hundred of us brought from all over North America to create this moment outside all the cul-tural norms and strictures to celebrate aspects of ourselves too long hidden, denied or negated. I remember Harry speaking eloquently of "shedding our ugly green frog skins" to allow our true spirits to shine forth.

The most powerful teaching was during my frequent pool breaks to seek refuge from the blazing sun. There I often found my brothers frolicking playfully, innocent-ly celebrating our naked male bodies. By diving underwater and blowing bubbles on one another's wands, we created a level of magic healing my soul had longed for, showing me at last how sex and spirit truly are one.

Now, as my sixty-sixth birthday approaches—certainly another milestone—I feel naturally reflective. That weekend stands out in my memory as seminal—pun intended. My new, true self literally *came* into being in the loving embrace of my tribe of wise elders and loving brothers.

I am deeply grateful for the guidance that led me home to the real me.

A Re-Membering

by David S. Cohen

THE FOLLOWING ARTICLE, WRITTEN IN *November of 1979, barely three months after the first Faerie Gathering in the Arizona desert, seemed important for me to recover and share as a result of a recent reunion of some of the men who attended that Gathering. We came together in a private home in Los Angeles to view in one another's company the wonderful slide and musical meditation on that event prepared so lovingly by Allen Page and Michael David the year after the original event—part of an effort now underway to preserve that presentation on video cassette or laser disc. I offer this written "re-membering" out of a sense that it is time for other reminiscences as well—so that newer Faeries can see our shared history as part of a continuum of experience. Also because, since the Plague of AIDS has begun its work of devastating the tribe, the impulse to recollect and to tell the stories of our youth is strangely accelerated. We in our mid-forties are prematurely elders, even as some relative neophytes must become archivists, while the whistling shimmer of the scythe still sounds just outside the window.*

I have been tempted to rewrite some of what follows from the perspective of the past fifteen years. A phone conversation with Harry Hay some years ago about our having imported the term "Patriarchy" from the world of feminist scholarship leads me to have come, with him, to prefer the term "Androcracy"—as, technically, it is not rule by fathers that is at issue so much as rule by men, a category which Faeries, in their "Third-gender" status (not-men, not-women) do not occupy.

The incident, toward the end of this article, about the dark side revealed by a stranger's horrifying story—and an untold tale of the Mourning Circle that preceded our departure from the safe and sacred space of the ashram—can both be understood as foreshadowings of what AIDS would one day bring unmasked into our midst.

And there is, of course, the temptation to say more about particular personalities who have since clashed and formed some of the myriad fragments created when we look into the mirrors we are to one another—and shatter. But let these things pass; or wait for another day. May this fragment of memoir draw forth others.

It was I who bore the *thyrsos*—through the Exile and to the place of Home-coming. What I wish to relate here is what that detail of Sunday night's ritual at the very first Radical Faerie Gathering meant to me. I want to explain what it meant then and what it means now and to affirm how because of that I am changed. If at times I seem to speak from out of the fabric of dream or memory or moonlight, so it is; I write not only for you but as an act of recovery. I am trying to rejoin the scattered limbs, to renew and re-animate what time and distance and the condition of another life have again torn apart. I am trying—like the gay and Goddess-blessed culture we came together in the desert to celebrate and to invoke—to piece myself back together.

I had almost not brought the thing. As tall as I am and always coming apart, it was probably just show-offy in any case and beside the point. I would feel silly carry-ing it. But the flyer for the "Spiritual Conference for Radical Fairies" had asked that we bring our magic and our items of ritual; so I thought again. The object in ques-tion was a five-foot branch. Attached to its top was a honey-dipped pine cone from which vines of ivy might be curled down toward the base. I had fashioned it some months before in conscious imitation of the sacred staff known as the *thyrsos* carried in ancient Greece on Mount Cithaeron by the Maenads, the frenzied female wor-shippers of Dionysos—a god whose ecstasy and passion had struck responsive chords in my soul even before books or teachers had brought his image directly into view.

Like so much else in my life that has at first seemed random, pointless, absurd, or nonsensical, the branch and the pine cone had been gathered separately and for no apparent reason on different moments of prowling through San Francisco's Buena Vista Park. One night I was looking through a book of plates of Greek art and dis-covered just such a branch depicted in the hand of the god himself—and realized, with the uncanny quickening that always accompanies such essentially unshareable moments, what archetype was informing me and what I was to do. I connected branch and cone with a length of rough hemp twine.

I understand now, in a way I couldn't have then, how much having that *thyrsos* physically present in my room, standing unobtrusively in a corner, began a process of inner transformation, a kind of approach to Dionysos that allowed him to instruct me from within as well as from without. The Greek historian Heraclitus called him "The Lord of Souls." Looking back I can glimpse how subtly those depths began to open upwards into me with the aid of that concrete symbol, much as the masks of the divinities must have taught and illumined from within the actors who moved across ancient *proscenia*. Holding the staff and feeling earth-energy move up it; sensing it as a rod that also brought down currents from above; reading speeches from Euripides as I held it in my hand to brandish like a spear or lean on like a staff; arching it out and upwards as a large stiff cock—I played it seriously, as a child plays.

One night remains vivid. I lie in bed next to a lover who is no longer there, on the eve of my finally admitting to myself—after months of painful longing and evasion and denial—that my hopes for a future with him are self-deceptive and futile. I have held to him too tightly and he has withdrawn what once he offered so freely and generously. I feel betrayed, panicked and abandoned.

He sleeps; I am more and more awake. His beautiful body, his serenity and quiet breathing become torment to me as I begin to let go of all the ways I've lost myself in him and in the fantasies of our merging. The panic grows—I want to wake him but know that it is no longer an option. That it would only be a hook to try to reattach. When I reach out, it is to that staff standing by my bed and all the thoughts and all that pain come coursing through my fist and into it, grounding me, comforting me as once I'd been comforted in happier times sleeping a whole night with his scrotum cupped in my hand. I last through the night.

With dawn comes the sense that I have transferred my clinging from the human to the god—where it becomes something else. Not that the mourning did not come, but that it shed a different light. I feel close to Ariadne, the Cretan princess in later versions of the myth who is abandoned by the hero Theseus on the isle of Naxos after she has helped him slay the Minotaur in her father's Labyrinth at Knossos. It is Dionysos who comes to her then too, as lover and as consort, taking her as his priestess, shifting her perspective from ego to soul.

It is as if an initiation had been prepared.

Bits and shards of my character and history assume new meaning when viewed in connection to this ancient deity. Is it that womb I seek in the laps of men? Does it relate to the birth of Dionysos from his father Zeus' thigh? What connection might it have to the past dozen years of struggle to keep my faggot sexuality growing and alive in the midst of a heterosexual marriage? Isn't it Hera—the goddess of wives—who eternally seeks to dismember the Horned Child, to drive him mad? She represents a principle of contained energy and order with which he in the wildness of the natural world is utterly incompatible.

And what of Dionysos' early years in hiding dressed as a girl, or the fact that he is a god of women who, unleashed from their domesticity, run with him on the mountainsides holding baby animals to their breasts? And what about the satyrs in his entourage who are always erect and bursting with life, or the bull or goat torn to pieces every two years at his rituals in celebration of his dismemberment, as stand-ins for the god?

Were these not, all of them, images for me of the mystery of my nature—this vibrant uneasy collage of the female and the phallic that join and fight and become one another within me? Dionysian androgyny, I discovered, is not the balanced and ordered conjunction of medieval alchemy's hermaphrodites. There is ferocity and devouring; real death; a different sort of coming back to life. But neither is it just unbounded drunken frenzy and release as simple renditions have pictured it, any more than Dionysos is just a god of wine. He is god of all vital liquids—of coursing blood, chlorophyll streaming through the leaf; the surge of sperm with shining sweat; mothers' milk. Overarching all the passion and deep within the heart of it there is a fugue of unbroken silence.

All this that I have written was background then, of course, at the conference. Talking about it here directly has made it more the focus than it was for me then where so much else was happening. Perhaps one meaning of that conference for me is exactly the way in which it brought that background into focus, helped me to discover during those three days how much of my own background I tend to discredit, repress and ignore. I am learning through it how I have participated in my own dismemberment.

What I re-member now is what it was like to sit in the Faerie circle that first morning with these two-hundred other gay men and to realize that each of us had grown up believing that he was the only one of his kind. I felt from the depths of that early isolation how much I longed for a community of other men who understood.

> I will plant companionship thick as trees
> along the rivers of America, and along the
> shores of the great lakes, and all over the prairies,
> I will make inseparable cities with their
> arms about each other's necks,
> By the love of comrades,
> By the manly love of comrades.
> —Walt Whitman

We were a tribe reconvening. For centuries we had been parted. Our ways had been lost in the ways of the foreign patriarchal culture which had overtaken us. But now the members were re-Gathering.

Such was the myth. I became part of the group which formed with the intention of evolving a ritual for Sunday night. My staff, far from being a point of alienation, had become a kind of identifying mark, a point of connection with which I could teach or play or bless. Away from here it was a symbol of shadow—of what I held, darkly, inside; here it became persona—how I greeted the world and made my place in it.

I hid behind it too, of course, as all of us, accustomed to hiding, found our protections. We were not the ideal community out there in the desert—though in those early and euphoric days, it was easy to allow our wish for that to imagine that we were. But it seems important to remember that the common longing that united us spoke through the anger of the dissenters as well, as it also spoke through our defenses.

The planning of the ritual was itself an event—and fascinating to be part of as I watched the splits emerge between the intuitives and the organizers. I watched the ways in which decisions were arrived at, conflicts opened and compromises found. One point seemed insoluble. Some of us felt the site of the event should be outside the compound, in the desert itself, in the wilds. Others found that jarring, feared rattlesnakes and scorpions and thought the central area had ample room. I believed that staying too close to the encampment would tend toward an event that was a clever exercise rather than an actual opening to the unknown and the unplanned and so went with two others to see if an appropriate area could be discovered that would meet both needs—the one for safety and the one for openness.

On the outskirts of the ashram, we found a large clearing where candles could be set out in the middle to create a central altar as well as around the circumference to define the "ritual." Adjacent to an area just behind it was a wash where once a stream seemed to have flowed. We checked with the monks of the ashram. Yes, we could march the whole Gathering out of the front gate, into the desert and then up the stream bed a mile or so before cutting across to the clearing which—after that walk under the nighttime sky with the mountains outlined by the waxing moon's light and the clouds and stars all above us—would feel sufficiently removed from the encampment to truly let the sacred in.

My task was to meet the Faeries at the front gate and lead them with my staff in hand through the desert to the appointed site. I was delighted of course to be able finally to act the shaman I'd always dreamt of being; and stirred as well, sensing how real was the possibility of becoming the shaman I've always acted. I knew how much power was in that desert and in that Gathering, that staff, myself. And as the day continued, I became even more aware of how much power we conjured already, every time I looked into sets of open unclouded eyes or overheard conversations or watched bodies move.

Often on a street in a gay section of town or in a locker room, I've had to take a deep breath to absorb all that male beauty around me which I find intoxicating, sometimes to the point of illumination. As a youth in a small town in upstate New York, or even in the city sometimes, I found that terrifying and used to be on the edge of panic. Here, that panic had a different face. Breathing freely in open confirmation of desire, it wasn't panic but Pan I saw and all of nature was alive with Him and my whole soul quickened. I prepared for the night.

Toward sundown some cars remained in the clearing. I went there to see about moving them and to prepare the space with candles, as well as to prepare myself. I began to talk with a group of brothers from Louisiana, men who had been living together in a commune and who had between them a palpable love I found empowering and nurturing. As we talked and struck up an easy fellowship, I became aware of another man standing near who clearly wished to speak but held himself back. When invited to come closer, he hesitated. Then he said that perhaps he'd come back later as what he wished to say would change entirely the mood of our pleasant conversation. We encouraged him to speak.

His story was indeed horrible and his telling of it was often overwhelmed by releases of deep and violent emotion. A former lover was in trouble, he told us, a boy of nineteen who was to stand trial in the Deep South for a terrible crime—he was accused of participating in the rape and murder of a fourteen-year-old boy. The speaker himself was a complex of contradictory responses. He was filled with disgust at the crime itself and with hatred for what his friend was said to have done. But, at the same time, he was fearful for his friend's life and aware of how much desperation must be part of his involvement in such a thing if the charges were true.

As we held his sobbing body and listened to what he said, sometimes incoherently and from the bottom of his pain, I was forced to look at everything the idealized conditions of the conference had kept away from me. The still hideous repression of homoerotic love and feeling that was part of the creation of such a situation; the guilt and fear which *still* surrounds us in this society where the possibility of witch hunt is still so close. And the grip of sexism and violence that still holds us and destroys innocent lives.

"Still," I thought as I held him and looked into the crying eyes of the man across from me who was cradling his sobbing chest. "*Still. Still.*"

There was stillness. We were quiet.

I had deepened; the mystery had re-opened. I went back to the clearing for my things where I'd set them. By the *thyrsos* a friend had placed a mask he'd fashioned of a satyr's face that I knew I was to wear that night. I was quiet. I couldn't stop thinking about that nineteen-year-old boy who was sitting in that jailhouse when he should have been here or about the fourteen-year-old victim who—maybe—should have been here too. I felt deep longing in my heart for a world in which they might have been connected as comrade-lovers in a womb of mutual support rather than this world of competition and brutality. I sensed the darkness that was in me and in all of us and at the same time felt some other thing: the dark wisdom of the Goddess. I donned my gown. I put on the mask. I picked up my staff. It was later than I knew. No sooner was I dressed than the whole procession was there before me, faces gaily painted, singing, dancing like the Israelites before the Golden Calf. I had to silence them and began to dance in a circle before them, first slowly, then faster and faster, then held up my *thyrsos* to bar their way until all noises had stopped.

Finally no one spoke or sang. There was the sound of wind on the desert. At that moment, I felt my familiar self leave me. It was as if the person known as *David* had been put on hold for a time while someone else had charge of his form. My role had taken me seriously and I knew enough to step aside and let the deeper self act. I waited another moment, then held up my staff and pointed the way.

As the men passed, I stood and watched them. They became a kind of concrete evocation of the spirit we'd come there to embody. ("Faerie spirit, Faerie love," we all greeted each other later.) My experience of the stranger's tale had opened my feelings beyond my own resistance to them. Other channels had opened as well and I began to imagine all the faggots who had ever lived walking in that line and I saw my role as being greeter and guide, the doorkeeper who beckons and admits. I invoked all the gay men everywhere who still live in fear or in terror of their own true natures, or in fear of the terror of their neighbors who would harm them if they should sense that truth. I invited all the powers of the sky and of the earth as well and the Faerie saints I worshipped, most especially, Walt Whitman who'd invoked all of us in the first place:

> Come, I will make the continent
> indissoluble...
> With the love of comrades,
> With the manly love of comrades.

I ran to the front of the line pointing toward the clearing. On my way I stumbled and cut my feet, holding the *thyrsos* over my shoulder. I did not know from one moment to the next what I was going to be doing. And yet I distinctly felt that my every movement had been carefully planned, even rehearsed many times. At the other side of the wash I stood quiet again and pointed my staff toward the central altar. In the moonlight I recognized Harry Hay wrapped in a white cloth. We acknowledged one another.

All night I'd been aware of a conversation we'd had the day before about his research into the less-reported aspects of ancient culture, into the suppressed history of gays and Faeries. We'd spoken of the young men who'd gone into the wilderness between the settled city-states and had "the wrong visions"— women's visions—and had thus been banished from the patriarchs' circles. It was these men, he indicated, who had formed a culture in the bush, who became the shamans and oracles.

We nodded now, silently. He moved on.

As the last man passed, I removed my mask and entered into the converging circle to read the Whitman poem I've quoted here and begin the next phase of the ritual. My offering that night was the pinecone that had topped my staff. Some claim that on the outskirts of the Gathering stood illumined a white bull who watched for a time, then bounded away in the glare of an exploding flare. Just such a bull had been worshipped in Thrace as a form of Dionysos.

That night I lived what before I'd only known intellectually: that the most personal places in our souls are exactly the places that connect to the most profoundly shared ones. Walking through the wash the next afternoon, I was full of the memory of a walk I'd taken years before—one Good Friday in New York City—to the spot on the corner of Greenwich Avenue and Christopher Street where I was first picked up by another gay man. I'd gone to the city on a lost weekend, spending four days trying to get up the courage to really "do it." Then, I finally met a sailor on leave, at nineteen a year older than me. We'd gone back to an apartment I thought was his and, as the television flickered a re-run of *Frankenstein Meets the Wolfman*, had sex on a mattress on the floor. I was surrendering my virginity—full of relief and excitement and terror.

Suddenly the door opened and in swept my companion's lover. The apartment was his, I later found out. I quickly retreated to the bathroom in confusion, guilt and anger, where I listened to the outraged lover shrilly demanding, "Who is that little bitch in there and what is she doing in *my* home?" I laughed, though inside I was devastated and ashamed. I felt doomed to eternal exile in this frightening demi-world. Sitting on that curb, years later, I was able through bittersweet tears to recognize that what had appeared then to be an exile was in fact the beginning of a homecoming and an affirmation of my Natural self. My *thyrsos*-bearing walk through the wash that Labor Day weekend became for me a way of sharing that journey through Exile with all my soul-bound brothers, a way of affirming that all of us, re-awakened, were coming Home.

The Faeries Gather

by David Cawley

"TIME HAS COME!" DECLARED HARRY the Elder. "He-man has gone too far! Though our spirited are ever-young, his evils wear away these fragile bodies. Before we are called to leave them, let us gather as once we did in days past. I long to hear the music of laughter from our kinfolk."

"Oh yes, my love, yes!" exclaimed Brotherjohn. "I, too, would see our Faerie brothers and sprinkle them with sweet kisses and hugs."

DonBushbeard, joined in. "I shall help send the call. Let us form a circle and sing out with our hearts and voices." He stretched out his arms, closed his eyes and beamed quietly.

And so it was. From coast to coast, from north to south, silent voices sang out. And everywhere Faerie bells tinkled softly.

In the cities, wearing their Manmasks and gaysexobject garb, Faeries heard the call. Whether alone or in isolated groups, country Faerie ears perked up. The outrageous ones, the Quiets—those Faeries who were almost totally invisible, even to themselves—even they heard the call and set out to join the Great Circle, the Convocation of Faeries.

Meanwhile, in an oasis, far away, in the desert, SwamiBill, heard the call. "Friends!" he shouted to his little family, "We must prepare! Our Sisterbrothers come!" In his big heart there were excited little flutters but he added gruffly, "Silly-sissies all over our chaste little Ashramsweethome! I can hear their cackling now." He mock-grimaced and put his hands over his ears, but no one missed the twinkle in his eyes.

Animals heard the tinkling bells, too. Birds twittered, donkeys brayed, butterflies flitted nervously. "Dear, oh dear! Will they remember us? Are we safe to welcome them? Some look so much like He-man. We must keep up our guard and be certain they are Trueheart Faeries." They all agreed to be courteous but maintain their own space.

So the Gathering was set. Dust fell from many stiff, little-used wings. Some had never stretched their wings to fly before. They shuddered with apprehension and anticipation. Others who had once flown, only to be shot down by Manstings, wept. Their scars hurt deeply but they held themselves and each other and their tears healed them. Patching their tattered wings, they resolved to try once more.

A few Faeries heard the bells as they glided and danced in the air. Smiles sparkled and their brightly-colored wings made a rainbow for all to see.

"O joyous day! Calloo, callay! Sing to the flowers, shout to the breeze. We meet again!"

One small circle of Faeries from the City of Angels fought their way across barren desert land. The dark work of He-man's magic turned against them. But these were smog-smart Faeries familiar with the freeways. Peter Rabbit suggested to Lady Day that they make an offering of their large water jug to appease the creature that bore them across the miles. Slowly they made their way to the sanctuary, stopping many times to slake the creature's thirst.

At the Sanctuary, the Elders convened. Even with the light in their hearts, their Maleminds gave way to tiny prickles. Even so, problems were soon solved as they began to feel the waves of love rushing toward them. They knew everything would be fine.

As the opening date approached, even the shyer creatures of the desert, the rabbits, snakes and birds, peeked out to see the arrival of the multi-hued Faeries.

Midweek, three Faeries from the Northlands arrived on a high flyer: one from the Creek of Wolves, two from the City of Saint Francis, lover of small creatures. Elder Harry and the Seer Mitch greeted them and all were transported to the sanctuary. Each brought with him, as did all the Faeries at the Gathering, gifts to share. And they were greeted by hordes of butterflies decorating the entryway. Carl brought the wonder of flute and dance, LaRee had packed an extensive wardrobe of Silliness and Dayvd held his magic wand.

The earliest arrivals shared in the preparations. The aroma of baked loaves of love perfumed the air; pathways were cleared on the land, signs painted to mark the way. Of course there were a few un-Faerie like plans and details requiring attention, but everyone pitched in to help and soon all was in readiness.

Bright Faeries flew in from all around, scores in all descriptions, big and small, short and tall, dark and fair, young and old, rich and poor. Faeries, Faeries, as far as the eyes could see! And although there were many who could not bring their hard-selves to the Gathering, their spirits wove a tapestry of light and love to make their presence known.

The first great circle was convened. Invocations were made from points around the circle. Faerie voices sang out. Into the center of the circle they stepped, one by one. Each offered a feeling, some hope or an idea for all to consider and share. Time slowed down to allow the variety of styles to emerge. Faerie facets reflected in the waning sunlight.

And with each voice from the great circle, particles of crust and calluses fell away from each Faerie. Sighs of relief and relaxation joined to form a refreshing breeze. Soon they were naked; stripped of defenses, of anxieties and worries, free from the ugly, green frog skin that had hidden those beautiful Faerie princes. They were free, free at last, free once more.

For three days and nights did the Faeries delight. Splash, splash in the water they played, or sang softly in the shade; all loving one, loving all. Some had a ball. Others balled. Bland masks fell from Faeries' faces. Colors sparkled in their places. Dreamers of love, lovers of dreams, sisterbrothers on the mend, healing, feeling, reeling, soaring upwards. Caring, sharing the same cup, spirits rose, up, up, up!

Some sat in little circles and spoke their hearts with each other's words. A band of Earth Ones scampered out into the desert, discovered a dry streambed and brought buckets of water to make mudluscious monkeyshines in the sun, covering them with a coat of mud and decorating their bodies with twigs. A time beyond time recovered in reveling. Others danced and sang, paddled in the pool or were just quiet and contemplative. Hugs abounded and kisses flourished. Work was play and play was more play. And as those in the know are aware, many Faeries are horned creatures and have magic in their wands. Be they large or little, the Faeries loved to stroke those wands and to drink deeply from each other's horns.

Murraybear brought forth a circle of Faeries to touch and heal each other with their sex magic.

Dayvd offered to share his worship of Ouroboros, the serpent that consumes itself.

"Use the meditation tent" said Swamibill, as he knew the value of the magic Dayvd shared. And so many seeds were sown. Freely and openly, the Faeries made love, on the carpet of grass, in tents, on covers on the sand, Faerie to Faerie, man to man.

Then, as in a flash, like the white lightning that lit up the night sky, the days disappeared.

A great circle was called for the last night together. All day the Faeries flitted about with expectant smiles and goofy grins. Flowing gowns were draped; flowers adorned each beautiful, unique Faerie body. Faerie dust was sprinkled from Faerie fingers. Song and dances were devised and a path was set for the grand procession.

The lavender sunset darkened to violet. Clouds floated and stars sparkled, the moon filled with the light of Faerie love and rose to show the way. Musicians led the procession out into the desert night. Instruments blended in harmonies with the music of the night.

For a time a hush fell over the procession. Wonderment and awe brought tears to Faerie eyes as hand in hand, one and all, they met in the night. From out of no-where a white bull appeared to see what was disturbing the silence of his land and just as suddenly, he disappeared. A circle path met with the circle of Faeries who stood arm in arm and gently rocked around another circle spiraling into the center.

Again, invocations were made. Voices filled the darkness. Blessings were sent into the night—to the shadows, to the light, to the trees, to the hills, to the birds and the bees. Magic spilled from Faerie lips; calls to the glad to the tragic, to the peaks and the dips and to the Faeries' hips!

Beloved Davyd, the mythmaker, intoned words of love from our Forebear, the Whitman. We were a community of loving brothers, now and forever.

Phillip of the Moon gave testimony. Sing hallelujah, give praise! I believe in Faeries! I do believe! I do! I do! Make offerings to the Great Goddess: from Aurora, from Oakleaf, from Crazy Owl. Hurtful energies were released, healthful ones ab-sorbed. There was ecstatic dancing and singing. True lunacy abounded!

When the procession returned, Smiling Gene led a sit down, monkey dance; sprites dancing, spirits swirling, faster and faster, side to side. Then there came the delicate waterbrother ceremony, with jugs blessed with Faerie spirits, Faerie love was passed from brother to brother. Each served the other equally. When the ritual finally wound down everyone drifted off to sleep.

In the morning, even before a farewell circle could be convened, some of the Faeries had flown away. Reluctant to depart, one by one, they came to realize their duty. The Sanctuary had provided a breeding ground for new hope and ideas for the world within and without. The time had come to take that energy back to transform the old "realities."

A last sharing, a final invocation was made.

Tears of pain and anguish mixed with those of strength and determination. Round and round a circle of Faeries from the Southlands turned. Sensitivity and empathy we feel for our sisters who suffer as we do under the bloody fist of He-man: "Let us scream and yell and vent the rage! Cry! That his power be diminished soon. His dominion over the Earth has been unforgivably abused. No more! No more! No more!"

As it had begun, the Gathering ended, with tears like crystal bells chiming as they fell from Faerie eyes. Hugs and kisses and addresses were exchanged as departures began. Into the Man's machines the Faeries folded their wings and disappeared into the desert's dust.

But, in truth, there is no end, only sweet fare-thee-wells till we meet again.

Standing on the Shoulders of My Ancestors

by Eric Lichtman (Toozy)

WHAT DOES IT MEAN TO be "radical" in the context of being a "Faerie"? I really don't know. I don't know, either—what it means to be radical or what it means to be a Faerie.

Nevertheless, I was drawn to the Spiritual Conference for Radical Fairies in 1979. My friend and mentor at the time, Don Kilhefner, was one of the principal organizers. The Call drew me and several of my friends as well. There was the pull of curiosity, adventure, as well as friendship. There was something mythic, tribal about the event. Who would come? What would we do? Where do I belong?

Thinking back thirty years, I was probably experiencing a blend of personal searching, loneliness, spiritual questing, mystery, romancing and even asceticism. I remember meeting Don after a significant primary relationship had ended and I was wondering whether there was more to being gay than eating in gay establishments, attending dance clubs, marching in the streets and sleeping with someone. Was there a unique spiritual expression that gay men could share? With grace, patience and a bit of magic about him, Don had introduced me to writings of Carpenter, perspectives on Whitman and threads of history that could evoke a gay, evolutionary and spiritual tapestry.

At the Gathering, I tended to be shy as I recall all of the varied garb and diverse intentions that assembled on that Labor Day Weekend. As I find myself in most groups, when I am not in the center ring facilitating, I tend to gravitate toward the edge and that's where I remember situating myself for most of the weekend—on the circumference of the circle.

The sacred circles are probably my most vivid memories. Harry Hay would often be the master of ceremonies, as he and John were held in high regard as elders of the Radical Faeries and he would speak about the Faerie inside each one of us. It was wonderful, really. He was a bit avuncular in his advice and for me he became the relative who had stories to tell that enlarged my sense of family and inheritance.

I remember the multitudes of talented people who shared the Talking Stick and expressed their truths in the circles that weekend, many of whom I saw only once or twice afterward during follow-up events in Los Angeles or San Francisco over the next year or two. But aside from these wonderful connections, that Spiritual Conference for Radical Fairies was a singular event in my life and I don't know what longer-lasting significance it has held in my life since.

I have followed my interests spiritually (largely Buddhist and Jewish), deepened my friendships and professional life (college professor in Miami the past twenty-four years) and am partnered in a significant, life-long, cherished gay relationship. I believe that having considered myself a Radical Faerie, even for that summer or more, has given me access to roots that continue to nourish me. I am standing on the shoulders of many ancestors.

Behind the appearance of what many in our modern, western culture may view as "homosexual behavior"—I suspect there is much more going on behind the scenes with those of us who are living these scenes. Perhaps it's a liberating path that many of us have followed, to chart our own course and find our way, after we have been brought up by heterosexual parents and a hetero-dominated culture, with all the trappings of religious and social institutions (classrooms and media) that reinforce weird norms of behavior. At some point, many of us say: "Stop. This isn't right. There are other ways to be."

While some of us have allowed ourselves to be engaged by prevailing trends in the political sphere—equality, gay marriage, civil unions, gay parents, adoption, gay clergy, et cetera, which are not negative trends necessarily and provide many positives—there often is much that becomes occluded from the discussion when we try to assess our social progress as a people, as a tribe, as a family.

Being radical, for me, means being beyond definition, beyond compartmentalization, beyond religion, beyond even beyond. In that sense, the Spiritual Conference for Radical Fairies was an invitation to love and find deeper self-acceptance. It was an invitation to dance, to celebrate, to tell the stories of our lives and to discover our common, rich threads. And the weave from that hot, Labor Day Weekend continues to be one of the garments that I can wear proudly: I was there. I don't know exactly what happened. I am glad that I made it, contributed to it, participated in it. I am glad that it is a part of my history and my lineage.

My First Gathering

by Orlando

I'M IN A SCENE FROM *Welcome to the Dollhouse*, Todd Solondz' adolescent-loser film classic. The cafeteria fills with animated affinity groups of varying size. I'm holding my tray, wondering where to sit, so nervous my breath is coming in short gasps.

No, it's not a suburban middle school and I'm not Dawn "Dogface" Wiener. It's my first Radical Faerie Gathering and even though I'm way beyond my teens I feel raw and nerdy and conspicuous.

I spot two men I noticed earlier in the parking lot. Both handsome, a tad scruffy, with big smiles. Something identifies them as kindred spirits. "Mind if I sit here?" I ask. I'm giving a performance of a functioning person while inside I'm dying.

"*Please do*," says the first Michael. "*Of course*," chimes in his friend, the second Michael. How could I know that I would hit it off with these two darling men, or that both would become lifelong friends?

That was the summer of 1995. The Northwest Radical Faerie Gathering at Breitenbush Hot Springs in the Cascades of Oregon. My first, long-overdue immersion in Faerie space. What took me so long? Why was I so apprehensive fifteen years earlier, when my friend Mark Thompson, one of the original Rad Fae revelers at the 1979 Gathering in Arizona, spoke so rapturously of that first celebration?

I remember one of Mark's pictures from that Gathering: a circle of naked men is clasping hands, covered in mud, grinning like fools and howling at the wind. It struck me as unhinged, druggy. I couldn't imagine myself in that context. I now realize it was my own fears of intimacy and being seen that stopped me. Growing up gay in the dominant culture, with a father whose disapproval shamed me, I learned to be cautious to an extreme.

A lot of men who find themselves in ecstasy at a Faerie Gathering initially have to be dragged and cajoled. Maybe it's that term—"Radical Faerie." It sort of flies in the face of everything we're supposed to deny, both outside and within the gay tribe. How do you re-embrace something essential to your spirit when it's been drummed in your ear that you'll be sexier, happier, more successful if you don't look or act too gay?

I've tried many times to describe a Faerie Gathering to people. It's next to impossible. When I talked about it with my dad, who mellowed and tried to under-stand my sexuality in his later years, he looked at me with a puzzled frown. "You mean it's an orgy?" he said. Even when the person is gay, you can't get it across. Like a Grateful Dead concert, you have to experience it to understand it.

"What's going to happen to me?" gay friends ask if I encourage them to get their Faerie groove on. "Am I going to get hit on constantly?" "Will everybody be tripping?" "Will I have any privacy?"

I have a Navajo friend right now, a very gifted man in his mid-thirties, who is so clearly ripe for this experience. So clearly a Faerie spirit in his creativity, he has an innate sense of play and a deep understanding of metaphysical dimensions. But he's afraid. "It's not my scene," he told me after months of persuasion.

I understand. I think back to 1979 and 1980, when Mark gently encouraged me and I balked at that Boschian image of naked, mud-caked faes in the desert.

In retrospect, it's curious that even though I couldn't say "Yes" to Faeries, I found myself in a similar, mold-breaking culture. In 1986 my co-worker and dear friend Regan McMahon drew me into the Grateful Dead commonwealth—a big, joyous, amazingly friendly tribe of seekers, magicians and mainstream exiles. I saw between thirty-five and forty Dead concerts over the next decade, all with a group of dear and wonderful straight friends.

I think it was in that world—held by its random and never-ebbing kindness, its alchemy of musicians and audience and intangible magic—that I found a training ground for Radical Faerie revelry.

In 1995, I got a phone call from my friend Ira Ono, an artist/dancer from the Big Island of Hawaii. "I've been to a Faerie Gathering at this place called Breiten-bush," Ira said, "and I think you really need to do this. You'll love it." I guess the time was right. When the next Gathering came around I was there, not knowing a soul.

The Northwest Radical Faeries meet every February and August. Breitenbush, located two hours southeast of Portland, is an isolated oasis that also draws yoga and massage workshops, meditation retreats and a lesbian hoe-down called Women in the Woods. A river runs through it. There are meadow pools fed by natural steam vents that at night draw enchantment from a vast canopy of stars. A cluster of cabins is shaded in a spruce grove. No cars, no television, no cell-phone reception.

In fifteen years I've missed only five out of thirty Breitenbush Faerie Gather-ings. I fell in love. I laughed until my sides ached. I developed a stage character, my

reincarnation of Tallulah Bankhead that I played for nine years and have since retired. I took long, luscious afternoon naps. I joked about the veggie cuisine of tofu
and twigs. I made a fool of myself pining for unattainable objects of desire. I cried
at the bravery of men sharing their grief and pain and love at Heart Circle. I made
delightful friendships that enrich my life every day.

A Faerie Gathering is a vessel for unexpected possibilities. When I facilitated the
summer 2006 Gathering I wanted very much to convey this and energize my fellow
campers. I wrote this description in the announcement/registration form:

> At Faerie Gatherings we often find parts of ourselves—essential but
> dormant—rising delightedly to the surface.
>
> As queer men, we live in a world circumscribed by heterosexual
> norms: a world that sees us, even when it sees us kindly, as a marginalized
> "other." At a Breitenbush Radical Faerie event we are the norm. We define
> our experience, display elaborate affections and manifest parts of our nature
> that we hide in the dominant culture. A Faerie Gathering is experimental,
> exploratory, open to improvisation.
>
> Freed from the judgment and confines of our real-world experience,
> surrounded by loving and affectionate men, we feel the shudder of release,
> the recognition of a part of ourselves that we held in abeyance. Creativity
> and humanity, generosity and warmth, the sense of play that is so essential
> to our gay nature, the two-spirit humanity that makes us unique on this
> planet—all those gifts begin to flow.

Okay, I'll admit it. I sometimes get bummed or alienated at a Gathering. It's very
tricky to arrive with expectations of new and wondrous connections and then have
those expectations unmet. There's also a *lot* of psychic energy flowing and one has
to be very careful with one's self not be overwhelmed.

But a disappointing Gathering can easily be followed six months later by something miraculous. In February of 2009 I went to the winter Gathering, emotionally
shattered from losing my father three months earlier. My wonderful mother had
died two years and four months before him. My brother and I had the job of closing
down their home, putting it on the market, liquidating their clothes and furniture
and other talismans of their fifty-eight-year marriage. The good stuff we kept; the
majority we donated. There were legal and financial details to work out, a memorial
to plan.

Following Christmas, for the first time in my life, I had panic attacks and had to be put on the anti-anxiety medication Klonopin. I was very, very scared.

It was a month later, at Breitenbush, that I started to repair. Frolic, a marvelous new friend from Vancouver, listened to me for hours. He held me, cried with me and through the kindness of touch—and through the loving act of listening—he helped me to begin healing.

The landscape was enchanted that week: snow had fallen just before our arrival and was still fresh and powdery. Then, exactly at noon on Saturday, while walking from the Breitenbush lodge to the cabins, the softest feathering of snow fell on Frolic and myself. I'd never seen anything more beautiful.

And what about those two Michaels I met on my first retreat in 1995, during my *Welcome to the Dollhouse* moment? They're wonderful. Michael Brooks, a Seattle Web designer, wicked wit and spectacular tenor, recently designed my website. He picks me up at the Portland airport en route to most Gatherings and at the end drives me back to Portland while we do inventory on the weekend: who was in good form, who seemed lost or lonely, who was belle of the ball, who was transcendent at the talent show.

Michael Henry (Faerie name: Peppermint), a Portland coffee *wallah* and master pastry chef, is still my favorite cabin-mate at a Faerie Gathering. I can say *anything* to Michael and know that he'll hear me, not judge me and honor my confidences. I like to outrage him with raunchy humor. Sometimes we laugh like preadolescent girls.

I can't imagine where else I might have discovered these men or developed friendships this sweet and lasting. It was that way in college, but we all know it becomes more difficult as we get older and our lives become insanely overbooked. A Breitenbush Faerie Gathering is the exception to that: a respite of warmth and camaraderie in our lives. An experiment in loving kindness.

Ascent, Lament and Admonition

by Franklin Abbott

waking up the next morning
the dirt of Roan Mountain still on my feet
I let go of one long sigh
not of relief
but resignation to the fact
I am back

I lie in my bed
allowing the city to soften
and fade away beneath my closing eyes
hastening my return
up the moonlit mother mountain
up through honeysuckle-scented, star-silvered
   hems of clouds
to a morning of running water, birdsong
and a bright sun climbing to its solstice

there will my brothers hold me
turn me loose, set me free
there will I be heard, listen
and in concert sing
to the opening of hearts
and the laying down of burdens

the telephone rings
I have no charm to stop it
and so I am dispatched
to walk the city streets
expected to be the same
but I am now a better lover
my gentleness refined, aligned
and dangerous

SANCTUARY

A Voice from Short Mountain

by Leopard

WE ARE LIVING BY THE wisdom of our ancestors that envisioned communities of individuated, heart-centered, political, radical, "rootsy," fun-loving and caring faggot, dyke-and-gender-flexible shamans willing to do what they can to support each other in a real and conscious ways.

It is a vision that led to the formation of our Sanctuaries, places where we may discover ourselves, exchange and enliven ideas and ideals, redefine family, extend our networks and find safe space to challenge each other. A place where we can develop a radical, queer sense of our lives as much as possible, outside of the heteronormative paradigm.

They found lands in hidden, often neglected places and lived in close proximity to each other with very few amenities and little money, working for nothing other than to provide for themselves and those to come. Our Sanctuaries have become a foundational core in claiming our birthright as multi-faceted, radiant and colored jewels, as passionate, authentic and shameless homo-lovers.

In a world where a life sustainable through non-destructive, symbiotic interactions with natural cycles has been genocided out of existence and the perpetual war has become more and more perfected to wipe out the lives, cultures and ways of anyone holding out against global domination, the individual has been put into a crisis of isolation-created insecurity. We find escape in all kinds of practice: alcohol, TV, music, drugs, sex, the usual distractions. We suck in poisons and excess in our slow personal destruction. We struggle with over-indulgence and our indulgences are often what kill us.

Sanctuary attracts those who live—at least in their hearts—on the fringes. These places of respite, which our Faerie elders and ancestors have carved out for us as safe havens, allow us to be ourselves, if we choose. We can connect with our full sensitivities, with the forces of nature, with the truth of the seasons, with a smaller, more immediate circle of life.

I first discovered Short Mountain Sanctuary in 1993. At the time I longed for a more rural existence after several years of urban gay life. Unable to imagine a place in the country without having to return to a more closeted existence, it was chance and magic that led me here.

I connected with the Radical Faeries at the amazing drum circle held the night before the March on Washington, then landed directly in the freedom and excitement of the Beltane Gathering that followed. I found a beauty that emanated from a love of being, without anything to prove or having to define ourselves.

Here we lived closely around the log cabin, many days unfolding entirely out of doors during much of the temperate Tennessee year. Discovering a seemingly mythical existence in this world of trees, I listened intently to hear, to feel the love I imagined they hold for us. The sunny days were inviting, the rains dramatic, the wildlife free. Living beneath the circling stars, the moon cycle having influence, finding divine connection in being open to the magnificence of the embrace of nature.

I had found the end of the road, with caring queer people to share this experience. The idea of Sanctuary intrigued me. A place removed where we could live intimately, in our own way. We were offered the chance to reinvent ourselves through the mirror of each other, through identifying and letting go of attachments to the way things should be, always trying to come up with a "yes" or a thoughtful and considered "no," accepting and seeing the love and sadness in everyone, the circle of life so close.

The needs of work responded directly to the ever-shifting seasons: caring for a herd of milk goats, tending the gardens and orchards and vines; digging, seeding, weeding and harvesting; chopping wood, making fires; baking bread and sharing good food; playing guitar and singing along; massage on bathhouse nights, sharing the heat and companionship of the sauna.

A greeting, often a hug, touch is not unusual. We speak from the heart in circles as a revolutionary way of sharing our hopes, fears and observations in a listening space. We feel the subtle power and presence of the spirits and invoke snake wisdom by hissing our approval in circles, instead of clapping.

Chanting in the Memorial Circle, honoring Native American traditions in the Medicine Wheel, we imagine the global ley lines firing with light from the center of the maze. Gazing at the sunset from the end of Halloween Ridge, as others must have for generations, we hear the bell sounding for dinner.

Short Mountain Sanctuary began as a gift and belongs to no one. A half dozen back-to-the-land hippies found the land as an abandoned family farm in 1973. They built the Yurt, which still stands, as a temporary structure for fifty dollars in six months using reclaimed wood, covering its steep round roof with hand-cut white oak shingles. They built a small stone house by the flowing water in The Bottoms, with split tin cans for a roof, used for meditation and as a sweat lodge. They reclaimed the old cabin from hay storage and built a tree house, a small gnome tower tucked back behind the fenced-in garden. They cleared, with machetes and goats, what is now the garden and knoll, the orchard and backfield and planted fruit trees. Water came from a spring several hundred feet from the kitchen.

After a few years this group began to disband leaving Milo Guthrie to call the "Short Mountain Re-Inhabitation Project." At the annual Southeastern Lesbian and Gay Conference in 1977 he attended a discussion on rural queer living led by Mikel Wilson of the newly formed Running Water community on Roan Mountain, North Carolina. The vision became a Sanctuary for queer folk wanting connection to rural life.

Johnny G was one of the first to respond and once recalled hearing discussion of whether or not to install a hand pump to bring water to the kitchen. Some said it was a bad idea because dishes would begin to pile up. He told me with a grin that, of course, the water was brought in and, yes, the dishes did begin to pile up. He lived as the Sanctuary's closest neighbor for the next thirty years, until his death in 2009.

He and other enthusiastic queer communards drove off to the 1979 Conference for Radical Fairies in Arizona and arrived home inspired by Heart Circles, working in consensus, sharing equality and developing a consciousness of infinite gender.

In July, 1981, Short Mountain Sanctuary was formed as a land trust in the State of Tennessee. Core values included: no one owning the land or any property within it, no one being in charge, working together, living simply so others can simply live. We also developed a strong, supportive and shared power that honors the individual as well as the community needs. Homesteading and awareness of environmental impact were included in the mission statement. The place has always been dedicated as a Sanctuary for both gay men and lesbians, with no lists of work expectations and minimal structure. This simple yet clear vision has informed a unique way of sharing space that affects anyone who finds it.

Over the years, the Stewards of the Land and the Sanctuary have sustained these loosely defined ideals primarily through regular weekly meetings and monthly Heart Circles, requiring an openness and honesty from all concerned. The intention has been defined by those who are living on the land at any point, with input occasionally about bigger issues from an extended community that cares deeply about the life of the sanctuary.

Inevitably as the Steward body changes, as one arrives and another chooses to move on, the group intentions and values shift, sometimes noticeably, sometimes subtly. This has allowed the initial vision to grow and be tested by real interaction and experience. At the same time, there has also been a strong core of long-term residents who have given many years to this blessed land, inspiring newcomers to the possibility of this way of life, sharing experiences and knowledge, creating strong continuity.

Occasionally there are moves to define the agreements by which we live and clarify what Sanctuary is. This can be helpful as too many gray areas can cause anxiety in the community mind and makes us vulnerable. We are occasionally reminded of the "tyranny of structurelessness." However, a willingness to listen to every voice and working with an organic process, on a case-by-case basis, allows us a lot of flexibility to address situations in creative ways. While making for more complexity at times, an exploratory, experimental style of relating—clear, careful and compassionate—allows for more realness as we find ways to better address issues and conflicts.

"Come be part of an experiment that's working," we touted for a few years. It kind of replaced "where the odds are good but the goods are odd!"

The first Gathering was held for the entire hot-and-buggy month of June in 1981. The next year the Gathering was moved to May. The May Pole ritual has happened every May Day since. It is an incredible example of the free form yet connected magical celebration that Faeries conjure so intuitively, a joy-filled witchery that can only be felt. In this intentional, prayerful winding of our lives together, we strangers, friends and lovers feel a part of something so much greater than our selves. We are affirmed in our beauty and crazy wisdom, our open heartedness and love brought up from our soul.

So as it is chanted: "We are the weavers, we are the web."

A slow, organic community was structured throughout the 1980s, appealing to a particular kind of faggot and dyke. The feel of the place was isolated, insular and remote. Money, for the most part, was tight. It was an intimate scene, still relying on kerosene lanterns for light for many years until a couple of solar panels were installed. Cooking happened mostly on a wood stove. Housing was basic and small. The shower was a makeshift arrangement in the common room and it was a full day's job just to have a hot bath before a small bathhouse was built in the late 1980s. When *RFD* moved to the land it was originally printed on a typewriter and laid out by hand.

Then, as everywhere in gay life back then, loved ones began to die: Purli Sudds, our first "Empress" and dedicated networker; Linda Luna, who encouraged drumming at our fires in the early years; Michael Mason, beloved poet and stone layer; Dale the spinner; Manfred Ibel, one I know only from a photo of him playing a flute in the sweat lodge; and many other beautiful poets and dreamers, builders and gardeners.

The pain of their loss was palpable to the wave of newcomers to the land that I was part of. We felt a serious loss for not knowing those who had been so integral to the growth and formation of the community over the previous ten years. Our dead Faeries are honored at the end of a ridge in a stony circle of carved, painted and handcrafted memorials.

The land began to grow in prosperity and dreams of a bigger bathhouse and even a new kitchen were beginning to seem possible. Long-term residents began to build houses in the woods, removed slightly from the "downtown" area.

Manfred left a bequest of $35,000 for building and land improvements. The covered octagonal pavilion, providing the great luxury of dry space for circles and dances, was built in 1992. The decision to extend the bathhouse was easily made. Where and what to do about the kitchen needed some further discussion.

There were still four people living in close proximity upstairs and a proposal was made that, before work started on the kitchen, the Sanctuary would fund a house that would be built as a communal house. The idea started as a whisper and so from the beginning became known as "Project X."

I remember holding on to one of the old oak four-by-fours that stood in a row holding up the porch roof to feel the life that this wood had witnessed, acknowledging and absorbing the laughter, loving and tears, the meals and casual relaxed life of the past generation. I felt anxious about what might be lost and yet through it all learned about the inevitability of change and the value of embracing it.

The Gatherings continued to grow. The numbers of folk living here doubled in a few years. It was a trend that was being cautiously encouraged in the spirit of sharing the magic that existed. More space needed to be created.

The building went on for several years. Wide decks and a covered dishwashing area, an enclosed back porch, a craft room and other new spaces were constructed. The tree house was deconstructed and replaced by the house called "The Temple of the Great Whatever," where many amazing and jammin' dances have been hosted over the years.

The new Millennium came and the Sanctuary found itself becoming more relevant to a greater number of people. Inevitably the nature of the Gatherings changed and there were growing pains. Ways of relating began to shift and the collective reason for being together seemed less certain. It became difficult to exchange information during increasingly larger Gatherings and to know what brought everyone together.

One response was to recognize the value of "off the land stewards," those living near the sanctuary, as well as lovers of the Sanctuary, who began to establish long-term relationships to the Gatherings on the land. This has strengthened the sense of purpose within the community as a place of sharing resources and heart space, giving what we can and finding a common vision. It allows fuller participation and awareness of our impact on one another. It also allows residents to come and go with more ease, bringing our sense and understanding of being Sanctuarians out to the cities and other Faerie lands and households.

The neighborhood has also grown significantly. IDA, an adjoining queer community, has held a focus of art, music, theater, gardening and political activism since 1993. In 2002, a network of women and trans-identified people held the "Plan Z" conference at IDA. "Z" acted as their gender-neutral pronoun. It was a powerful addition to a scene that was largely male-oriented. It was encouraging to see how a group of people at first coming with a desire for separatist space—to which we were willing to cater—soon felt safe enough to be themselves within the flow of our existing culture. The "Z-ers" wanted to build a bridge over the creek at IDA to the part of the land that was intended to be for women-and-trans-folk-only. Help was offered in a non-threatening way and by the time the structure was completed more than a physical bridge had been built.

Plan Z introduced a fresh energy to our scene. In return, we gave others a chance to explore their connection to queer history, the joys of drag and play and an open door to our family. "Idapalooza," a queer music festival in the woods, became a homecoming of sorts for many of our trans friends and has enabled IDA to grow and to recently begin to buy their beautiful creek-side land.

In the late 1990s Faeries bought four hundred acres adjoining the Sanctuary. They built a large house, named "Sassafras," designed as home, studio and an event space. A community based on providing space and support for resident artists is now beginning to establish itself on this land. Land to the east of the Sanctuary was bought and then resold with a conservation easement to those who wanted to establish their own backwoods homesteads and communities, distinct from the Sanctuary.

Ha!, who had been one of the founders of IDA, by some miracle of money magic, was able to step in and buy one hundred acres immediately to the west of the sanctuary that was threatened by logging, which would have had a negative impact on the psyche of our Sanctuary. Later, the generosity of supporters of the Sanctuary enabled us to buy much of this land from Ha!.

Other Faerie community land projects in the area include the Creek View Retreat, Pumpkin Hollow and Whim-Away. There are now almost two thousand contiguous Faerie acres on the north side of Short Mountain, guaranteeing a wildlife and environmental preserve, as well as a creative queer space.

Most recently the ideal of sustainability has moved forward with the formation of Little Short Mountain Farm. In 2009, its first year, the wider community has come together to produce food for local families and supplement community gardens, while bringing renewed inspiration to those gardens and allowing the participation of many younger people wishing to learn how to grow food and work with livestock. "The Farm" is also the site for a new fermentation kitchen. These projects all grow out of the original inspiration of our forebears and long-term residents and equally reenergize it.

Everyone here is holding a gateway for others to experience the land and the life-enriching opportunities for social change that exist here. We are, as Crazy Owl once observed, as much a nexus as we are a community. Differing flows of energy meet here, energize and cross-pollinate. People of different classes, races and genders can find a mutuality within the context of this community and in the close relationships that form, challenging each of us to be more authentic, loving, human beings.

There is still much to do. Even the most far-seeing Faerie back in the early days would have found it difficult to imagine the Radical Faerie web and the role of Short Mountain in this very different world thirty years later. Yet by trusting their dreams they formed the necessary groundwork to give us the foundation and framework to bring forward a generous network of creative, life-affirming and diverse queer folk.

And so, may we inspire the creation of more Sanctuaries throughout the world. Both those of land and home and those we hold in our hearts. Each generation comes with their own understanding of what makes our queer consciousness more whole. Through example, respect, openness, consideration and cooperation, we will maintain this spirit home, this spiritual home and this real and earthy place of healing, social activism, magic and play.

It is fragile. Everything beautiful is.

It is only ours as much as we give it away with love.

Living on the Body of the Mountain

by Jan/Nathan Falling Long

Between trekking up to the 16,000-foot base camp of Annapurna in the Himalayas and entering a Buddhist monastery in Chang Mai, Thailand, to meditate for twelve hours a day, I received the first telegram of my life. My parents wrote to say I'd been accepted into graduate school.

So three days after I returned home—after six months in South East Asia—I dove into the high-paced, hyper-theoretical world of a late-1980s cultural studies program (think *all* the "isms'") at Carnegie Mellon University.

I had been involved in Radical activism—from no nukes to queer rights—and was excited about learning Radical theory. Yet soon after I entered the program I learned that the more you spoke with long and obscure vocabulary words, the more likely you were to be seen as brilliant; the less you knew of the real world, the more likely you were to float to the top.

I also realized I felt silenced as a queer person. The only other out person—a cool, tough, elder dyke—and I whispered our concerns and plotted our revolts, but they often fell on deaf ears. For a year I tried to play along, and though the university gave me a Masters degree and welcomed me into the Ph.D. program, I'd grown too critical of the program to stay. Most of the women students had left, the only African-American student had left, and as the only out gay male I knew it was my turn to leave too. But what would I do if not study?

During my second semester a queer-friendly friend from Baltimore named Peter Pan told me about a Gathering of the Radical Faeries in upstate New York. I didn't know much about the group, but something compelled me to hitchhike five hundred miles to spend a weekend on Blue Heron farm with this group of strangers.

I set up my tent, then fell silent, stunned by the ease of the people around me: they wore brightly colored drag and practiced yoga on rocks, they cooked communally and danced naked around the fire, they meditated in the field and had sex

106

in the woods. That is, they were actually living the ideals I had been reading about at college.

At the end of that semester I quit grad school and hitchhiked down to the Short Mountain Sanctuary in central Tennessee. This was in the spring of 1990. Except for a year my family lived in Alabama I'd never been to the Deep South. All I remembered about that year was learning nursery rhymes and being locked in a tool shed by older boys who threatened never to let me leave. My third night hitchhiking, I slept in an abandoned dirt road outside of Smithville, Tennessee wondering if I'd be found by rednecks and killed during the night.

In the morning I woke unscathed and looked over the endless green hills. Then I stuck out my thumb, getting rides from a series of locals, afraid to tell them exactly where I was going. Would I ever find the commune with the vague map they'd sent me? With luck, I was dropped off at the base of Short Mountain. As I walked up the gravel road, beneath a lush canopy of poplars, I was struck by how much this place felt like where I grew up, on a small farm on the side of a mountain in rural Maryland. For almost five years my family of five lived in a tiny three-room log cabin with only cold running water, a small wood stove and an outhouse across the yard.

After I walked for a half hour I paused at the lane heading down to Short Mountain Sanctuary to examine a geode I'd found along the road. I heard the sound of many voices rising through the trees. I looked out over the canopy of leaves to the hills in the distance, which seemed to roll on forever. This place seemed as remote as the mountains I'd climbed in Nepal.

I nearly ran down the lane, both excited and nervous, my backpack pulling me down faster. Around the corner, at the bottom of the lane, the trees opened up to an old log cabin and beyond it a farm yard with a huge tobacco barn and several outbuildings. Mish, a man with a white beard braided in pigtails, greeted me at the door and showed me where to find breakfast—hot pancakes with fresh goat yogurt, local sorghum syrup and strong coffee.

I sat on the back porch among a dozen other people, with my plate of food and mug of coffee. As I ate I heard a bell and a strange collective yodel from the crowd, which I could hear spreading all around me. It was morning Circle.

I started to eat fast, but someone stopped me. "Don't worry, that was just the second 'Yoo-Hoo,'" adding, "There are usually at least three and you have about ten minutes after that."

After eating, I handed my plate to a burly man wearing only a yellow apron and black army boots who was washing dishes in plastic buckets under the porch. On my way to the Circle, I stopped by The Chapel, a four-seater outhouse with no walls, but a domed, church-like roof. A few porn magazines and gardening journals rested against the divider between the seats. I looked out into the woods where a few old white goats grazed on the underbrush. One looked up, staring at me with sagacious gray eyes as if to welcome me. In the barnyard, men and women lingered, in punk or hippie attire, bright drag, or nothing at all. A few smiled at me, like they could tell I was new to the place.

I spotted someone in The Greenhouse and popped in to say hello. It was Greg, a man with flowery cotton pants, wireframe glasses and two pigtails. He invited me to garden with him after Circle. Beyond the barn, where over fifty people had already gathered in a rough circle on a grassy knoll, and beyond the knoll, stood a small wooden building, a large fenced-in garden and a path along the top of the narrow ridge that led into the woods.

I sat, trying to become invisible by concentrating on my breath. Someone announced a Tantric sex workshop in the afternoon. Then someone held a wooden flute, proclaimed it the "talisthing," then began talking about getting lost in the woods the night before and what they had learned from the experience. The next person talked of caring for his lover who was dying of AIDS and could not afford to come to the Gathering. Another spoke of the transition from city life to being in the woods these past few days. Slowly the wooden flute made its way around the circle to me.

I can't recall exactly what I said but I know I talked about my long trip to the mountain, the truck driver who had picked me up the night before and sleeping on the side of the road. But mostly, I felt unable to speak, my year and a half of graduate school filling me with a language that seemed to have no meaning here. I cried, feeling embarrassed and overwhelmed, trying to understand how I could feel at once so foreign and at the same time at home.

After Circle I found Greg and we walked through the garden, eating mulberries and picking greens for the Gathering lunch. We discovered we were both interested in meditation and decided to sit the next afternoon. We walked to the kitchen with a basket of greens when someone asked if anyone could help with lunch. I volunteered. But when someone came through the kitchen that afternoon and said the Tantric sex workshop was about to begin, I stopped peeling apples.

The workshop took place in a half-finished house in the woods. The walls and roof were up, but the windows and skylights had yet to be installed. About thirty men gathered and after some explanation and ritual we broke off into groups and slowly undressed each other.

Then we divided into two groups, one lying on the floor, the other standing. Those standing spent a few minutes erotically touching a guy who was lying on the floor and then moving on to the next person. The goal was not to cum but to stay in a prolonged aroused state.

Then we switched roles and I lay on the floor while fifteen men, one by one, touched me. For two hours we massaged each other while trance music played from a solar-powered boom box. We were told to pay attention to our breath, to breathe through whatever we were feeling or thinking, to let ourselves enjoy the sensations, but not to orgasm.

The Tantric Safer Sex workshop was supposed to be about exploring the erotic, but mostly I felt anxious. I was shy and private about my body and, at twenty-six, had been in only a few brief relationships. Still, I'd forced myself to come to the workshop, to undress in front of the other men, to touch these strangers and be touched, thinking it would help me grow more at ease and less self-conscious around other men. In an hour I'd experienced so many "firsts" I didn't even both trying to count them. Through it all, I remained focused on my breath—for as radical as it seemed, the practice was not all that different than meditation. By the end, I was in such a state, I achieved a few seconds of complete mental silence, a sublime state.

Then my mind began to generate thoughts again—*Are other people feeling this? Should this have felt more erotic than it was? What in the hell am I doing lying naked with thirty other men in a shack in the middle of Tennessee?*

For a moment, I could see these thoughts without attachment. They were endearingly familiar and amusingly petty—products of my worried mind I'd always been too close to recognize. Watching those thoughts and worries enter my consciousness, like drunken flies, made me laugh out loud. The rest of the room was silent, which made me wonder: *am I being rude by laughing?*

That thought—even more petty and more endearingly *me*—made me laugh harder, until I had to get up, leave the house and puke behind a tree. And even as I lay on the knoll after vomiting, I was glad I had made myself go to the workshop. I knew the next time I was naked in front of others—in the sauna or the bathhouse— it would be easier.

I spent the next three days of the Gathering as low key as I could. Though I talked to a few people, I was too shy to flirt and would eventually go off to sleep alone in my tent, listening to the beat of the drums late into the night. Days, I spent walking in the woods, gardening with Greg and otherwise hiding out in the kitchen making bread.

With a huge ceramic bowl of dough between me and everyone else, I felt both productive and safe. It was on the fourth day while in the kitchen that Gabby, another man with a long white beard, came in and said something that changed my life.

Out of the blue, he said, "So I hear there's a rumor that you're going to move to the mountain and bake bread for them."

"Yeah," I said, kneading the dough. It came out of me as effortlessly as a breath does every moment of our lives. And as soon as I had said it I knew it was true, though I hadn't thought of the idea before that moment. But once it became a possibility it felt a certainty.

I left the Gathering by the end of May to gather my things in Pittsburgh and earn a bit of cash. I returned in mid-September with all my possessions, excited to start this new life, only to learn as my ride drove away that there were no living quarters available for me.

"I told you when I left I was going to return," I said to a couple of residents on the porch. They seemed surprised I'd come back. "Hundreds of people who come through here say that," one said. "You should have written."

"If you want to stay," added another, "you'll have to sleep in the barn loft."

At that moment, I learned several lessons about communal life. To survive you have to learn the rules and customs. It's easy to be forgotten. There is no collective goodwill, only individual kindness.

Still, here I was. Sunlight poured through slats between the boards, illuminating hay particles suspended in the air above. A late-summer wasp droned overhead and chickens squawked below. I dropped my duffel bag beside a double mattress in the center of a large open space and lay down on the bed, staking this place as my new home.

I'd been a part of a lot of alternative communities—a food co-op, an indie punk band, group houses—but none had combined nature, alternative living and queer culture like this commune did. So, despite not knowing where I'd sleep come winter, I began the year-long process of becoming a Resident. As my membership project I organized the 3,000-volume library and spent my spare time baking bread, milking goats and helping to collect firewood. I worked hard, whether alone on my projects or helping others with daily tasks. But working jobs I'd chosen for myself never felt laborious.

At the end of each day the nine of us would circle in the one-room log cabin we used as a kitchen, for dinner, and hold hands. Our faces were illuminated by lantern light, the warm, fragrant air steamed up our glasses. Then we'd sit around the large wooden table to eat, telling stories as if we had spent the day far apart from each other.

After dinner we played an elaborate, invented card game called Crazy Queens, sang songs and talked about our pre-commune lives. Once a week we'd see a movie, out at the yurt, on a VCR powered by a gas generator. Occasionally we'd dress up and throw a party, even though we and a few neighbors were often the only ones who came.

After each long day I would crawl through the pitch black maze of the barn, settle under the covers and take in the scent of hay. I thought how wondrous it was to be living deep in the woods again, in a place where I could dress, act, cook, work and play however I wanted. Then I'd fall asleep to the sound of barn planks creaking and goats shuffling or rain tapping on the tin roof high above.

Mornings, I'd wake to footsteps crunching the gravel barnyard as residents headed up to breakfast. Within a month I could distinguish each person by the pattern of his or her step or the resonance of their voices.

Living on an isolated farm—without cars, electricity, phones or television—made every moment feel more vivid, and without visits from old friends, my previous life soon felt like an underwater dream. Greg and I spent the most time together, meditating, collecting wild plants for dinner, going into town for beer and sweets.

Like any family, the nine of us had our squabbles—usually over a dirty kitchen, neglect of a duty or collective money spent without consensus. But generally we got along, though at times I still felt so isolated, even during Gatherings, when hundreds of people would be on the mountain. My older friends or family would rarely visit and though I loved this life I wondered how to integrate my past and present, my Faerie life with the rest of my interests and history.

Winter came. We began weekly wood runs and I moved into a large dome tent at the end of Sex-Change Ridge. I slept on a mattress elevated by pallets and sat at a makeshift desk, writing long letters by lantern light to college friends who were now finishing grad school, getting married and buying houses.

At times I worried that if I left the mountain I would feel lost. I had no career, savings or even knowledge of popular television shows. But my life seemed freer and richer than the lives of my friends, the proof of which was the time I had to write long letters about making wine or tofu from scratch, or about how lovely the moon shone through the thick Tennessee fog.

A month into winter a resident left and I got a room above the library. Some mornings, I'd wake up early, bring a bucket of warm water down to the milking room and lead in the goats—Paranoid, Solenoid, Psyche and Sensei—one at a time.

Then I'd feed them enough grain to distract them while I cleaned their teats and squirted all the milk out of their udders into a steel bucket. Those moments were among the simple best, leaning against the goats' warm bodies in the cold morning, singing songs I'd made up for each of them, watching the steam from spilled milk rise off the frozen milking stand.

I didn't have a partner and I didn't hook up all that much. At times it was lonely. More than the queer literature in the library or the porn in the chapel, what made the mountain a radical place to live for me was how we behaved: we kissed when greeting each other, dressed in playful clothes, and talked candidly about sex and everything else. Between that and living off the lush, wild mountain, nothing mainstream culture offered was worth the trade.

Once a week we'd go into the nearby town to do laundry, eat catfish sandwiches and pecan pie at Kathy's Kountry Kitchen and hunt at the thrift store for warm sweaters and socks, or for dresses large enough to fit us. In winter, these trips—with their glimpses of electric lights, central heating, hot running water and flush toilets—were both respites from our simple life and reminders of why we had chosen it.

We agreed never to wear drag to town, but our long hair and bright clothes made us easy to spot. Some locals were friendly; others looked at us funny, guided their children out of our path, or even heckled us. A truckload of local boys once threatened to beat me up as I walked home. Another time someone piled a stack of tires at the top of our drive and set them on fire. But we were never directly attacked. Rumors circulated that we were part of the Manson family or that if someone descended our lane, he'd never come back. Although none of this was true, we didn't dispel those rumors. They seemed to keep us safe. This seemed a strange and wondrous form of Faerie magic.

That first winter, Greg left for several months, as others had, to make money and visit friends. In the coldest, shortest days just four or five of us remained to milk the goats and keep the fires going.

One particularly cold, clear morning, feeling a little stir-crazy, we all decided, as a meditation, to hike through the snow in silence to the top of the mountain. After breakfast we bundled up, damped down the stoves and headed out, shooing the goats back when they tried to follow. Then we hiked through the snow to the mountaintop. As we rested and ate sandwiches someone pointed out a bald eagle soaring in the sharp blue sky. Though I'd hiked through the Himalayas and had meditated in a Thai Buddhist temple I'd never felt as still and connected to the world around me as I did at that moment. We later learned it was the farthest south eagles had ever been reported.

The residents often said the true test was to survive winter. The constant cold, frozen pipes, long dark nights and isolation made many give up. But then spring came. The trilliums, daffodils, violets and harbingers-of-spring lit the forest floor. I could almost hear the buds push open on each branch of every tree on the mountain. The underground springs gushed and filled the streams and the goats rubbed themselves against us to shed their winter fur.

By April we closed down the wood stoves, opened the windows and doors of the main cabins and began preparing for our spring Gathering. I wasn't yet a full Resident, but I worked like everyone else, repairing the road and parking spaces, printing up and mailing flyers, ordering enough food for a hundred people over two weeks.

Then, finally, I got to greet new visitors as they came down the lane. I led them into the kitchen. I showed them where to set up their tents. I organized a drag show, cooked a pizza dinner for one hundred and twenty-five people, guided hikes through the woods and met a boy who became my Gathering date.

In less than half a year, I had learned how much responsibility and work it takes to live with others and sustain ourselves without most modern amenities. I had come to see the mountain itself as a quiet, unwavering friend, who might surprise me at any moment with a snake or a jack-in-the-pulpit, an ice storm or a sky full of shooting stars. And I had become comfortable enough with myself to find a boyfriend, who stayed on after the Gathering in the only space available—the barn.

I felt part of the land and the community. I would remain there for another four years until my partner and a creative-writing program called me away. Transitioning back to the outside world—owning keys and a wallet, dealing with traffic, having people stare at my pink or purple overalls and plastic daisy hair clips—was even more difficult than adjusting to Faerie communal life had been.

Now it's been more than ten years and I live, teach and write in the Philadelphia area, but I still don't feel completely a part of this culture, with its bright lights, cell phones, credit cards, car alarms and so many rules about how to behave. But I have become a part of it in many ways. I could imagine living on a commune again, though I would want one with a greater gender balance and a place where fewer people poured through.

Still, I like sharing meals with friends and housemates. I still like to pee outdoors and garden. I am a part of the Radical Faerie community, though for me, the Faeries have always been more about nature and the particular intense experience of living on the mountain than about simple ritual, Gathering, or queerness. When I meet up with a former Resident of the mountain we're usually drawn to each other in a particularly strong way, reminded of a quieter life.

And we realize how easy it is for all the lights and noise in this world to swallow us up.

Flight to Neverland

by Jonas (Peterpansy)

"WHERE ARE YOU GOING?"

"A Faerie Gathering."

"A *what*?"

Oh, how to answer such a question. Just what on Earth is a Faerie? Who are the Radical Faeries? My usual short answer: a nationwide and beyond community of queer misfits.

What is Faerie sanctuary?

My Dr. Seuss answer: Faerie space is a place to be. To be who you are; to be what you feel; to celebrate one another; to touch what is real.

My maiden voyage to Faerie-land happened to occur during the same year that I started working in a state institution for the severely retarded. Feeding, changing, bathing and loving people who were never able to learn fear and shame and repression of self, I was learning a lot about who we are as humans, as beings, as Earthlings, in our pre-socialized natural state. At the same time I sought out the Faeries and my imprisoned self came bursting out to play.

My first exposure to the Faerie community had occurred one year prior. It was 1993. I was twenty-three years old, barely out and in Washington, D.C. for the Million Queer March. I was living in a hippie co-op in Madison, Wisconsin, and had heard of the Radical Faeriess when Rainbow Gathering-goers mentioned Faerie Camp. I was curious. I was intrigued. But I was not ready.

As I danced along the Washington march with a drumming contingent from Pittsburgh, the Faeries came flitting and fluttering and bouncing and beaming…and barreling past us…and I shriveled…the flamboyance…the flaunting…the color… the confidence…the nothing held back. It was a circus. For me, it had to be Other. Still trying to hang on to more masculinity than I needed, somewhat of a macho hippie bisexual wannabe, I let them pass, not wanting to associate myself with such shameless gender-fuck.

Exactly one year later I was ready. I was fed up with the alienation I had felt all my life in general and as a sexually frustrated queer-commie-hippie-freak in a small college town in particular. Sure, there were plenty of alternative folk I got on with, but only to a limited extent, as my sexuality was mostly repressed. The town had queer folk, but I related to them even less. Basically, the other freaks were straight, the queers were normal and I was in a black hole. At least so it seemed.

So I went to New York for the Stonewall-25 anniversary celebration, intent on finding the Faeries. I was ready. And there they were, gallivanting up Fifth Avenue in a frenzy.

Drumming, dancing, circling, chanting, giant puppetry, nudity, fabulous drag... the creative spontaneous ritualistic energy I craved.

I was stunned. I was moved. I was ecstatic.

It was a magical whirlwind that sucked me in. With QUEER written across my chest in lipstick, it was time to come way-the-fuck out and get my freak on. I knew I was home.

I went to Short Mountain Sanctuary for the first time a few months later for the fall Gathering. Fifteen years later, I haven't missed a fall or Beltane Gathering since. Gatherings are where I fuel up for the year. It's summer camp. It's a family reunion. It's a reality check. It's where I thrive and where I shine and where I remind myself of who I am and whom I love.

Living in New York for the past twelve years, I have been lucky enough to experience Faerie space at home as well as at Gatherings. Many events bring us together throughout the year, my favorite being the Drag March, an annual commemoration of the Stonewall Rebellion. (And sometimes, more than others, of Judy Garland's life and death.) It was a collaboration of the Faeries and Church Ladies for Choice.

The current tradition began in 1994 during Stonewall-25 as a reaction to the ironic exclusion by Heritage of Pride (i.e. the main march organizers) of anything that didn't "look right." Like drag.

No drag queens? Hello? Who made Stonewall happen?

Since then the Drag March continues to bring back original visions that have been lost as the Pride Parade (which was originally a "march") becomes less political and more assimilationist and corporate.

So, on the Friday of Pride Weekend with a police escort—but without an official permit—we Faeries circle in the park and ritually march to cheering onlookers from Tompkins Square in the East Village. We head to the West Village, circling and singing "Over the Rainbow" as we make our way to the Stonewall Inn on Sheridan

Square where the rebellion occurred, where the modern queer liberation movement began.

In our best Faerie gender-fuck drag, we drum, we dance, we sing, we chant, we frolic…well, you know what Faeries do. But this time it's not hidden in the woods, but out in the city streets, which is more empowering and affirming than I can possibly say. A highlight of my year, it is moments like this that I am incredibly grateful for and oh-so-very proud of my Faerie family.

Thank you, Faeries. I love you.

Faerie Gathering

by Trebor Healy

Wolf Creek is one big 80-acre faggot
I've got a crush on

These ten days   have been
like one   long   slow   delicious   fuck
looking into that lovely faerie face
I can feel the smooth friction of the muddy land entering me

I see the shadows of his faerie wings
flitting across the moonlight
My body has become a pattern of magick tokens
offerings to this Great Faggot Spirit

My asshole opens like a rising sun to receive his hot Oregon day
Each morning   I open my lips   to kiss his faerie skymouth
and out rolls a purple moondisc from his smile

Oh my Whitman cock
sings like a cricket in his sweatdrenched night
and paints a jackson pollock out of blackberries and limestone

All the daylong I lick his drygrass chest
and hold his treebranch limbs
I watch him piss the clear coolness of the spring

I run through his red earth
like tears and blood and cum and mud and honey
  I like the bees that swarm around him
They're the faeries
Comin' for to carry me home

118

My chest is an altar
I've erected to my Wolfboy
and my heart dances under his moongaze
My arms move like my tongue through his breath
I whistle the pipes of Pan
rolling like an echo through the woods
I contort my body into a kiss inside his meadowmouth
All these forested hills are his goatee

I squirm around in his warm muddiness
I sing to him with my blood
My orifices echo with his laughter
—they are the pores of his skin

I bathe in his eyes
like cool waterholes in the 100-degree heat

I can barely contain the love of this iron cockring
of trusting faggots
faerie circle molten

Wolfboy heart
an opening timeless meadow
80 acres of sanctuary for fae ones
Our collective body
where we can sit and cry and fuck and share
and gather his magick seeds
—There are too many to count
falling from my open cupped hands
I feel like a big messy fruit
—And I am!
spilling my seeds and sweetness

Wolf Creek is forever

A   great   ripe   mango of joy
in my heart

SexMagick

A Faerie Falls in Love

by Mockingbird

Do you feel more beautiful because of my love for you?

You said you loved the shape of my jaw and the feel of my cock and my perfect ass as well as the softness of my hair and skin. You said you thought my voice was lovely and that was before you ever heard me sing.

The first time I noticed you, you were dancing by the fire, with no shirt, and I thought you were pretty. I was all whacked out and dancing and you told me you liked watching me dance. I thanked you and kept dancing and you told me your name was Jonas. I told you my name was Mockingbird. You told me later you thought that was a wonderful name and you'd been trying to meet me for days. And you didn't know I was trying to meet you too.

Mark said you were faun-like. I guess he meant "faun" and not "fawn." I could see that and I was worried I wouldn't be wild enough for you. I think you're more cat-like and when I'm with you my cat comes out. And I want to purr.

When I couldn't stand the smoke from the smoldering wet logs anymore I went wandering and I hung out with little Jeff in the smokers' tent. And Jeff told me about you and I thought "*Hmmm.*"

He had a crush on you (and on me, too, he said) and he told me a rumor that you'd said you wanted to be with all two hundred and fifty Faeries at the Gathering. If true, I thought that was a little extreme and was both repelled and attracted. And yet, I'm sure that was the moment I decided—or knew—that I wanted you.

I hoped for nothing more than a little sex. Who looks for love anymore? Perhaps when we don't realize we are looking for love is when we find it. How was I to know and how were you to know we were being woven together in intricate strands? Becoming more inexorably bound with each glance and each turning away of the eyes to avoid the other's glance in the paralysis of fear, the fear of naked revelation. How were we to know?

I was possibly the last person to find out that you wanted me. I told one or two people that I wanted you but was trying to keep it hush-hush because it hadn't happened yet. I really had no reason to think it would. I had no way of knowing except I thought you were looking at me. I just thought you were, and god damn it I should at least try to talk to you. At one point I walked up to you and gave you a hug. It was so tentative because I was so afraid and I wanted to hold you so much tighter and so much longer because somehow you'd already gotten under my skin.

You responded tentatively and we let go quickly because we were afraid. I didn't want it to look like a cheap come-on. But it was so much more than just a friendly Faerie hug. But that was all it turned out to be. And I wondered how long I would let my growing desire for you sleep inside me.

I loved the stony-faced expression you carried when I looked at you. I don't know if you gave that look to anyone else; a look that hid so much more than it revealed; the way one side of your mouth turned up as if you were just keeping it cool and under control.

I thought I'd been in love so many times but never like this before. When I left the Gathering all I could think about was you at the bottom of the hill and how I could have stayed in your arms forever.

One of Short Mountain's trucks came up the drive and Mitch was in the back of the pick-up. I got one last chance to say goodbye to him and to this Faerie land that I love. And he told me you were down at the bottom of the hill *melting* and I was melting too.

I told Mitch I was in love with you and I told him how I had heard you say that you don't like to admit to someone that you are in love with them. But I said that I thought you loved me even if you wouldn't say it.

Mitch said, "Well, he told *me*." You told Mitch that you were in love with me and I held on to that confession as I would to a raft in the ocean. If I didn't have that I felt sure I would be swept up in the waves and drowned.

Yet I already knew that. I knew it from your sighs, which were equal in passion to mine, and I found myself in a greater state of ecstasy than I've ever known. I was overcome that I could feel as I do about you and that you could return that to me. Together we were a new being neither of us had seen before. I already knew it.

When I asked you if you loved me that morning in your tent in the blissful moments we spent together there, you evaded the question. You said English was inadequate anyway and you distrusted it. Yet English is my business and so I must find the words and I shall gush words upon words for pages and pages in hopes of finding some kind of release, some kind of peace to quell or ease this passion inside that I am afraid will build up so much that I will burst.

And now I smoke cigarette and cigarette and see your beautiful face before me and see the love in your eyes and wonder what I will do without you. I shall keep wondering and I shall keep wandering until I should find my way back to you. What shall I do till I find my way back to you? How I adore you and how I crave to be with you.

How beautiful you are and how brightly you shine.

My First Saturnalia

by Michael Rumaker

In the back room on the way to the Faerie Circle:

Men continued to move by me in a slow, careful walk, still funneling through the half-light of the doorway past the jukebox, faces expressionless, solemn—lust appeared grim and unsmiling here, just as at the baths—not much different from the faces I'd seen on my first visit, yet each pair of eyes having that same alert watchfulness as the eyes of the young man leaning in the booth and the other by the jukebox, an intensity of scrutiny and swift appraisal that gleamed with an unmistakable light out of the heavy darkness.

As I watched him go, I could've bitten my tongue, thinking how foolish it was of me to spout on about the Faerie Circle and its Saturnalia celebration, extending invitations to utter strangers, idiotically trying to share my own excited anticipation, here, of all places, where interests focused chiefly on one thing only and much of it fast and not too choosy either. It was as preposterous as if I popped into the McDonald's over on First Avenue on my way to the East Second Street loft tonight and went randomly among the male customers munching on their Big Macs and fries, inviting any and all to join me in the evening festivities.

Here, any extreme taken, in ultra masculine drag, in stiffly posturing attitudes of apathy betraying the circular and receptive spirit, the curvaceous earth itself, not to be like women at any cost, to be free of the abhorred taint of women's blood, erasing the mothers in murderous denial, erasing the prints of their hands on us, the incredible gift of their breath and blood.

I thought of our little Faerie Circle, of all our past Gatherings and our Gathering again this night in the Saturnalia ahead, of our raised energies moving sun-wise from joined hand to joined hand, as in all the previous circles I'd been to and suddenly had a sharp physical hunger to be there, right that very moment, to feel that clear strength and unity again, that indefinable glow of affection, the bubbling excitement and levity that lifted me out of myself into airy regions of inner and outer space and awareness I'd never dreamed existed before.

What deserts we make of ourselves, I thought, watching the dim figures circling in the corridor, what aridities of flesh and spirit, the gods and goddesses, dead in these desolate worlds, dead to women, to men, to children of all ages—dead. This darkened booth in a darkened backroom of a porn shop in lower Manhattan, a desolation, a desert of desire, an illusory oasis and mirage of sensual wellsprings, a poor substitute for the forests and fields we played in in other days, in the fragrant nights of trees and grasses, still remembered and revered in the dangerous brambles and bushes, the dark places in parks we commandeer in service to Eros, as guardians of Eros; and womankind and womanspirit absent from center, daughter-renewal absent too; and the dry, inflexible hands of the fathers gripping us all; myself held too, forever thirsty, forever unsatisfied and always told, the hand on my throat, the boot, the foot, it's myself to blame if I cannot breathe.

Betray the fathers! Faggots, get up off your knees and learn sedition! Learn treason! Learn the reawakening of the heart, of affection and merriment and playfulness in service to the dark hags of ancient earthly wisdoms, bow down and listen, kiss their warts and leathery faces, kiss them on your knees and love them and the frozen spirit will crack and the meadow of the heart will be miraculously carpeted with violets and snowdrops and the first silver spears of the grasses of spring, when we are all made new daughters again.

At the Fairie Circle:

For centuries our circle, broken, the backs of women, broken—all under the marching feet of those who have forgotten how to dance. Now at long last, in this long turn of the year, our circle is whole again, these thirteen sons, faces like thirteen moons, remembering forked-root Cernunnos and the best of leaf-trembling Dionysus, in wine-drunk sperm-ecstasy entwined among each other, in senseless and sensual celebration of the shaggy musk of loins, of pot-high, the sweetly intoxicating singing of seed like the roar of a sea in our ears; that roaring loud in a room suddenly transformed into a huge prismatic conch shell, in the inner spirals of which our ears, held fast, are listening; hearing news of women truly loving one another again and that's a revelation and a revolution; and news of some men now, as here tonight, beginning to have love for one another, too, feeling totally alive in our bodies and that's also a revelation and a revolution and not the same old turn where nothing changes: changes everywhere in the air like pollen flying.

More and more I let myself be taken by their hands, turned from one to the other in a gentle and pleasurable turning, only once or twice having a flicker of doubt, when the mind asserted itself, wanting to take over again, the fear of losing control returning and I wanted to take back my will, which made me instantly lose my footing and stumble into their arms rather than sliding easily in and away on the palms of their hands. But I called on Kali again to help me, her picture among the candles vivid in my mind's eye and got my feet centered again, felt centered by her, placing them firmly on the floor, imagining, instead of my ego ruling, the suppleness of a snake coiling into my limbs, for the second time this day, letting myself drop again in lazy, rubbery loops, a black snake weaving its body around and through and from limb to limb of a yielding and sturdy tree of flesh, their arms the human branches I dipped and wrapped around in my snake-hipped gliding, trusting myself to the certainty of their vine-like hands, having renewed confidence that their wait-ing fingers, like tendrils, would be there to catch me and they always were, hands and arms as excellent snake-handlers as they were limbs of trees and knew then, in that moment of total surety and trust, the game was over and stopped my swaying and falling and stood perfectly still with eyes closed for several minutes till I sensed the circle begin to move apart and opened my eyes and saw the others looking at each other and grinning and I grinned myself…and we all burst into spontaneous and gleeful applause, as children will, in exhilaration after the game, several of us hugging and clapping each other on the back in an equally impromptu sense of high-spirited camaraderie.

And as I concentrated with the others on the healing of the earth, of its air and land and waters, the healing of the Earth Mother, my mother's own face appeared before me and when it seemed no one else had anything more to say, I mustered up my courage, saying that I, too, didn't want anything for myself, only wanted to speak to them of her, of a face now seamed with fear and anguish, reflecting a mind, a spirit, suspended and wandering in a shadowland where I cannot follow, try as I will each time I visit her, can only sit with her and hold her hands and comfort her as best I can with soft, encouraging words, the shadows deepening in her cataract eyes each time I see her. My father, her husband of forty-nine years, dead now six years and her behavior so unpredictable, walking around the little town in her nightclothes in the early hours of the morning, lost, confused, knowing less and less of who or where she is, forgetting who I am, forgetting all her children and all of those around her.

Her whole life given over to others, she has none now to give herself and none of us able to give her what she needs, or know what it is we could give her. Although she cried to me in a breathless, angry voice as I helped her get undressed for bed one night, "I wish I had my husband back!" because she is nothing without him, not ever knowing any other way—so that my sister and my other brothers, having tried to keep her and look after her as best they might, could no longer handle her, nor the one brother now living with her and decided, after many family meetings, she must be in some safe place, each of us finally facing that hard decision and agreeing to put her in a nursing home. And I knew she understood this without understanding, knew what was coming, even though she didn't know and can see the fear grow larger in her eyes each time I visit her, as the time approaches for her to go and the light gradually drains from her eyes as she slips deeper and deeper into the twilit place of shadows where there are no more names and I can no longer follow, having stepped out of my own shadows, for this day, anyway.

Much as I wanted to, it's hard to comfort her and make her feel less alone, less frightened in her going, which isn't just her going into the home, we both know that. I try to see her gathering darkness, which I know will also someday be my own, so that I might give her stronger solace and understanding, however awkward or useless, in this growing lightless place she's in in her mind, where she's screaming out the truth of her life at last, an illumination, as I listen and listen hard, not wanting to forget any of it. And the best I can do for her most times is get her to sing fragments of songs she still remembers, because she always loved to sing and help her along with forgotten words, phrases, the two of us singing "Oh, You Beautiful Doll" and "I Found a Million Dollar Baby at the Five and Ten Cent Store," sitting side by side on the front porch of the house where I grew up and where she has spent much of her life, songs I heard her sing as a kid and learned from her, following her around as she did the wash or cleaned the house and still remember.

The Devil's Prayer

by Tim Doody (Query)

My parents converted to The Church of Jesus Christ of Latter-Day Saints when I was four and I began lusting after boys.

I'm not saying the two things are related, just that they happened concurrently. I don't recall liking, in any but the big brotherly way, the two nineteen-year-old missionaries who knocked on the suburban door of my childhood home and promised salvation. My parents reacted to them far more strongly than I. Within weeks we were Mormon.

During the following years, we absorbed "gospel principles" and dedicated increasing allotments of time to church activities. When I was seven years old, my family got "sealed together for all time and eternity" in a Mormon temple. The stewards dressed us head-to-toe in white—even our belts and shoes—and they all smiled. We walked down a corridor filled with painted clouds and knelt in a ceremony room I can scarcely remember but for the white, the gilded gold and an altar of some type in the center. Afterwards, in the cafeteria, we ate saucer-sized cookies. When I asked Mom if this was what Heaven was like, she said, "It's got to be pretty close, huh?" And I nodded.

Back on Earth, by age thirteen, I started to grow underarm hair. My seventh grade friends and I tried to adjust to undressing together in the school locker room, casting furtive glances at each other's bodies and talking in amazed voices about how big Nate Shellinski's cock was. My hand brushed it once when, during wrestling in gym class, I scooped between his legs to toss him on his back. When we grappled again I felt tingly as he scissored his legs around my torso.

The same year I wrestled with Nate, the bishop asked me to speak during a Sacrament Meeting, the main Sunday Gathering for Mormons. I stayed up all Saturday night getting my words together. I walked, on wobbly legs, up to the pulpit and spoke about faith, the importance of belief in things not yet seen. I said that we could all access God, just as my band teacher told me everyone could make music, but if we're musicians, then Prophet Kimball, the leader of the Church, is like a composer with perfect pitch. I said I was glad for his guidance. I said that even though Grandma and Grandpa were no longer in this world I had faith that they were watching from above and coming closer to God.

With armpit hair came libido and in bed, day or night, I couldn't keep my hands off my cock, even if I still wasn't sure what to make of the corresponding fantasies involving wrestling and athletic clothing and sinewy chests. During a dodgeball game, I went to get a drink of water from the fountain. I walked by the open locker of the school's star soccer player and, after looking both ways, swiped his Umbro shorts. I hoped my grandparents weren't watching me *then*, or worse, when I got home that night.

Judgment Day terrified me as much as Nate Shellinski captivated me. Whether I read it in Prophet Kimball's book, heard him say it during a closed-caption television broadcast from Utah or got it secondhand, during a priesthood lesson, I was very aware of Prophet Kimball's council on "perversion." Masturbation could lead to homosexuality and homosexuality was a "crime against nature," a "deep, dark sin" that could even cause sinners to seek "satisfactions with animals."

I was sure he was right. My bizarre longings were my own fault, brought on by a complete lack of discipline. No matter how many pledges I'd made to God, I couldn't stop my sexual routines, not for more than a few guilt-ridden days at a time.

Soon after the Umbro Incident my priesthood teacher shared an anecdote passed down from Mormon pioneers which seemed to illustrate my predicament. He said that if you try to cook a frog by putting him in a boiling pot of water, he'll jump out. But if you put the frog in cool water that you slowly turn to a boil, he won't jump until it's too late. "And that," he said, "is how it is with you and sin."

Most days, I prayed to God at least once. I prayed to get through school speeches I hadn't prepared for and gym classes, which, despite the boys, I hated. Occasionally my prayers were more heartfelt—I expressed gratitude for my family and asked God to heal a girl at church who suffered from a brain tumor. During the rise of prime-time movies about nuclear war, I begged God to guide us towards global peace.

In fact, my prayers covered just about everything except the boys in gym class. The one time I explicitly mentioned boys in prayer, I wasn't speaking to God. What good would that do? He'd only get in the way. Instead, at approximately fourteen years of age I turned to the only one who would listen. "Satan," I said, "if you could make it so I can get with one boy, just one boy, I know it's what you want, too."

With that deep, dark prayer, I finally acknowledged, even spurred, the split between body and soul, between sweaty teen-aged locker rooms and transcendence.

While I had faith in the unseen, the Holy Ghost just didn't shout *"Here"* like Nate Shellinski did when the gym teacher called out his name at the beginning of the period. Besides, Heaven was a long way off. Far. Even after high school graduation. And so I waited on the Devil, entranced by the thrill and terror and awe that must have also overpowered my parents as they anticipated the Lord's return.

In 1992 I went to college in a northwestern Pennsylvania town two hours away from my parents' home. During freshman year, when I discovered the good-time qualities and numbing potential of alcohol, I stopped going to church, impersonated a frat boy and got a girlfriend. Always drunk, I never had to do too much with her sexually—except some late-night groping and early-morning apologizing.

During the time we went out, I watched my roommate John transform from a tormented closet-case—whose journal entries I read in secret—to a flaming artist who openly dated a composer and painted canvases of pop art bunnies and pastel-hued cartoon divas. Finally, in the first semester of sophomore year, I broke up with my girlfriend and told John I was queer. A month later I also told my ex-girlfriend.

I painted my fingernails black and finished growing my hair past my shoulders. I wrote "Recovering Christian" on the dormitory door in drippy red paint to emulate the lamb's blood of the Passover spattered on front doors to protect first-born sons from destroying angels.

I confessed to John that I'd read his journal entries. He laughed.

"I'm sorry, darling," he said. "If I'd known there was an audience, I wouldn't have made them so maudlin." Then he asked me if I'd met Trey yet. "He's a film major. Smart. A bit nutty. You two would get on smashingly."

John and I went to a party filled with the kind of misfit students that populate small college towns: renegade geeks, poets with drums in tow, budding radicals snickering about The Man, and hippies dressed in hand-stitched clothes. From the center of the packed room, I heard a voice that sounded like it belonged to a game-show host. John dragged me in after him, closer to that voice so obviously used to entertaining crowds.

The boy who was speaking had a full head of Greco-Roman curls, colored a Grover-from-Sesame Street blue. He was cute in a slightly cherubic way, as if he'd been unaccustomed to work. He finished an anecdote about failed sex by saying the only thing coming was the morning papers. Everyone laughed. Then he blew a stream of smoke from his clove cigarette and I inhaled the sweet, foreign scent. John nodded to him and then gestured his thumb in my direction. The boy with the blue hair grinned and said, "I'm Trey. And you must be Tim."

Trey and I went back to my dorm room sans John. We crouched into positions that Trey had clearly been in before and connected our bodies in ways I'd never even seen, all on the lower bed of the dormitory bunk. In the morning my cheeks were raw from whisker burns.

Several months and many sexual exploits later we sat in his bedroom on either side of an end table covered with burnt candles, stalactites of wax dripping to the floor. Trey looked directly at me.

"I love you," he said and I knew it wasn't true. He didn't know my favorite food or even my middle name.

"What do you…like about me?" I asked.

"How you see the world. Your legs in those corduroys. The way you jump into fire. Which is why—I'm dropping school and moving to Pittsburgh. To make films. Come with me?"

I leaned over the table and stuck my tongue down his throat.

On our first night in Pittsburgh, Trey sucked me off on the rooftop of his favorite club while the tenants in an adjacent building yelled "Faggots." And we laughed. That summer, we danced dervishes to New Wave tunes and stared into the flickering screens above the mostly empty seats at an art-house cinema. We perched in diner booths for incessant conversations as the sun set and then ducked into red-bulbed back rooms with designer kids on designer drugs.

Through it all, Trey displayed that incessant game-show host ebullience: the bawdy quip, the knowing smirk, each moment calibrated for maximum mirth, his and yours. If his routine seemed a little forced, I didn't notice, at least not at first.

Shortly after we'd moved in together, we went to his childhood home in the middle of a weekday. His mother returned home from work early and I had to hide under the bed because she'd already discovered enough clues to suggest that I was more than Trey's college buddy. Out of sight, I heard her fume about End Times and the need for a Christian Nation. Trey disarmed her with a quip, even made her laugh, if only for a moment, before the ranting resumed and I escaped out the first-story window.

I waited tables. Trey worked with a temp agency. After a few office gigs, he was assigned to a university bookstore. The third day on the job he came home with $400 in stolen cash, which we promptly spent on eight new CDs and dinner in an upscale restaurant.

Trey pocketed more and more money from the university job. The scam involved pretending to ring up students who paid for their textbooks with cash. His thieving was a habit, he confessed, that predated the temp agency. Several weeks after our initial shopping spree, Trey suggested that we use more of the money to go to Graceland the next day, no later than the one after that, why wait, why? I called in sick to work and we popped ephedrine and drove over the mountains of West Virginia, talking a thousand miles an hour.

We stayed in a hotel with a guitar-shaped swimming pool, wandered Beale Street, Elvis shades perched on our faces, and sucked down a bucket-sized bourbon and ginger that cost eighteen dollars. The wear and tear of that trip ripped a hole in the floorboard of Trey's car, near the gas pedal, and eroded the brakes. Back in hilly Pittsburgh, the only way to slow down was to pull the emergency brake. Trey still drove but kept it very local.

My relationship with my parents had degenerated to a bi-weekly phone call, usually with my mother. In our conversations she typically talked about everything but what she once called my "lifestyle change," which was fast becoming the defining element of my twenty-one-year-old life.

Trey organized the sixth house party of the summer. Over a hundred people arrived and it wasn't even 11:00 yet. The DJ began to spin trance records in our living room and when the LSD hit I swayed back and forth like a snake. The whole house shook. Knife-blade-thin boys and girls in baggy pants danced with robotic gestures while their eyes rolled back in their heads. A drag queen named Fifi re-applied her makeup in the kitchen. A mutual friend writhed on the floor and shrieked about the bugs crawling out of her head and the nearby answering machine.

The refrain of an old Sunday school song started to play in my head like a skipping record: "The Iron Rod is the Word of God." In Mormon scripture, the Iron Rod is a railing the righteous must cling to as they traverse a narrow pathway over the Devil's traps and into the Gates of Paradise. During each repetition of the lyric one of the Devil's traps flashed before me: a house of carnal delights, illustrated in a children's version of the *Book of Mormon* with fiery colors, people clutching each other and carousing, almost pouring out of the windows. They wore wicked grins that wouldn't—couldn't—last.

Later, Trey and I fucked in the bathroom and on our way out heard something in the shower. We pulled the curtain back and saw a naked man staring at the tiles. He didn't even flinch. In the living room, puddles of people writhed in the corners and the beat from the turntables pounded like a gavel.

"I've got to get out of here," I said to Trey.

On many nights in Pittsburgh, I walked the streets for hours at a time, past sidewalk drug dealers and souped-up Cadillacs and winos hunched in doorframes. I walked to release my jangled nerves and ease my stomach, which frequently got nauseated for three to four to more hours when night came on. The only way I could begin to calm down—and it often took most the night, despite my best efforts—was to try to think of nothing, nothing at all. Just breathe and walk.

While I paced the streets under the haze of a July smog one night, the moon appeared to be blood red, which is supposed to be a sign, a precursor to the Second Coming. My stomach twisted tighter than ever before and that was when I knew I needed help. The next day, after a phone call, my mother came in from the suburbs to drive me to the doctor. The doctor told me that extreme anxiety caused the lower muscles of my stomach to clench and block food from passing through. He gave me mild tranquilizers.

"Homosexuality is a sin," Mom said as she drove me back to my house. "It leads to great unhappiness." She used to look like Cher in the 1970s, but after joining the church she wore chaste dresses with floral patterns and wide belts and got plump. "You know I love you. I'm just worried about your eternal life."

"Okay, Mom," I said. "Thanks for sharing."

We passed through the orange darkness of the Fort Pitt Tunnel and emerged in the white of day, high up on a bridge, above the buildings of Pittsburgh.

"I've gotten some books about your condition," Mom said.

"Oh good. You've been studying."

"Do you know the vagina has three linings and the anal canal only has one? It's not as protected against disease."

"Really?"

"I want you to know you can change," she said. "The books will tell you how. They're in the trunk." She glanced over at me and I saw tears rolling out of her big, chocolate eyes. "Please take them."

"Okay...okay," I said.

In front of my place, she got the books out of the trunk: *Desires in Conflict, Homosexuality: A New Christian Ethic*, an entire stack like that. We kissed good-bye and when I went upstairs I stuffed the books in the back of my closet.

Over the next few weeks Trey and I ran in the same circles, to the same clubs, and coffee shops and parties. We were like Trey's car post-Graceland: there was no safe way for us to slow down. Staggered sleep, missed work days, drugs, film projects discussed extensively but never written, the ebbing and flowing of people who I'd dig or hate or feel intimidated by but who, ultimately, I'd never see again.

"I need a break," I finally said to Trey. A year after he first said he loved me we split up. We spent an awkward couple of months in the same house and then I moved out. I didn't see Trey for another month, not until a friend called and told me to watch a news broadcast on the television. Yellow tape and flashing police lights filled the screen. Trey, his hair now a closely-buzzed platinum, walked towards the camera with hands cuffed behind his back and cops all around him like he was a famous star and they his entourage.

"The twenty-three year old approached a tollbooth window, aimed his rifle at a clerk and demanded money," the anchorman said. "Lucky for the turnpike worker, a state police cruiser happened to be in the vicinity. The suspect tried to flee into the nearby woods. Dozens of officers responded and the suspect's weapon discharged during the chase."

It seemed as if Trey had decided that, instead of talking through another madcap scene from his film script, he'd perform it. I later learned that Trey had cut eyeholes into a pair of paisley boxer shorts to create a mask and had stolen a rifle from a mutual friend of ours, an NRA-supporting, drug-dealing writer. As the police chased him, he accidentally pulled the trigger of the rifle. Then he tripped on a branch and fell, which like everything else about Trey had a certain luck to it, as a state trooper had his back in the scope of a rifle and was poised to fire.

The guy who whisked me away after Trey and I broke up—I'll call him Boyfriend Number Two. I met him on a dance floor, where we moved closer together until his long blond hair got caught in my stubble. When I left the house I was sharing with Trey it was Boyfriend Number Two who drove me away, my possessions, including the books my mother gave me, crammed throughout his car. We left the city, bound for a western Pennsylvania town where billboards implored you to accept your Personal Savior with open hands and an open heart.

I lived hours away from friends and family. Just me and Number Two and the money from his parents. I had no job and neither did he. We did have lots of sex. His lanky limbs and mine, on the bed, off it, we spanked and cursed and fucked.

After the flood that summer, during which parts of town sat under a dozen feet of water for days, Number Two began to change. At midnight, he'd speak to the ghost of his dead grandmother, begging her not to hurt him, not to say she hated him. He screwed in a blue light bulb for these chats.

My stomach started to churn again. One night, while Number Two was crying and pleading with his grandmother, I dug through the closet, deep into a bag I'd never fully unpacked, and pulled out a book titled *You Don't Have to Be Gay*. Jeff Konrad, the pseudonymous author, said that he wasn't writing for guys who enjoyed their "lifestyle choice." The book was intended for those who were experiencing difficulties and would like to change. That sounded like me.

Konrad said that men have a legitimate need for intimacy with other men, but in cases like mine this desire for camaraderie gets warped into sexual cravings. It's envy, he said. You really want to have the character traits and body parts of the guy who arouses you. He is the person you wish you could be.

I devoured the rest of the books and their promise of a more peaceful future, one that might finally merge my spiritual and carnal thirsts. I didn't tell Number Two what I was reading and he didn't ask. But you should have seen us a few weeks later, when his grandmother made nightly visits and my re-emerging religion kicked in: him all wailing, "No, Grandma, please don't say that," and me holding the *Book of Mormon* in front of him, saying, "Put your hands on this and pray, God can help you."

A ring of men in beige and pinstriped suits stood in a tight circle around me. The bishop, who often wore a Santa Claus grin and had the belly to match, sprinkled sacred ointment onto my hair. My neck gave slightly under the weight of seven pairs of hands laid on my head. I closed my eyes, smelled soap, aftershave.

"Heavenly Father," the bishop said. "If it be Thy will, help Brother Timothy Patrick Doody to overcome his developmental struggles. Help him to walk righteously and find joy in his life." He said that I had many talents to offer, that youth was often a time of great trial and error, that the way forward may be difficult. When the prayer ended, everyone said Amen.

About a month after my attempted exorcism of Number Two, I'd returned to college and the Mormon Church. I knew my ex-boyfriends were crazy and wasn't too sure about myself. Still, Konrad offered me hope when he swore that he no longer liked to stick it in other guys at truck stops and had begun to perceive girls as the more attractive sex. I tried to follow his instructions: pray, learn to enjoy sports, don't masturbate. He said it was just a matter of time and faith and even if you didn't feel one-hundred-percent straight for a while, the act of trying would begin to make up the difference. Eventually.

Back at my parents' house, after a big pasta dinner one Sunday evening, I sat in the family room with my father. He said that John the Baptist, who was one of Jesus' closest followers, had been long-haired and wild just like me. He talked about his own past—the alcoholism, the whorehouses in Vietnam, the directionlessness. "You can't know what religion's really for," he said, "until you live without it."

That spring, church members spoke of the latest Mormon phenomenon from Utah—singles wards, or churches dedicated to worship services for eighteen to thirty year olds as well as to activities and socials designed to turn singles into doubles. Our leaders had just given the okay for a singles ward to be built in Pittsburgh. This caused me no small amount of anxiety, as a singles ward would be the fastest track to marriage and children, neither of which I felt quite ready for.

As the buzz heightened, the bishop asked me to speak during a Sacrament Meeting. Just like the other times I'd spoken in church, I lost another Saturday night to procrastination and preparation. The next morning, from up high on the pulpit, I looked down at the familiar, carpet-padded pews packed with people, some of whom I'd known for more than a decade and a half.

"Forgiveness is part of God's great plan," I said, "which is a good thing, especially for prodigal sons like me." The congregation laughed.

Then I talked about William Blake and his *Songs of Innocence and Experience,* explaining that the poet begins this sequence of verse by portraying a world of wholesomeness. After reading some passages depicting cotton-ball clouds, pastures and grazing sheep, I said that Blake then transports us into cities where poverty and vice and cruelty expose innocent people to the machinations of sin.

"But because Blake ends the series by again describing the cotton-ball clouds," I said, "he symbolically returns us to that sky where we started." I said he was showing us that we don't just move from wholesomeness to sin but that it's possible for us to cycle back to that initial state of innocence. I was stealing an interpretation from a freshman lit class, yet many church members leaned forward in their pews, interested.

Then I described how "my friend Trey" robbed the turnpike. Legs re-crossed and brows furrowed. My voice trembled. I said that even though he had to serve a two-year prison term, he could still repent and return to the path of righteousness. "It may be difficult," I said, "but everyone can change. Prophet Kimball told us, 'How can you say the door cannot be opened until your knuckles are bloody, till your head is bruised, till your muscles are sore?'" I didn't mention the context for this quotation: Prophet Kimball's "revelation" that homosexuals can be cured. Tears dripped down my cheeks as I spoke, dripped for bloody knuckles and Trey's heartbreak, for a future I didn't want to know and a past so difficult to escape.

I looked down at a couple in the front row. Gesturing in my direction, the man whispered something in the ear of his bride-to-be. Her mouth dropped.

Six months after the bishop blessed me, I sat down on a toilet, pants around my ankles. I'd just finished a semi-successful semester back in college and was visiting my family for a few weeks during Christmas break. As I sat there, I read a few paragraphs of an article titled "Same-Gender Attraction" in the *Ensign*, a Mormon monthly: "Whatever our susceptibilities or tendencies, they cannot subject us to eternal consequences unless we exercise our free agency to do or think the things forbidden by the commandments of God."

Then, beneath the magazine, something caught my eye: a scab, like a squished caper, near where my upper left thigh met my torso. Odd place for a scab, I thought. I scratched it off, dropped it in my right palm. As I lifted it for inspection, six little legs extended out like six live wires. My scab started to walk. I jerked back, an inflated balloon caught inside my chest.

When I looked more carefully at my groin, I saw dozens more "scabs." I jumped off the toilet and took one of my parents' cars to the emergency room. After a two-hour wait and a brief, embarrassing exam, the doctor told me I had pubic lice. He prescribed Nix lotion and instructed me to wash all my clothes and sheets in hot water. Worse, he suggested that I should probably tell my parents because I might have infected them or my three younger siblings.

Driving home, I reconstructed what had happened. I'd still been reading my aversion therapy books at college and contemplating their words daily. But one night at the end of the semester, with nothing to do in that small, beat town, I'd violated the Mormon prohibition on alcohol and gotten pretty tipsy playing a drinking game called Asshole. I was losing. And this scruffy frat boy had put his hand on my thigh and said, "Too bad, baby," and just the way he'd said "baby," I knew. When he grinned, I exercised my "free agency" by asking him back to my apartment for more drinks.

That fucker. I drove back from the doctor's office in a state of panic. I was convinced I'd infected my entire family. *Your twelve-year-old sister with crabs? Diseased faggot,* that's *what you are.*

After my mother came home from work that evening, I approached her—without getting too close.

"I slipped," I said.

For a moment, her eyes filled with tears, but she encouraged me to try again and said she still loved me. Then she collected the sheets and blankets while I got my duffel bag of clothes. We met in the basement and began stuffing the machine.

Even though my family remained louse-free, my face burned red around them for the rest of Christmas vacation. There I was, a decade after the onset of puberty, completing a distorted version of Blake's cycle: instead of returning to innocence, I was re-experiencing all the awkwardness, embarrassment and self-loathing that I'd felt during middle school gym classes—and all because I couldn't fathom a life unsanctioned by Mormon leaders. The crabs offered the kind of accident I needed, not because they scared me enough to escape the pot of boiling water that my priesthood teacher had warned me about, but because they made me give up trying.

It took me two more years to graduate from college; during a semester abroad in London, I walked into my first gay ghetto. When I returned to the States, I packed a rucksack and hopped a Greyhound bus to New York City and came out to my parents a second time. They'd suspected as much, but I wanted to make it official.

As for my relationship with the Divine: during the spring of 2001, shortly after turning twenty-seven years old, I traveled to Tennessee again, this time along back roads and byways, until I reached a wooded, remote holler whose residents claimed they dwelled and played "under the buckle of the Bible Belt."

It was under this buckle that a lanky guy, the traveling kind, painted mud on my back with his fingertips. I remember tingling as he traced interlocking swirls and dots, Dreamtime designs, a mandala that remained on my goosebumpy skin as hundreds of gay or gender-variant men, along with dozens of dykes, transgendered folks and straight people joined hands around a May Pole. In that moment when our hands connected, or seconds afterward, the sky clapped thunder, a kettledrum so loud, so close that everyone jumped and some squealed and others joked and didn't joke about magic and the magnetism of bodies.

"Merry meet," said a barrel-chested Walt Whitman wearing a habit, black eye shadow and pancake foundation. "Merry part. Merry meet again. Mary Tyler Moore."

He looked around the knoll at every face he could see and then threw his head back to laugh long and hard. He welcomed us to the Beltane ritual and encouraged everyone to take hold of the motley ribbons that dangled from the top of the fifty-foot May Pole.

We pulled them out from the center as far as they would go, until we formed what looked like the skeleton of a carnival tent. Then some participants began to orbit the May Pole to the left or the right while others zigzagged or simply pirouetted in place. Whatever our respective directions, the ribbons we held inevitably began to cross, to weave a web high above our heads.

Every aerial intersection of fabric drew us closer together and this increasing proximity triggered the eternal awkwardness in me, made me avert my eyes even though I desperately wanted to experience everyone. But the ribbons that stirred us around this cauldron on a knoll bound us even tighter, until I had no choice but to interact, to look directly at ecstatic faces coated in glitter, at kohl-lined eyes wilder than a wolf's, at crusty-punks in stitched pants and gender-bent gentle men wearing frocks and Lakota beads and flowers in their hair.

I stared at a platform-heeled queen and a slender boy wearing only a bedazzled skirt. I stared at a muscular, blue acolyte of Shiva and an elderly man whose hands perpetually shook while his smile spoke of second chances. All around me, a tribe who'd clearly grown accustomed to dwelling on the margins, to going beyond, to re-inventing and re-interpreting. It became impossible not to first receive and then give kisses on cheeks and lips and shoulders. Impossible, as our ribbons tangled and then we followed suit, not to touch and embrace.

The May Pole, a tree trunk we'd stripped of branches and shoved into a hole in the ground that morning—it was a fairly straightforward and ancient ode to fertility, to birth and re-birth. But then what of queers? How did we fit in the ritual, let alone the universe? "Don't you see, my pretty," the bearded nun had said to me earlier. "We're the ribbons."

Maybe it was the psychedelics coursing through me or the heartbeat of dozens of hand drums, but I couldn't just walk around the May Pole. I crouched to touch Earth and sprang up and spun. I whooped. When the skies began to pour, when my ribbon snapped from my fingers and the web above contracted and lowered, other ribbons began to gently ensnare me and I palmed the May Pole and gazed up this umbilical cord to the cosmos. Then, there he was beside me, now in my arms: another long-haired guy—so many John the Baptists here, so many unruly worshipfuls. We rolled together on the soggy ground while all around us rivulets of rain and glitter, mud and sweat and costumes-come-undone dripped down the knoll.

The Beltane ritual spurred on my evolving identity, but it wasn't the only encouragement I received. Eventually, I'd learn that, in countless cultures on six continents for over ten thousand years, the spiritual and the queer have been as intertwined as a double helix. Before the burning stake, before the stomp of empire, long before Joseph Smith started his religion, queers—the third and fourth sexes, the two-spirits, the *izangoma* and the *qedeshim*—nurtured and mediated and guarded and visioned and walked between worlds.

While I still occasionally think of Prophet Kimball and the religion I've left behind, more often I find myself thinking of Trey, the boy who saved his life by falling down.

The Faerie High Gathering

by Mac Del Ray

WE WERE TOGETHER JUST THAT one night and in the group for two days, as I had to get back to town early. It was the Gathering which Saul had always attended in its entirety, being a longstanding Faerie from the onset of this Faerie group. They were celebrating their twentieth anniversary.

It was my first big Gathering, although I had attended two other smaller Gatherings that year. I noticed him immediately. He cared about people and was always "taking care" that they were all right. Mainly, he seemed to be fussing over the owners of the land, a mature couple who seemed very devoted to one another after many years together. I didn't know why he was making me wait so long that night, while he checked on Ben and Tim up in the main house.

I had arrived in the late afternoon and drove up to the dining house, which everyone called the Erection. I stowed the grub I had picked up on the way, before setting up a tent that I had borrowed from the storage barn alongside the road. I decided to sleep in the cedar section, which was a secluded, shady area adjacent to the kitchen. It was hot and sultry that Friday in August. I was happy to shed my duds and wearing only my straw cowboy hat I joined the others.

It happened that I faced him in the Heart Circle. I hadn't noticed him before. He wore his usual yellow sarong around his slim waist and held a parasol. It occurred to me that his fair hair had, somehow, disappeared overnight. I soon learned, as Saul took his turn with the talking stick, that he had felt inspired to ritually shave his head at midnight the night before, to mark the changes he was about to undertake in his life. He had just completed a course of studies and would soon begin teaching in another town.

When the talking stick came to me I presented a gift to the community. "I have attended Gatherings for a very short time compared to most of you. It is my third Gathering and it is my first year here with you. I want to congratulate you all and to honor this land, which is holy, with this gift on this twentieth anniversary year."

I handed Tim, who was seated close by, a Buddha head of Thai design. "It is a Bodhisattva and I believe it can be a symbol of the holy and the Eros coming together and co-existing in this place, among us."

The talking stick eventually found its way back to Saul, who commented on the gift. "It's not something I know very much about," he said. The implication being that there was an interest there.

My turn to speak came again and I elaborated. "I must confess that I have an ulterior motive in presenting this gift. What I find is needed here is a space where one can go and sit quietly and contemplate. I need a meditation space away from the bugs and the rain where we can get in touch with the holiness inside us and all around."

Then a lengthy discussion began around the subject, each speaking their truth, according to who held the stick. Louie-Lou, with his belly sticking out round and pointy, as if he was about to give birth, was well known for his nicotine habit. He reminded Fry-Pan that he had been expressing his wish for a screened-in gazebo for a number of years, for the purpose of smoking and relaxing in nature, while not being bothered by it.

When it came time for Pilgrim to speak, he took the inverted bell which was filled with water and being used as a talking stick and, walking over to the Bodhisattva, he pouring the water over its head.

I beamed at the sight of this spontaneous act and commented. "In India, a ritual of devotion called Puja involves pouring water over sacred objects for veneration purposes."

Tim summed up. "Often a gift to the land brings a project with it. We'll wait and see."

The circle discussed at great length how we would proceed with the day's chores, which included moving the outhouse over to its new hole. I learned that Saul had taken upon himself the task of digging this new hole.

After the Heart Circle, most of the men convened to the outhouse where able ones joined in to lay it on some heavy slabs of timber. After some heavy breathing and concerted effort, it was done. Next, men on all sides raised the structure up and over the new hole. We placed large rocks and boulders all around to steady the structure firmly in place. Others found a wheelbarrow and shovels and covered the first hole with soil that had been prepared for that purpose. Saul and I both kept to these tasks. I noticed him carrying out all of his tasks in a quiet, methodical, cooperative manner.

When most of the work was done I went to the kitchen for a cool drink and returned to find that Saul was still hard at work. He was quite alone and his face was smudged with dirt. He had taken on a different, earthy persona. His bald head was sweaty and shined in the afternoon sun. He was placing sod where the outhouse used to be.

"You've been working so hard," I exclaimed.

I touched him on the shoulder from behind. I placed my hand on his belly and held it there. It felt warm and so I circled that area and passed my hand up to his chest and held it there for a time, lingering on the firmness of it. I eased my face up to his cheek and felt his energy close to mine. I started to break away, then heard him whisper, "You don't have to stop."

Saul turned around and we held one another for a long time, our lips lightly touching. Then, close to my ear he whispered, "I like you." I felt all new and special in my heart and I could only keep silent.

We walked up to the Erection and I served him a hearty bowl of homemade soup. Six or seven of us ate together on the porch.

Afterwards, a few of us went outside to the fire pit. Saul was there and I couldn't keep away from him. Approaching him from behind, I held him and then turned him around. I kissed him on the neck and cheeks and mouth. I didn't care if anyone was around, but I soon realized that people had cleared away and there were only the two of us left.

"I want you," I sighed.

Saul was quiet and kept kissing me.

"Let's go somewhere," I said.

"Later." He kept kissing and hugging me.

I didn't want to give up and said, "Later never comes."

Saul promised that we would be together later that night and broke away to take a shower outside next to the sauna.

The evening meal started earlier than usual because there was a show planned that night. It was one of the highlights of the Gathering. We began by holding hands in a circle around the table, giving thanks to the cooks and to Mother Earth. I said a silent prayer for Saul and me that we would be together later. I was very aware of him at table as he was sitting at the Foreskin (a section that had been added to the Erection.) He was at the head of the table and I was a few seats away, so we were unable to speak. Secretly, I was hoping I was on his mind.

Saul and I had prepared numbers for the talent show and earlier he asked me to be the MC for the show. I succeeded in finding a low-cut orange dress which went way down over my knees, practically to my feet; it showed my bare shoulders. I felt provocative in the warm night. I refused to wear a wig because of yesterday's heat but I did wear a pretty little pillbox hat with a net, a string of pearls and some comfortable, low-heeled shoes.

Saul and I did two numbers. I started with a Joni Mitchell favorite, "Willy," with as much fervor and passion I could muster. Saul sang a duet with another man named Saul, "Me and My Shadow." Both Sauls wore complementary black and white outfits. After a couple of good renditions by talented Faerie performers Marilyn and Miss Fi Fi, it was Saul's turn again.

This time he entered looking like a genie out of a bottle. He did an old Frank Sinatra song I had never heard, warning the audience of the dangers of falling in love on a starlit night. He was a great performer. As MC, I chimed in after the number, telling the audience to beware, as there were a lot of stars in the sky that night.

Reno did a number about California and I introduced him as "coming all the way from out West to be with us tonight." He played the keyboard in a melancholy kind of way and did a husky Willie Nelson song that was a crowd pleaser.

At the last minute I decided to get the gang singing along to an old Janis Joplin favorite, adding a stanza at the end: "*Oh, Lord, won't you buy me a meditation space. My Bodhisattva head needs a good place.*"

It was a hit. The finale was provided by Marilyn in a dazzling white gown. He did "Diamonds Are a Girl's Best Friend" followed by the sexy Miss Fi Fi, who lip-synched a lively number, inviting everyone to get up and dance.

I changed out of my costume and made my way to the blazing campfire. It was past midnight and there was no sign of Saul. Why did he need to be so caring towards everyone else when I needed him here beside me now?

Soon after he was beside me, saying he'd been up at the house checking on Ben and Tim. Shivering in the cool night air, I took Saul's hand and together we made our way, under the stars, to the evergreen grove. My life would never be the same again.

His tent was an exotic oasis, like a desert man's abode, tall enough to walk around in and spacious enough to sleep fifteen people. Saul stripped off the yellow sarong. Soon, I was naked, too. We caressed and my body melted into his warmth. I felt waves of energy moving from his body into mine.

I gratefully kissed his lips. They opened for me and I sucked on his tongue, hungrily. We went on and on in a slow deliberate manner.

We rolled over to the opposite side of the tent and unzipped the flap and stepped out. Standing naked under a moonlit, star-filled sky, I stood there with him holding me. The land was sacred and we were the holy sons of the earth and sky, joining space and time as one.

I felt blessed to be sharing such a blissful time. I could feel Earth Mother Namura pulsing through my feet and sending me her energy.

Returning to the tent, we had little time for sleep. But we did doze off. As sleep fell, I thanked my Archangel Michael for sending me such a handsome man. I felt from the depths of my being that something very important had happened.

When we awoke, Saul left for breakfast, and I meditated quietly in my dome tent. By the time I joined the group and had my breakfast, I was still quite tired. At Heart Circle, I felt pangs of separation, as I had previously decided to leave that afternoon. I expressed the need to hug everyone at the end of the Circle, but secretly wanted to hug Saul. At the end of the Circle, we ritually went around and had a hug from each man. It was painful for me to leave so soon and to hug Saul just like anyone else after the previous night.

I was dismayed that we did not have the chance to properly say goodbye. Had he said, "Stay one more day," I would have. But I did not—could not—have any expectations, as he had told me that he had a longtime companion—who wasn't a Faerie— waiting for him back home. As I drove away from the land my eyes filled with tears. I suppressed crying when I saw two Faeries standing along the road waving their goodbyes.

The next day, in the sunny garden at home, I was overwhelmed with thoughts of Saul and his whole being which had filled me with so much joy. It was a powerful feeling that had been dormant in me for many years.

I found watercolor and paper and brushes and painted Saul, in his freshly shaved head, with his bright parasol and me in my straw cowboy hat, walking together towards a field of summer flowers.

How I Got My Heart-On

By Michael David (Mykdeva)

I GOT IT. THE SEX GODS *came through and gifted me with revelations beyond anything I had expected.*

So I wrote in the afterglow of the first SexMagick Workshop I attended, in 1999, and those revelations have continued to inspire my journey ever since. Two decades after the life-changing experience of attending the original Spiritual Conference for Radical Fairies, I reflected on the impact that Harry Hay's work had on my life and I found myself wanting to go deeper in my exploration of commingling the energies of sexuality and heart.

Packing for the workshop, my mind races on about the possibilities—what situations will I encounter? What should I be prepared for? How far will I go? How many condoms should I take? Which sex toys?

In years past I had hesitated, but now it was time to go. More than once my dear friend David had visited me after attending SexMagick workshops, fresh from that heart space that I really only fully understood after I had been there and done the work. I was always amazed by his openness as he told me about his experiences and those sharings with him transcended how we had ever related before. Yes, I felt some apprehension, because I knew it would be about sex and so much could come up. But at the same time, it was precisely *that charge*—the knowledge that sexuality would be at the heart of things—that primed me for the work and inspired my preparations.

I know that what gets packed for a SexMagick Workshop is much more charged than what's needed for a generic Gathering. And if we don't bring that spark in our luggage with us, there won't be any smoldering coals to coax into flames. Those physical things—and the nebulous inner realms that they connect to within us—need to be brought to the circle, if only to serve as fodder. They're put in the crucible of the talismanic circle and brought to a boil over the flames of passion, so that they can be alchemically transformed into the pure gold of heart-and-dick-connected Faerie sexuality.

147

Apparently the charge around sexuality was felt by others as well. I had joined with one of my fellow participants to do some erotic massage after circle one afternoon. In clearing space in his tent and spreading out a blanket I came across a bag containing a variety of sex toys. I imagined that these items were a collection of his own sexually charged objects—what *he* had packed as he prepared to face the fire. A workshop titled *The Daisy Chain: A SexMagick Workshop for Radical Faeries to Explore Sexual Rituals of Healing* certainly impregnated my imagination with endless possibilities as I considered where it would all lead.

It was well after the workshop that I realized how some of my earlier life experiences had influenced my encounter with SexMagick. It was as if I had brought together all the most precious threads of sexuality that I'd accumulated through my life, whereupon the constant circling of the Daisy Chain spun and catalyzed them into some exquisite fabric.

The process had begun with my initiation into the Radical Faeries in 1979, which set me on the path that I had been searching for. I soon found myself studying belly dancing with an eye to shamanic ritual and its connection to the divine feminine. This led me to a dance partner, Inanna, a reticulated python, with whom I studied snake moves and communed with the cold-blooded reptilian brain, priming myself for the eventual Kundalini awakening within my own body.

In ritual practice and ceremony I learned how to pull cosmic energy into the circle, down from above and in from the four directions and started to experience palpable changes in the physical environment as a result. In addition, Ashtanga Yoga connected me to the life-force in my body and to the power of breath and the *bandhas*.

This physical practice brought forth a spontaneous heart opening and allowed me to experience profound compassion. In 1986 I became interested in diet and nutrition and the concept of dietary practice as a path to spiritual development. Healthy living enhances the vibrancy of one's nervous system and contributes powerfully to moving energy through the body, making it a natural precursor to ecstatic sexuality. These are the threads—the attunements and practices that I had developed as a Faerie—that I brought in my luggage to the SexMagick workshop.

As I danced around the sense of sexual *charge*, I made two resolutions for the upcoming week. I promised myself that I would do my Yoga series each morning. I decided that I would be open to any one-on-one sexual encounters available, but I would not take such activity to ejaculatory orgasm because I knew I could experience orgasms throughout my body, separate and distinct from ejaculation.

I understood the workshop process was to create a ritual space as a group and so I resolved to save my semen, to gather, to build and to hold my sexual energy for use in that group ritual setting, intent on having all that available for some ultimate release. With these things in place, I arrived at Wolf Creek and surrendered myself to the process.

The Heart Circle has been at the center of what the Radical Faeries do from the very beginning. The SexMagick workshop uses the Heart Circle as a key process for the work that goes on during the week. I have memories of Heart Circles in past Faerie Gatherings where my heart was coaxed open by a compelling story. Memories of being blessed to witness the spiraling of the circle as sharings built on the ones that went before, spiraling open the collective heart of the group. This was all in play in the Heart Circles during the workshop. But at the SexMagick Heart Circles another thing comes up. I wrote to one of my comrades about this.

After that Heart Circle under the maple tree, early in the week I came over to you and said, "Everyone's sharing has deeply touched my heart—but yours gave me a hard-on." I didn't mean it to be an enticement in any way and I sensed that you might have been taken aback, or perplexed, by my comment, which probably seemed like it came out of left field. So let me tell you what was coming up for me:

As we went around the circle that day my heart was opening up big-time. During your turn with the talisman you were sharing some of the incredible situations you have encountered during your life and I was witnessing your strength and your ability to learn, move on, grow wiser, more powerful—to become even more the unbelievably wonderful person that you are. My heart was embracing you fully. I was taking in your aura—your goatee—your forehead— your arms—your torso—your legs—your shoes and skirt. It was a full embrace.

In my heart I heard the words, "I could really love this man." Just then I felt an energetic connection with my groin and that warm tingly rise of attraction in my cock. This surprised me and brought me pleasure and it enabled me to see you also as a fully sexual being as I embraced you with my heart and cock connected.

Why is it so hard for so many of us to stay in heart space when sexuality raises its head? Why not embrace the sacred connection to the life force that having an erection provides? If only we all could be more present with these moments (me included). I wish I had lifted my skirt so you could have seen my erection across the Circle.

It would have been as natural for me to be flashing you with my hard-on as to be hissing in support of your words. I feel like we should lift the veils off the magic of our sexual pulsations. Maybe this could become a new Faerie tradition from the Daisy Chain. In addition to hissing or applause one could flash a hard-on if someone's sharing has really made the point.

Then the speaker could gracefully acknowledge the display and perhaps look around to see an entire circle with that reaction. Ah, well—work for future SexMagick Workshops.

As the daily circles continued I could feel the sexual energy within me growing. The heart space was really expanding and some of the difficult group dynamics were melting away. Outside the group process other activities gave participants time to share one on one or in small groups. One thing that contributed to my experience of the growing arousal within me was my decision to accept an older man's offer of an erotic Tantric massage after dinner one evening. This was a blessed gift before sleep that night.

On the next day we exchanged massages in his tent—which is when I found his bag of sex toys—and I learned some specific genital massage techniques from this man, whom I fondly remember to this day whenever I bust out some of the strokes he showed me. I had also brought one of my dance costumes and I did a seductive belly dance for the assembled group one night for the birthday of one of our facilitators. All of this sensuality, physical exercise and the heart processes of the workshop started to feel like foreplay setting the stage for something to come.

As Harry Hay had written on the flyer: "We achieve our vision by collectively creating—as the core of our workshop, (and for its duration only)—a Ritual Space within which safe and sacred precinct we freely empower ourselves and each other, to set aside our boundaries in order to experience the same total loving sharing with one another as we do in loving ourselves."

Our group worked hard that week, but try as we did, there were some boundaries that couldn't be set aside, and our group could not arrive at a full consensus about moving together into Ritual Space. This meant that I would not be experiencing a group culmination as I had thought, but it in no way diminished the power of the weeklong group process, which brought us all so much closer to real intimacy with each other. Here's what I later wrote to Harry and John:

Although our group didn't reach Ritual Space, by our last day together I was fully sensing the potential of what that experience would be and I was basking in the warm embrace of the heart space we had created. It was in this place that I had a connection with another Faerie that triggered an event in me that was so incredible, unexpected and SexMagickal that I've had a hard time putting it into words. After consulting several books with accounts of similar occurrences, I've concluded that it was a spontaneous Kundalini awakening. What a gift this was, another piece of the puzzle revealed and the crucible of the workshop facilitated that for me. I could not have done it on my own. I'll share some passages from a letter I wrote to that Faerie. I'd like you to see how your work is rippling out into the world in deep and profound ways as we, the workshop participants, integrate SexMagick into our lives.

On the last night at Wolf Creek I made it a point to visit that particular Faerie, whom I wanted to acknowledge for his repeated sharing about his difficulty with the gap between heart space and sexuality. I had been very moved to see such a sweet-hearted loving man struggling to find heart space in his sexual encounters with various men. I wanted to wish him well with that and I was touched by his obvious arousal in our exchange on the subject.

After our sharing, I tucked him in and retired to my tent. I tossed and turned that night and decided to rise early, hoping to find him as he was waking up. I found him in his sleeping bag and held him and caressed him and told him of my feelings toward him. I later wrote him about what had gone unspoken that morning. I am including some passages from a letter I wrote to that Faerie. I'd like him to see how his work is rippling out into the world in deep and profound ways as we, the workshop participants, integrate SexMagick into our lives.

When we were sitting across from each other, both very aroused from kissing and heart sharing, I was aware of our connections: our lips meeting, our hearts on the same level, each feeling the other's beat as we embraced, our cocks throbbing, the awakened serpent energy coiling in our loins.

I felt compelled to move my charged genital region to the proximity of your heart to make that energetic cock-to-heart connection. So I raised myself up on my knees pressing my erect cock into your sternum and holding it there. It was in that very moment that the culmination of the entire week started to unfold and what happened next became a peak lifetime experience. I felt a wave of compassion for you. I had images of your "acting out" activities that you had shared in circle, coupled with my perception of the bigness and true-spiritedness of your heart and I was pained by your struggle to come to terms with integrating the two. I sensed that moving my sex-center at full erotic attention right to your heart might be a way to energetically help you make that connection in your body.

What I wasn't prepared for was how completely on-target my impulse was. As I pressed my cock against you I felt this overwhelming urge to fuck you in the heart—to penetrate it sexually—to feel my hard cock squishing around deep inside the chambers of your heart. I moved my lips to voice those words to you and at the exact moment when I whispered to you, "I want to fuck you in your heart," something opened up inside of me. It felt like an explosion of energy went off in my lowest chakra—as if my spinal cord had become a shaft, a perfectly smooth cylindrical tube about three inches in diameter and the energy from the explosion had sprouted powerful wings and fluttered right up the space of my spinal column and flown out the top of my head.

"After the rush I had an eternal moment of feeling the complete unblocked path connecting all my chakras and I felt my body completely open for the flow of unlimited energy. I had

a tinge of fear that I could have accessed something so powerful that I might have been harmed somehow. It felt like I had literally jumped out of my body. That's why I said, "I just jumped out of my body." And then I collapsed like a rag doll because the energy release was so complete.

It was incredible, but what was that fear? I had glimpsed the face of the Goddess in a life-changing ritual at the Colorado Gathering in 1980, so I had been in this place before. This was a normal reaction when faced with the awesome power of Spirit in a much larger dose than we normally get in everyday life. In essence, it was the fear of God.

As I recovered from this jump into the spirit realm, I was faced with a bit of a quandary around the limits I had set for myself for the workshop. I wouldn't engage in sex to the point of ejaculation with anyone outside of group ritual space. My letter continued:

After collecting myself for a moment and assuring you that I was alright, I had to decide whether to disengage completely and leave you there (much as I had left you the night when I came to tuck you in) or to remain present to see where you wanted to go and to give you space and permission to go there. So I pulled back a bit energetically from my cock. I remember shifting my attention to my heart and to yours and just riding the mounting and rising sexual heat from our loins. I remember I was making motions with my hands moving my heart energy across the space between our bodies and pulling yours across the space to me. My mind went to thoughts of how to be the most fully present for you that I could be, at that moment.

I didn't want you to sense that I was holding back, that I would be holding and retaining my semen. I tried to think how I could help you past that, if on any level you were picking up on my restraint. The words that came to me were "you can go there" because I wanted to give you space and permission to take your energy where you would. It was a joy for me to be present with you in these moments—not having a direct way of knowing what you were experiencing but just trusting the space that we'd created, the work in Circle during the week leading up to this moment and letting all that come together to the point of orgasmic release for you.

Ten years after that culminating experience and thirty years after the first Gathering, I now find myself assessing how this all fits into my life. I've come to some conclusions about how to keep my cock-to-heart connection strong. I've largely gone back to masturbating as I did as a child, without porn and just a mirror, my own self, my own body, my own soul. I use breathing techniques and exercises and practices of semen retention. I enter sexual encounters with more heart and loving regard than most situations can bear and have learned much from this approach about avoiding interactions that block integrated spiritual-sexual development.

I've taken to heart one of my mother's favorite maxims: "If you can't fuck your friends then who can you fuck?" And try to leave the door of erotic possibilities unlocked, or even wide open, to those I consider friends. I've learned how to reach full body orgasms separately from ejaculation to the point that shooting is no longer the goal. I'm using the words "ecstatic" and "ecstasy" more than ever these days and that state is so present in my life that a *mula bandha* contraction and a few deep *ujjiyi* breaths can bring on a body shudder that feels like a harbinger of orgasm.

I remember saying flippantly in 1999 that I was on a spiritual path whose ultimate goal was to live life fully engaged erotically (with a hard-on) twenty-four hours a day. Obviously, this would be problematic in many social situations, so the revised concept is a spiritual path whose ultimate goal is to live life fully orgasmically engaged (with HEART-on) every waking hour of every day and I'm taking *this* approach more seriously.

Many Faeries have been on this path of heart-based sexuality, which is an important part of subject-SUBJECT consciousness. First, we have to work on ourselves to be that "subject" with heart and cock connected within. Let each of us enter the temple of our own body to do the work of self-love and self-pleasuring, so that we can find the ways these personal sex practices access spirituality and transform consciousness. By harnessing the spark of life that drives the universe, this essential life force that is the sexuality within us, and being able to move it up and down our spine, from genitals to the inner heart and then move it at will to circulate through another person's body, there we can find *subject*.

There was something, something building, in the entire group during the Workshop. I believe the power of group ritual can work in strange and mysterious ways. I think that more than just my energy was moving up my spine that last morning. It felt like somehow my body became a vessel for a larger group release. Was I a conduit for that energy to get where it needed to go?

I can't really know if, indeed, that was what was going on, but it certainly was one of those extraordinary moments that offer a really good look at what lies on the other side of our existence here. It left me with a deeper knowledge of how we, as Faeries, can use this SexMagick work to find the paths to ecstatic states in our group rituals and personal sharing.

I know that subject-SUBJECT consciousness can be our vehicle on this path of spirit and flesh connection and the merging of dick-to-heart energy. This is the realm of Faerie procreation and Faerie midwifery, as we spiritually inseminate each other and then birth each other anew as ecstatic Faerie beings.

A Coming Out Tale

by Carol Kleinmaier

IT WAS A RADICAL FAERIE Gathering in the summer of 1988. In the depths of Gaia's forest at Wolf Creek, Oregon, a dozen or so Faeries gathered at sunset, apart from their fellows. Amidst the huge old redwoods stood a circle of trees that had formed around the grandfather tree.

Here in their temple, Alain, Daddy Bear Rings, Daffodil, Ganymede, Harry and Mark formed another circle and joined hands. They were dressed, if at all, in colorful sarongs, flouncy bits of Faerie drag and leather jock straps, harnesses, or chaps. Most had adorned themselves with tattoos and multiple body piercings.

Each man took the talisman and spoke his intention or his prayer for the revels about to begin. They made music with drums, rattles and bells. They danced, they chanted and found themselves, spirit and flesh, in that timeless space "between the worlds." What might unfold here was unknown to the celebrants. But they stepped off the edge into uncharted parts of themselves.

By the late 1980s, a few Faeries had begun bringing leather clothing, harnesses, floggers and other accoutrements to Gatherings. For the most part these items never left the tents. In coming out as leather Faeries, this small band risked the opprobrium of their fellows, including Harry Hay, for whom leather and leather sex perpetuated an image of hard, even violent masculinity, antithetical to the ways of gentle-hearted Faerie folk and, well…a different kind of *radical*.

At that time leather sex was often viewed through a set of distorted stereotypes and, consequently, condemned by many in the gay and lesbian community. Radical Faeries were all about embracing "androgyny and the aesthetics of men-who-are-not-men" (one of the meanings of the name of the sponsoring group, No-men-us).

So, the leather was rarely exposed in public and leather Faeries grew increasingly frustrated by perceived limits to authentic expressions of self. Even at a Faerie Gathering, this safest of safe places, some "felt like outcasts among the outcasts," remembers Ganymede. But as Radical Faeries true to form, these leather folk de-

154

termined to follow their deepest inclinations, even if that took them into a new, controversial realm of Faeriedom.

When they wandered out of their forest temple in the early morning hours, they couldn't articulate, even to themselves, the mind- and body-altering experiences of that shadowy night. But they sensed that the night had been a transformative moment and was a turning point, a coming out for the leather Faeries.

A Blessing from Harry

What happened at breakfast the next morning wasn't wholly unexpected. Many in the camp were furious; some were very casual about the whole thing; others seemed shy when the topic came up. Much later, the joke went like this: A third of the camp was fuming, enraged that they had been forced to listen to shouts and shrieks and the heavy thuds of floggers on backs. And a third was peeping through the trees, straining to watch. Another third were in their tents jacking off all night, turned on but not quite knowing what to do. Between the anger and the joke, however, there was the wisdom of Harry Hay.

Harry took Mark Thompson aside at breakfast, saying, "Mark, we have to talk." Harry's friend for almost a decade, Mark had tried from time to time to tell Harry about his experiences South of Market in San Francisco. That day Mark tried to explain that someone could be into leather *and* be a Faerie. They talked on and on there in the Great Meadow at Wolf Creek. Finally, Harry conceded.

"Well, Mark..." (in his deep voice), "well, I suppose you're right that there are Faeries with black leather wings." Harry suggested that the leather Faeries might find a time and place for their own Gathering where they could focus entirely on being leather Faeries together. Harry was beginning to see a more integrated picture of Radical Faeries who are also leather Faeries. He had given the group his blessing and inadvertently, a name: Black Leather Wings (BLW). The first Gathering of BLW was held the following summer, 1989, at Rancho Cicada, a private campground in Northern California.

Black Leather Wings Unfolding

By the 1990 BLW Gathering at Wolf Creek, the first woman, Carla, was invited to join the group. By 1991, I and several other women (Stacey, Sharon and Neon) had gratefully followed in Carla's footsteps and were there, as well. A Radical Faerie Gathering had ended just before the BLW Gathering was scheduled to begin. A number of Faeries expressed interest in experiencing a BLW Gathering. They were invited. They attended and were a bit astonished to see women and, at mealtime, to find nothing for hungry vegans to eat.

Daffodil remembers it this way: "At that second Gathering, the one where Stacy cooked for us, some of the vegan Faeries were astonished to find 'Nothing to eat *and* women on the land!' Something very interesting happened. BLW had become known as an offshoot of the Radical Faeries that was so powerful and inclusive that some non-leather Faeries were drawn to the magic."

After the Faerie Gathering, almost thirty people stayed on at Wolf Creek for the BLW Gathering. They joined in with the leather Faeries and had their first experience of BLW. Ganymede also commented on this event: "That was amazing to see. Young men who wanted to experience what it was from us people who didn't know what it was but were busily doing it anyway."

A Very Harmonious Convergence

The leather Faeries who walked into that ring of trees in 1988 would probably agree that they were Radical Faeries to the bone, then and now. Just as early Radical Faeries rejected stereotypical gay male masculinity (think "the Marlboro Man" or the mustachioed "clone" look), BLW rejected the humorless hard edges and machismo of "old leather" ("Take it like a man!"). Instead, both groups adapted consciousness-altering techniques from various cultural traditions: powerful ritual, drumming, chanting, dancing, making music and the occasional judicious use of organic entheogens assisted people on paths of self-discovery and healing.

A uniquely Radical Faerie spirituality was sourced in a reverence for Mother Earth, the celebration of sacred sexuality, Wicca, paganism and shamanic traditions. Perhaps most importantly, there was a denial of spirit-body and male-female duality. Theirs was the land of both/and, where a multifarious ambiguity held sway and magic was afoot. Leather Faeries did not leave behind this rich spiritual tradition.

BLW continued the traditional Faerie Heart Circle, the living, breathing center of a Gathering. The land on which Gatherings are held seems especially blessed, a sacred space where connection with Gaia deepens and we walk with assurance that we are in the right place.

As Mark Thompson explains it, Faeries must find a private place, apart from others and free of reminders of mainstream culture lying in wait somewhere beyond the gate.

"A safe place to do unsafe things," says Ganymede.

Consider the enchantments of Wolf Creek, a mesa top in New Mexico, an abandoned mining camp in the Sierra Nevada foothills, Short Mountain, a desert just outside Benson, Arizona, Julie Andrews Point in Northern California and many more. These spots, too, invite processions, always a part of Faerie realms.

BLW processions, absent the wild creativity of Faerie wizards who sew and weave, are often central to BLW body ritual. It seems, too, that we usually travel a very long distance to get to a Radical Faerie or Black Leather Wings Gathering. I often think of this journey as a ritual pilgrimage consisting of three phases: the Departure (time for meditation on intentions, the gathering of sacred objects, packing the drag and other spiritual preparations); the Homecoming (reaching the destination and the great relief of hearing "Welcome Home"); and then the Return with its demands for reintegration into mainstream culture inhospitable to Faerie folk. We all know the feeling.

The Faerie Body

The emergence of the Radical Faeries in 1979 marked an evolution in gay male culture. Radical Faeries cleared the brush for the emergence of BLW, which brought together various strands of queer sexuality and shined a new light on leather sex. Both the Radical Faeries and BLW are deeply counterculture and take the body as a site of personal and cultural transformation and transgression.

The Radical Faeries play with kaleidoscopic expressions of gender and, it could be said, have passed on many of their idiomatic sartorial characteristics to the leather Faeries: fanciful drag and genderfuck looks, sarongs, jewels, feathers, the naked body itself and more atavistic adornments such as little goat horns peeking through curls.

For Radical Faeries, the gendered body became an experimental playground for the elaboration of new identities, new ways of living as gay men. Androgynous, duality-busting adornment of the body became the very image of transgression for the Faeries.

However, in BLW, particularly in recent years, the expression of identity through androgynous drag has morphed somewhat into expressions of *transgender* identity. Transfolk have been drawn to BLW Gatherings in large numbers. We span the gender continuum from crossdressers to transgendered persons who have chosen minimal or no medical intervention, to female-to-male (FTM) and a few male-to-female (MTF) transsexual folk.

Of course, there's always genderfuck and extremely festive over-the-top drag looks, for both men and women. For example, butch women in high femme drag. Gender fluidity is an essential source of Faerie magic, whether Radical or leather. Identity is not fixed. Definitions of "normal" do not apply. Boundaries give way to transformation.

For BLW folk, the body itself is a **means** for transforming consciousness. "Maybe it was possible to fly as high when tethered to a tree by a rope and flesh hooks as it was flinging about in a dress to the sound of drums and rattles. Both are shamanic practices, So why not employ both, perhaps incorporating one into the other?" Mark asks.

BLW is the resulting hybrid. In a 2006 interview, Fakir Musafar picked up Rajneesh's *Book of Secrets 1* and declaimed with great emphasis, "So Rajneesh says we 'pierce our nectar-filled body.'" Then he added almost in a whisper, "You can't reach spirit without doing *something* to the body."

The standard tools of leather sex—floggers, canes, ropes, blindfolds, clamps, et cetera—can provide a level of sensation to the body which can alter awareness and facilitate personal discovery. However, BLW folk wanted to move beyond typical implements of leather sex and reach deeper levels of transformative experience. This journey demanded that practitioners reconsider the phenomenon of pain and its consciousness-altering properties.

During the 1989 BLW Gathering, Fakir Musafar introduced adaptations of several body rituals from Southeast Asian and Native American traditions. The Sun Dance is a Native American ritual occurring in community over several days. Dancers are pierced once or twice on the chest. One or two hooks are inserted into the chest and attached with rope to the tops of tall trees. Celebrants pull on the hooks until they break through the flesh.

Hindu body rituals, the Ball Dance and Kavadi, also involve piercing. In the Ball Dance celebrants are pierced on chests, backs, arms, or legs. Objects such as fruit, bells, or brightly colored balls are hung from the piercings. Participants dance until the fruit flies free.

The Kavadi involves celebrants placing a wooden or metal frame across their shoulders, representative of an altar, through which as many as one hundred sharp metal rods are inserted into the flesh. Body ritual is practiced by BLW with heartfelt attention to the sacralization of the environment, spiritual intentions of celebrants and to awareness of the origins and cultural significance of the ritual. For BLW folk, body ritual and intense sensation—or pain—constitute a chosen path to spiritual awareness, personal transformation and a reintegration of body and spirit.

A Darkening Sky

In the early 1980s, only a few years after the first Radical Faerie Gathering in Benson, Arizona, there came the specter of HIV-AIDS and with it unrelenting loss of friends and lovers.

From the beginning, Faerie and BLW folk recognized the healing capacities of community and Heart Circles, where pain could be spoken out loud, screamed out loud and the burden taken up by the entire community. For BLW, extreme body ritual became an act of survival.

In my experience of body ritual I have found that for a moment or hours there is no fear, no uncertainty, no loss, only aliveness in body and spirit. The chosen pain heals the pain over which I have no control. My surrender to the spears and piercing needles gives me a sense of power: if I can make it through such a powerful, consciousness-altering experience, perhaps I can also support my friends through their deaths and go on living without them.

Of the Sun Dance, Mark writes, "The Sun Dance, holiest of all Native American ceremonies, was reenacted as a life-affirming sacrifice during the worst time of the HIV-AIDS epidemic. Experiencing these 'little deaths' helped make the terror of so many permanent ones more palatable. Baring spirit and the flesh in such audacious ways inexorably strengthened us for the grim days still ahead." This was Mark's direct experience of the Sun Dance, as well as responses observed in others.

How Faeries Dance

Dancer Redflower tells his story of Thanksgiving weekend, 1984.

"I found myself at my first Gathering of Radical Fairies in Mendocino. One night I went down to the lodge to dance, expecting the sort of dancing I had seen in gay bars. But I got one of the most profound shocks of my life. There was a wooden cabin, candles, drummers, people dressed in everything from full drag to nothing, wild bacchanalian energy. It scared me to death. I spent a lot of the Gathering on sidelines.

"I considered the taking of Faerie names. Some are deeply felt and permanent, some are probably changeable like drag. But nothing connected to me.

"Fast forward to the 1988 Faerie Gathering and the coming out of leather Faeries. By then I had definitely drunk that part of the Kool-Aid (the taking of Faerie names). When we leather Faeries went into the ring of trees that night, I remember Mark sacrificed me. There was no physical violence. I was blindfolded and bound to a massage table. Mark took me on a visualization, murmuring in my ear to bring me down to the underworld. I found myself instead in the forest of God. Mark looked at me and I looked at him. He reached out his hand and I took it and went dancing down His paths. And there came to mind an old comic strip, Pogo, 'We has met the enemy and they is us.' I stopped being afraid of myself that night and took the Faerie name Dancer.

"One night a few years later, Alexis showed me what SexMagick and pain sensation was all about. He gave me the most sensual whipping I ever had. At one point Daffodil whispered in my ear, 'Let the red flower of pain blossom in your mind.' That night I expanded my Faerie name to Dancer Redflower."

Not the magic of Radical Faeries dancing, not the wilder magic of leather sex... neither experience without the other could awaken the whole self to itself.

Now I understand why the Angels envy the Humans:
We live where the worlds of flesh and spirit intersect.
We are graced with the capacity for unlimited pleasure as well as universal consciousness.
While many men and women remain ignorant of the divine potential of these gifts,
We Faeries know—they celebrate this exalted state,
    and remind us to rejoice in who we really are.
They are my inspiration for the future.

—Ganymede

WINGS

Faerieland in Oz

by Marissa Zaknich

I CAME TO FAERIELAND OVER THE Christmas holiday of 2003 in Australia's Tweed Valley area of New South Wales on the night of the Summer Solstice.

There were men in drag and women in white feather boas, about forty smiling people getting ready to start the ritual procession. Though I was still in jeans and the t-shirt I wore on the plane, I made an easy and quick transition from the city to this relaxed and cheerful atmosphere. My time for renewal had already started.

There was a huge circular clearing on this vast property, close to the main house—a beautiful home on a hill with wrap-around verandahs and magnificent views of the distant volcanic Mount Warning.

We walked, holding hands—a graceful procession where people were calling up the nature spirits. The spirit of the East was said in a beautifully deep resonating voice. At the conclusion, a baby frog appeared in the light of our candle lanterns. This was an auspicious sign for creating abundance in new beginnings. It was even more promising as we were in a time of little rain throughout the state. But there was really nothing to fear, as the Faerie residents had built a pump to bring up spring water from the bottom levels of their land.

I slept in a former piggery in a "princess" bed with netting and concrete floors. The silence in that place gave a restorative chance for deep, uninterrupted sleep and strong dreams that were recorded in my journal every day.

Afternoons and nights I was in conversation with beautiful Faerie men living here such as Jay and Lars (one of the founders of OzFaeries). Jay talked about lost love and his happy time in the Tennessee Black Mountain Faerie community, where he was like Pan, tending goats. He talked about turning nineteen and falling in love with the young Dalmatian guy who sang old Dalmatian songs of the sea. How intensely sensuous he was but burdened with guilt from keeping secrets from his family about being gay. They were so in love, but the guy called it off. Jay's eyes welled up when he spoke of him. The intimacy in the sharing of these moments made me feel so complete.

Faerieland was large and lush despite drought conditions in the rest of the state. There was a mist coming over the valley and I was well prepared, walking with a big black umbrella and yellow plastic raincoat. Tim was walking with me after the Christmas lunch, which included fresh fruits of many colors. He spoke of troubled family scenarios and catching both parents, at different times, in compromising situations.

In the moist air, I breathed softly against the big tree at the end of the clearing. Tim said that there weren't too many big trees on the property. We see sexy Lars with his blond dreads and partly shaved head, looking like some Nordic warrior king from long ago. Everyone desired Lars in his happy self-containment.

What a privilege it was to be surrounded by this green abundance, the color of new beginnings. In all this greenery and great conversations with the Faeries, as a straight woman, in predominantly male company, I realized what it's like for gay men to be living in a mostly straight world. It must feel quite lonely at times, like you're missing a fundamental energy, even if you do fit well into society. There is an outsider quality that becomes part of you in the mainstream. Here for ten days, I was one of the few women—a minority. Roles were reversed. But as Tim said, "At least the difference here is that you are accepted. Those of us that aren't accepted have to keep pretending on many levels, not able to disclose our frustration or the truth about our lives."

The Tarot cards to my unconscious in a prelude to my trip revealed potent symbols of my truth. The Nine of Swords was the weeping woman, sitting up in bed with a quilt of patterned roses. The Empress was abundant nature and nurturing; and the Four of Wands depicted happy people in a processional dance, weaving their way around an open field while in the near distance stands a glorious castle.

People came from all over Australia to share some time at Faerieland and to talk about finding inspiration and self-worth. The shared life stories of many were like the warm circle of fire on New Year's Eve. People lit up their hearts from the calm and loving acceptance of the OzFaeries.

The New Year bonfire melted discontent, a perfect moment to watch time pass into the next year.

A Radical Journey

by Gregory Barnes

I FIRST BECAME AWARE OF THE Radical Faerie movement in the late 1990s when a good friend of mine told me about a group of Faeries he had met up around the Nimbin-Lismore area in Northern New South Wales. Subsequently I got to meet some of those guys through him. I stayed with one of the group members in his house in Lismore one night during 2001. This was just before his group purchased Faerieland and started their communal-style community.

One of my fondest memories during that first meeting was accompanying a few of the Faeries to a local market at Bangalow and then swimming nude with them at Kings Beach one Sunday. They were a very friendly bunch of men with a refreshing outlook on life not that dissimilar to mine: warm gentle souls with a curiosity for spirituality and things slightly off the beaten track. We got on just fine. I made a very small contribution to help them buy their land and get started.

I live in Canberra and it's not often that I make it up to northern New South Wales. So the next time I had the pleasure of the Faeries' company was at Sydney Mardi Gras, 2003. I joined a few of them again, this time dressing up in frilly frocks and gold lamé, and ran around squirting the huge crowd with giant pink water pistols. We had the best fun and the crowd loved us!

I had the pleasure of their company yet again at one of Body Electric's workshops on erotic massage for men in February of 2006. Rob Anderson (Sparkle) ran the workshop. It was a real eye opener into the world of male sensuality and one of my first experiences with Taoism. I loved the massage and have been using it ever since.

Recently, I met up with a few of the OzFaeries and a couple from the United States at the 2009 Easter Gathering. There I had another experience of a Faerie Heart Circle. That was a lovely opportunity to share some of my inner emotional world with caring like-minded souls. And, in the process, get to know a few of them at a deeper level as well.

I had my second Body Electric experience with the six-day Dear Love of Comrades retreat on a private property near Grafton, New South Wales, later that same month. This time I met more men and got to know them at an even deeper level. I was blessed to meet up with another Yoga teacher with whom I enjoyed practicing my morning *sadhana* in the temple space we had set up for the retreat activities. Puck had been living with the Faeries in their community for about a year.

So it was interesting to hear his stories about his experiences. One of my fondest memories of that interaction was painting my new friend with ochre-colored mud that he had collected from the creek bed on the Faerieland property. It was very nice to have that connection to the land. One day soon I would like to visit Faerieland and see it for myself. I hear news from time to time about various improvements they've made and it all sounds very enticing.

Notes from EuroFaerie Lovestar

by Marco Shokti

IN THE EARLY 1980S BRITAIN'S Jimmy Somerville and Bronski Beat sang of the Small-town Boys who were leaving family and friends to find life and love in the big city. I was one of those boys, coming from the Suffolk countryside to London in 1986.

I met many of my kind and we reveled in the huge number of men around us, available to kiss, to fuck, to love. We found unimagined pleasure in the abundance of passionate affairs and ecstasy and we found pain came alongside it too: the broken hearts, the atmosphere of fear that had grown from nowhere over the recent years and what we were afraid of—disease and death.

By 1995 I was preparing to die. I was five years into a seven-year prognosis of a nasty HIV-AIDS death and was starting to get symptoms. Suddenly all the joy and pain of my short career as an out and proud gay man came rushing to a crisis point. For the first time in my life I found myself ready to drop atheistic presumptions and search for answers. I opened my mind to Spirit and discovered I could fly.

Visions of celebration came my way, of circles of fabulous colorful creatures singing, drumming, dancing. The energy in these visions was astounding. The promise in them felt very real. Suddenly I became aware of a hidden history of queer kind as shamans, healers, mediums: a history that linked our kind across the planet, a spiritual function that a rational modern world had not embraced. There was no sign of awareness of this history in the mainstream gay world and there is still so little.

My visions became manifest when I discovered Queer Pagan Camp in the United Kingdom and heard of the EuroFaeries, meeting somewhere in the North Sea off the coast of the Netherlands. I soon became a regular face at these Gatherings, where my recent discovery of spiritual dimensions of the universe exploded into wild and amazing experiences: drumming at the fire, sharing deeply in Heart Circle, creating our own rituals that reflected our lives and experiences, meeting people who accepted spirit, love, magic as normal parts of life.

I found myself in environments where my very sexuality, my embrace of myself as male and female, my determination that my sexual nature was both natural and magical, were honored and explored. Where they could lift me into ecstatic communion that went far beyond what gay club land had ever offered. I came to see the constant reaching of many gay men for extremes of sex and highs through drugs and dance as a spiritual calling to know the deepest and most real essence of ecstasy within us.

The EuroFaeries met every summer for ten years on the island of Terschelling and held winter Gatherings around Europe. After some time they had saved enough surplus cash to put down a deposit on a mortgage for a piece of woodland in the Vosges Mountains of eastern France. Folleterre was born—land of the crazy, land of the fae—in fact the name was already there as the name of a local piece of woodland. We have Queer Sanctuary space up and running in Europe, holding five or six Gatherings there per year. And this has been alongside the continuing expansion of Faerie consciousness across the continent, with Gatherings cropping up in Berlin, in Greece and in the UK, where we rent out a genuine medieval castle named Featherstone for a truly atmospheric winter get together around the hearth fires.

At Folleterre we have a farmhouse and barn for accommodation, plus lots of camping land. We have acres and acres of forestland; there are streams, lakes and marvelous magical spots. And of course we have EuroFaeries, who come together from across the continent and beyond, speaking many languages and from many diverse cultural backgrounds. We're all united in common cause of love—for each other, for nature, for life itself—and embracing the mystical power in our sexuality to open us to communion and freedom.

The EuroFaeries are a great proof that humans can relate and love, whatever our backgrounds and beliefs. It's not so hard to get along and indeed to make space safe enough for all. Through our language diversity we have had to find ways to listen to each other with deep care and compassion and the rewards for this have been presence and intimacy beyond measure.

I still live in London, feeling more a global Faerie now than a smalltown boy. The country roots of my lifetime serve me well as I combine city life with time on the land in Sanctuary or visiting other wild places. Sometimes in the city a group of Faeries is pulling together. Known as the Queer Spirit Circle, we meet to create space where the essence of free Faerie brother-sisterhood and love is honored. This helps us to spread the word by being a visible presence of queers who are embracing the heart and healing properties of our nature.

This is a time when little sense of "community" exists in the gay scene and where trans, youth, ethnic and spiritual groups feel disconnected from the mainstream white gay middle-class male "norms" that currently define Queerdom. The

London Faeries are providing a deep and transformative experience of the spirit of community, showing always that we are not a set clan with fixed dogmas and practices but a tribal force with a spirit energy that is little known in the modern world. We're a force emerging as something new, but connecting to something ancient that stirs things to life in the souls of those who participate.

I love being a Faerie. I often meet guys who have heard of our Gatherings but who resist them, putting up any number of reasons why they won't come along. I see in their eyes the sadness of the magical boy whose dream of a perfect loving life was squashed, usually at a very early age. They cannot dare to dream that magic boy could live again, that the universe could feel as connected and wonderful as it did once to him. But I say to them it can.

We are Faeries because we are natural, magical and ancient, but our message and our hope is very much for today.

A Dialogue with EuroFaeries

by Efthimios Kalos, Junis and Eliendes Wasser

IN THE FALL OF 1994 *Efthimios Kalos met gay community organizer John Ferguson. Kalos had been to several Faerie Gatherings at Short Mountain and was part of the Faerie Circle in Chicago before moving to Paris with his partner earlier in the year. Continuing a tradition of Persephone worship rituals begun in Chicago by Kalos, he and Ferguson scouted a location in the Bois de Vincennes on Halloween and conducted the first EuroFaerie ritual: an effigy of the Greek Earth goddess Persephone was buried, covered in seeds and surrounded by bulbs which will be brought up from the ground on Beltane. The Persephone rituals are still performed twice a year.*

Efthimios Kalos: I'm at my parents' house right now in Greece where the weather is absolutely perfect and there are flowers everywhere. Here are my questions:

The Faerie movement began in the United States, but it was initially based on Harry Hay's intercultural studies of the social and spiritual function of third-gender men in various societies around the world. So, in a way, Hay imported and developed a notion of gender- and sexual-orientation-based spirituality into a context that was typically American. This context, in general, echoed the growing exploration of native, pagan and nature-based social and spiritual experiences in the 1960s and 1970s. It has evolved over time, as has the Radical Faerie movement.

What is of interest to me now is how the Radical Faerie phenomenon, inspired as it was by an international vision, yet taking root and developing on American soil, has interacted with non-American cultures as it has been introduced into Europe and East Asia.

What parts of the Radical Faerie vision have been adopted and what parts have not? Has the Radical Faerie experience in general evolved differently since it was introduced into Europe in the early 1990s? How universal is Harry Hay's vision? The Faerie movement is incredibly inclusive and flexible. Are there limits to these qualities as it meets new social contexts? What new and perhaps unexpected things arose from the introduction of Radical Faeries into Europe and Asia?

170

Let's start by asking how it all happened? How did you, Junis and Eilendes, be-come Faeries and how did you bring Radical Faerie spirit to Europe?

Junis: After a number of years repeatedly dismissing the Faeries as a bunch of hippies dancing around bonfires, I finally decided during a stay with Matt Whitney in Florida to drive up north to Tennessee just after Christmas in the winter of 1994 and spend a few days at Short Mountain Sanctuary.

It was a very cold winter, at night ten degrees below zero. When we arrived at the end of the day, darkness swiftly fell. No electricity inside the main house, but soft yellow candle and oil lamp spots here and there. To keep it warm inside, three, wood-burning stoves were blazing. I have often thought back to this very moment, arriving at Short Mountain, and why it made such an impact on me. I can only explain it as a homecoming experience. I made an instant connection with the residents, their lifestyle and their connection with the land. Men stripped of all things superfluous, in tune with their authenticity. No hollow phrases, no importance connected to social position or economic background.

Of course, there were also similarities with my own life back home which made me feel at ease: my little cabin just outside a small town in the country, also heated by a wood-burning stove, land around, half a dozen chickens, a dog, bees and a vegetable garden. The next day we got involved in the routine—cutting wood, carrying water, inspecting the cottages under construction, climbing down the frozen creek, doing kitchen work and preparing for the New Year's party—all while more visitors arrived. I enjoyed the liberty and flow of things, no questions asked. Everybody was just doing his thing.

This first experience with the Faeries left a deep impression. There was community life, a connection with the land, the Circle before dinner, singing and music at night. Inspired, we traveled back south.

That summer Matt came to visit me in Holland and he suggested a visit with John Ferguson, who at the time performed in Europe and lived on a farm together with his boyfriend Alfredo in the west part of the country. Matt and Habibi (John's Faerie name) had met at a Faerie Gathering on Short Mountain a couple of years before. We fantasized about finding Faeries in Europe and Habibi pointed out that there were already three of us, enough to create a Circle. Behind the farm in the field on that sunny day we closed arms and we had the very first Faerie Circle in Europe ever.

Habibi and I became friends, the Faerie topic kept coming back and one day the two of us got in the car to meet Geert Oetken (known later as Trish Trash and currently as Eilendes Wasser, or EW) in Oberkassel. Habibi knew that Geert had been in contact with the Faeries in the United States so most likely he was still affected by the Faerie spirit and also on the lookout.

This turned out to be an important step. About one hour or so after arrival, we got in the car and spent the whole afternoon in Geert's office in Bonn. He showed us some photos of the island Terschelling, which he had visited the year before, and the Wierschuur location looked like the perfect spot for a small Gathering.

Tasks were quickly divided, addresses of gay organizations all over Europe were found, a Gathering call was created. The copy machine multiplied what we needed, envelopes were addressed and stamped and everything was sent out that same day.

We had no experience and no clue what to expect and what to organize exactly. Habibi had met poet Franklin Abbott in the United States, a great Faerie Circle facilitator and an Atlanta-based psychotherapist, and I had happened to have read some of his essays. So we decided to invite him to the first Gathering in 1995 to lead us into Faeriedom. An advertisement in one of the national Dutch newspapers generated another two participants. Together we called together thirty-four newborn and old time Faeries to the first EuroFaerie Gathering.

Eilendes Wasser: I acknowledge Harry Hay's vision about subject-SUBJECT consciousness as a fundamental base of the Faerie movement. *RFD* gave me a good connection to the Faerie world in America. I felt that every single issue was a wonderful gift to me. It was and is a reading Heart Circle for me and it is my connection to overseas and the Faerie world there.

I came to the Faeries when my friend Rocky invited me to the summer Gathering of the Northwood Faeries from Minnesota, in Wisconsin in August 1989. This was the year when they also found Kawashaway, which is now their Sanctuary.

I went to the Gathering with my partner Gerd. We did not know at all what to expect. After a long drive we finally passed through a sandy forest road with ribbons tied to trees. We parked our car well before the Gathering site and walked the last stretch. The first sight we had was a circle of hugging, laughing, excited men of all ages—naked and gleaming with oil. My partner and I looked at each other in shock, ready to turn around and drive back right then. But miraculously enough we were also drawn to the site and it only took a blink of the eye to overcome our fears and let go.

We had the most wonderful and unforgettable time with the Faeries. I felt so welcome, so whole, so safe and so very happy to be with all those wonderful men in the most beautiful natural setting. It was almost unbelievable that this could be real.

The Heart Circles were breathtaking experiences. It was such a joy to be able to just play and be silly together. It was a spiritual experience to walk naked with other men, hand in hand, through a clear creek to a pond were we painted each other like tribesmen, laughing and hugging under the roof of the trees of the forest. The Gathering was an initiation for me, a strong feeling of having come home.

I missed the Faerie spirit a lot coming back to Germany. It felt like a big void. The only thing I could do was to put an ad into *RFD*, listing the "Rheingold Faeries," although there was only one Faerie I knew of in Germany—me. It took a long time until Habibi answered this ad in 1994.

In 2001 I went a second time to a Faerie Gathering in the United States. I went again to the Kawashaway Sanctuary. I saw many Faeries I still knew from my first Gathering. I realized how similar our Circles in Europe and in Minnesota were. It felt like family and it was so easy to be part of it again.

Drawing from this, I think Faeries coming here and Faeries going abroad will feel at home equally there and here. This is an amazing experience because one might think that the cultural differences could be remarkable. But they are not. I think that proves that there is something you can call a "Radical Faerie culture" that you should find at any Gathering around the globe. Heart Circles, ritual, play, loving companionship, sexual freedom, respect and awareness, subject-SUBJECT consciousness in an anarchistic non-hierarchical environment connect us with our roots and with nature. It proves the principle of Faerie unity.

For me, the date of our first ritual, recorded by our dear Faerie Karl of Albion, on June 24, 1995—when we celebrated the Return of the Faeries—was the beginning of the Faerie movement on the European continent. At the end of the ritual we were standing in a circle in the middle of the dim barn of De Wierschuur and I could strongly feel a shining energy radiating above our circle, connecting us all. It was the most magical feeling I have experienced in my life. I had the feeling that something very beautiful and very powerful had been reclaimed among us on our continent.

But this is not all that I believe Radical Faeries are about. Before I came to the Faeries, I was active in an environmental activist group in Bonn, Germany. Our main focus was the fight against nuclear power plants, which was partly won. We also were active in the peace movement opposing the stationing of middle-range nuclear rockets in Germany. It felt very good being a part of this.

I know Harry Hay and the Radical Faeries in America are rooted in the same grassroots movement, sharing the same ideas. To my knowledge, Hay came from a political, communistic background before he became a Faerie himself. And after reading the 2009 spring issue of *RFD* and a story by Covelo about the involvement of the early Radical Faeries in the fight against the Diablo Canyon nuclear power plant, I identify Faeries as also being politically progressive.

An essential idea of Hay was that being gay means more than just having another sexual orientation. He claimed that gays have a certain role in society as caretakers, gate openers, healers and so forth. This suggests an active role for the Faeries in the healing of this devastated planet.

I believe most Faeries in North America and in Europe share ideas about the unity of all, the respect for Mother Earth, social responsibility, a universal spirit, unconditional love and celebration of the life force. All of them can be profoundly political. Knowing Faeries from North America, talking with them at our Gatherings, reading their stories, I got the impression that there is much more energy to make the Faerie vision come true in society: to take a stand, to make a political statement, to be committed and thus to be Radical Faeries.

I hear this said, "There is very little such spirit within the EuroFaerie movement." It might be that being a Faerie is already more or less a vague political statement. But in my impression, there is no visible political impact from the Faeries in Europe, there is no Radicalism. There are almost no Radical Faeries in this sense at this time on this continent, or at least those who are active do not identify this as being "Faerie." For me, this is a big void. I do not want to be pessimistic, as the Faerie movement in Europe is still young. The Gatherings *are* truly beautiful and a big value in themselves. But this planet is changing, especially with the ecological crisis we are all facing which needs solutions fast.

I believe that if our Faerie vision could become more real in our daily lives, it would give Faeries as a circle so much more spirit, strength and happiness. Making us much more a tribe on and for this planet, taking a position of healers, caretakers and gate keepers that I believe we are.

Efthimios Kalos: Perhaps the relative lack of political engagement of Euro-Faeries can be traced to the general separation in European culture of the domains of politics and spirituality. But I think that even in the United States there is a veritable rainbow of attitudes concerning political activism within Faerie circles. I think the difference is in the willingness to receive motivation and go out and act politically when the calling sounds, whether that calling comes from within the individual or from agitation arising from Faerie organizations.

The exception to this is the interface of Faerie spirituality that is very much in tune with environmental concerns and the environmental impetus of the ecological movement here in Europe. EuroFaeries in general are much more likely to be concerned with environmental questions than social questions as spiritual beings. I think that spirituality is considered more of a personal matter here in Europe and in many ways so is sexuality.

You hear a lot of American Faeries talk about witchcraft and magic. But are they really talking about the same thing that Europeans think about when they think about magic? I think there is a difference. The magic discussed in America may be a mixture that arose from a variety of sources that may include back-to-nature spiritualism, feminism, Native American spirituality, Aleister Crowley-ism and a good dose of pop culture. I think this is not so much the case in Europe. And yet, the American magic may be more potent as it is more integrated and more alive to a greater number of facets of human life.

My limited experiences with the Asian Faeries, the three Thai Gatherings I attended, is that they take the strictness of definition of spiritual practices even more seriously than the Europeans. In the Thai Gatherings, the typical polymorphic and inclusive exploration of ritual and spirituality that can characterize American Faerie practices is not very present. There is a willingness to go along, out of respect perhaps or curiosity, but I rarely have seen initiative being taken to create and explore new, synthesized, or syncretic expressions of spirituality.

But then again, the people of Southeast Asia may be perfectly at ease with their spiritual traditions, not overly politicizing them as in America, nor marginalizing them into a separate realm as in Europe. Perhaps the world of spirits is simply present and all-permeating there. And what can a bunch of Faeries from the West possibly add to such a spiritual environment?

I love to go to both EuroFaerie Gatherings to experience the multiplicity of European cultures filtered through Faerie ways and Thai Gatherings to explore the outer edges of the Faerie phenomenon as well as its correspondences in eastern cultures. I also love to go back to Short Mountain to reconnect with the mothership and to see how American Faerie mentalities have evolved or not.

Eilendes Wasser: Sorry if I want to share some unpleasant thoughts and feelings with you, but you just brought up what I have been recently feeling. Actually my impression of the Faerie movement in Europe is that it is—to say the least—not very dynamic after almost fifteen years. This makes me sad because I think it is needed more than ever before and the Faeries are very dear to me. I do not know what happened. Probably we are missing something Faeries can hold on to. For many it might be too vague, not having an impact on their life, not supporting them or giving them a feeling of solidarity.

After we acquired Folleterre the enthusiasm about the real chance to build a Faeric sanctuary in Europe in the middle of nature seems to be very diminished. I miss many Faeries that are no longer involved. Our many requests for support of the Sanctuary have been answered by few. This may appear cynical, but it seems to me that to a certain extent the Faerie movement in Europe is more a spiritual vacation club than a tribe or movement offering a liberated spiritual path, an alternative lifestyle and a new connection to Mother Earth.

For me, having a place of our own was essential to the growth of our movement. But probably this whole land-search idea was a misunderstanding or misconception. I think we have really tried hard to involve most of the Faeries and ask them for their permission to start the land search and acquiring Folleterre.

I feel a lack of commitment and continuity. Many words have been spoken, many promises made without consequences. My feeling is that only very few Faeries have shown a constant interest in our movement during these last fifteen years and it seems to me that it has not grown. It might be that the Faerie idea, whatever that might be, is outdated.

Probably I have been and am expecting too much. I know that this can cause a spiraling into dark feelings…spreading dark energy. If this is the case, I have to learn more and I will. A very good experience during the last summer Gathering for me was to drop the feeling of responsibility, which put too much pressure on me in the last years and kept me from really being a part of a Gathering, really being able to enjoy it.

I am very thankful for the many dear and close friends I made being with the Faeries in the last several years and the important impact of the Faeries to my life, which I wouldn't want to miss for anything. This also gives me a lot of energy to stay with the Faeries despite these negative feelings. For me, the Faerie movement is one of the most important things in my life.

Junis: Maybe we expect too much engagement from Faeries who, after a first Gathering or longer Faerie experience, express their excitement and connection but in the long run refuse to commit themselves and to share a common goal.

Perhaps we also expect to harvest the fruit of our efforts after almost fifteen years. There must have been more than a thousand people passing through our Gatherings. What has been the effect of Faerie experiences on their lives, their personal development? Or should we not care at all for something like a "harvest," focusing more, perhaps, on what has been shared?

This last year I stepped away from direct and sustained involvement with the EuroFaeries and I have been thrilled by how things have continued thanks to the efforts of many other Faeries: networking, website improvements, house improvements, organizing of Gatherings and workweeks by Notre Dame, Shokti, Lappi,

Dee, Wolf, Dimitri, Nico, to name a few. I do feel Faeries are engaged now, even though sometimes it is on small-scale projects or for short periods of time. Does longer commitment carry extra value? Eilendes, maybe you can answer this question. Perhaps you are expecting too much?

I do see lasting results, but not necessarily in big numbers, not in quantity. As a result of one of Michel's Tantra weekends in Utrecht, for example, a participant created a shamanic discovery group. In that group another participant discovered the gay spirituality of Faeries and organized a gay spirituality discovery weekend this spring.

I introduced the Heart Circle at the gay Buddhist meetings in Amsterdam and it's still done to this very day. Freny took the Faerie experience to his sweat lodge sessions for straight and gay people in his village. Many more examples can be found, I am sure of it.

From maybe a small number of Faeries, many threads are spun through various layers of society. One individual can make a difference. I'm reminded of Strijder, the summer of 2008, feeling so stuck. He moved to Australia, where he found his grounding at a Queensland Faerie sanctuary.

Talking about finding and creating a new life experience while honoring the land, about sharing deep-rooted ideals in a Faerie community, I truly believe that this will only be possible by not talking and dreaming about it, but by actually doing it. Take for instance the time during and after the land-finding years. Folleterre initially proved not really suitable for long-term residence without requiring a large amount of monetary and labor investment. Yet now we have a house open to all Faeries, which is so much more inviting.

The Gatherings are well attended and inspire people to come back. There is a steady flow of newcomers. So the house has a true inspirational value for these Faeries. But Faeries who considered long-term residency faced the dilemmas of commitment. They lost a sense of balance by becoming conflicted. I personally went through the stages of this process, wanting to make it happen and at the same time unable to do so for a range of emotional, practical and financial reasons. Of course, you can say these are excuses, but I feel it is so much easier to give up the security of an established life pattern in your twenties than it is in your late fifties.

Eilendes, please do not let yourself be overcome by dark ideas up there in Lamontagne, 650 meters high. To a great degree, thanks to your expert and plentiful efforts, the Folleterre Sanctuary exists, perhaps still serving modestly but with occasional great impact.

Feel proud of it. Don't let the cold temperatures outside affect your heart. Short Mountain was founded in 1973, soon after the Stonewall Rebellion and the first development of gay rights. Consolidating and uniting the tribe then became most important. Now this tribe is scattered around the world. Its members Gather together whenever possible.

Others choose to blend into society. They have no need for a so-called "gay identity," feeling free to adopt children, live in suburbia and organize the weekly senior-citizen Bingo night.

Yet at the same time, perhaps because of this, spirituality grows and becomes more part of daily life. The Faeries may slumber at times, but they never vanish. One might just cross your path tomorrow, setting you aglow on your path.

A Folleterre's Faerie Tale

by Vyvyan Chatterjie (Notre Dame des Arbres)

Harry Hay asked us these questions: Who are we and why are we here? What role should we play? When stuck or while asking the question, I accept the reality that I *am* here.

Connecting with this world, my environment, Keats'Vale of Tears, I make soul. Together in good company we make group soul. Much of my role now is working my spirituality in this world as a soul-maker. The path is that of us all, I suspect, in acceptance and in forgiveness, most especially in *self*-acceptance and *self*-forgiveness. There is, as outside the window of this library room where I sit, much soil to till.

So, this is where I am as I write. And I will remain with the improbable reality that I am a Faerie. As with many realities this defies description as well as probability, but to the last first. I am of English upper-middle-class family, social background, behind the cultural split of a Celtic (Irish and Cornish) mother and Bengali father. As with the EuroFaeries, our *lingua franca* was English. What Englishness is (aside from a façade of charm and ironic self-deprecation) is so immediately illusory that it has been an immense prompt to self-enquiry in my life. That good old question: Who am I?

A seeker like many others, I took interest rapidly, however, not in gaining the answer, but in interesting ways of finding out. Those included the devout Catholic schoolboy, aspirant Jesuit priest, Cambridge history scholar, drinker and *roué*, British Army officer, businessman, chef, hotelier, screenwriter and wine merchant. As with most wisdom systems of the world, one aspect of that "who am I" question is always found to be: This, but also this and that and that. All of these personae are *me*.

A radical and questioner of establishment and hierarchies, I have a strong conservative streak and can seem imperious in the unconscious exercise of authority. I've wrestled with paradox, but if I combine the gay anthem of my Manhattan nights at the Anvil while AWOL from the Army ("I am what I am") with the motto of the Royal Military Academy at Sandhurst ("Serve to Lead") I learned that it is the slightest shift of interpretation to move from "wrestle" to "embrace." I always

179

believed Paradox to be the underlying structure of this world. Now I read scientists who assure me it is so.

Two such scientists are Peter Coveny and Roger Highfield, who wrote in *Time's Arrow*: "The improbability of man's existence is dwarfed by that, for the existence of the universe itself." Why am I here? Why in the universe? And why at Folleterre Faerie Sanctuary in eastern France? Here with my Faerie brothers and sisters when they come soon to join me?

At the start of alcoholic recovery in 2000, I found in gay community a place to grow, to be vulnerable and to receive; permission to be myself. With Faeries, however, I seem to find not only permission but encouragement to be the fullest possible version of my self. I work with this to help others feel that there is room enough for all to do, to be this.

Fear contracts. So as Faeries we work to love and expand the heart, to overcome resistances. I have never ever been able to conquer fear totally. I thought I had, but it was so much *hubris*.

What I can do, as a Fabulous Faerie, in my pomp and power, is to draw in so much love that it drives out fear. If the love recedes, the fear returns. My first route to enlightenment is to practice what I preach. Yet I learn this every day of my life.

There seems, in Faeries, a yearning for Paradise Lost and at Gatherings and in Sanctuaries we witness attempts to build Paradise Regained. Play God, start from scratch: create. All these Edens have their snakes. We cannot *un*-invent technology. Most of the human race no longer sees and feels Nature as animistic.

However there is a wonderful humor that shrugs its gowned and glittered shoulder at inconsistency when we parade in Technicolor plastics made by workers who do not dare to dream of a minimum wage, while we sit at table, eating our organic vegetables, healthy beans and grains cooked by sustainable energy.

We should maybe not look to Faeries for answers, but for style—which after all is a dance with content. It is said that in commercial terms, the "straight" world of fashion and music follows trails blazed within gay society—anthems of light born in dark clubs.

I follow author Will Roscoe's assertion in *Jesus and the Shamanic Tradition of Same-Sex Love* in believing that during the height of the HIV-AIDS pandemic in the United Sates, gay men offered an enduring demonstration of subject-SUBJECT relationships. That is, of *agape* rather than *Eros* or *Erotiko* in caring until death for so many who were "just" friends.

My view is that of the Sanctuary as a therapeutic container. Andrew Ramer, author of *Two Flutes Playing* and others, has encouraged us to heal together as a tribe.

I have listened to this; ran experimental gay mens' and queer events building intentional community. But the outside is always there and I hear the call of the Faeries to
take it out further: "Heal ourselves, our brothers, our land and our culture."

Just as the analysand will sometime leave the analysis, with alchemical work that
resonates inside him, so I look to the larger world outside to find what we, from our
collective hurt and wounds, can offer as healing gifts.

A Faerie symbol is, of course, the butterfly—signifying transformation. The
Sanctuary here, with my background, feels like the Celtic Cauldron of Plenty which
bubbles away all ingredients, transforming them into the magic broth needed for
renewal. In ritual, in some unique moments, spellbinding transcendence may overshadow workaday transformation. These safe spaces, containers within the container,
if you will, let us speak our feelings in vulnerability but in real trust.

By staying the course with many fellow travellers whose values and motivations
I found quite opaque to my imagination, I have always been rewarded. Paracelsus,
that maverick master, ever reminds me that to understand is to see; to love, and to
"understand" is to delve beneath the surface, always.

Besides the Heart Circle, consensus is key to Faeries. My interpretation is that
any one person can hold out against a decision, but that in fellowship we say to him
or her "you are certain that we are making a mistake. Nevertheless, can you respect
us enough not to withhold consensus and 'live with it'?" The Zen Master, when
asked what his career as a master was like, replied: "A life full of mistakes." The process of consensus is too exasperating for some. But like a long slow fuck it also can
be so rewarding.

To close on the same serious note, I would like to offer my answer to this question: "What is the one single thing without which Faeriedom would be impossible?"
Consensus? The Heart Circle? My answer is "the Bad Faerie," the contrarian, that
mordant Touchstone. The Trickster, Winged Hermes, Loki or the baby Krishna who
curdles the milk. That irritant without which the oyster grows no pearl.

Don Kilhefner never fails but to sign off our conversations with the injunction:
"Make Holy trouble." Fear of conflict can be fatal in a community. Friction creates
energy.

So whenever I feel it is time to throw that pebble in our pond, I invariably find
a large rock to hand. The "doing" versus "being" dilemma is solved for me by experiencing all as "becoming." So when personalities resembling tectonic plates slide
together I look lovingly on the collision, knowing that gifts, invitations and fresh
insights will come after all has been settled.

Groucho Marx said he wouldn't wish to join any club that would have him as a member. If all Faeries sang from the same book, then maybe I'd quit. We are of many colors—as am I.

I sit in my old Glastonbury rainbow jacket, gleefully anticipating growing old disgracefully, happily claiming my place in Folleterre's summer sun. Aged fifty-four now, I plan to celebrate my eightieth in a leather miniskirt—not mutton but crocodile dressed as lamb.

ISSUES & IDEAS

Heterowashing Gay Liberation
and the Radical Faerie Antidote

by Jerry Berbiar (Jerry the Faerie)

WITHIN TEN YEARS OF THE Stonewall Rebellion, which served as a symbol for the already emerging gay liberation movement and the soon to be founded Gay Liberation Front, the movement was already endangered by conservatism, commercialism and assimilationism. The roots of gay liberation were in feminism, the African-American civil rights movement, the anti-Vietnam-war movement and other organized efforts to achieve social and economic justice.

Many gay people who were activists in the 1960s, with the exception of unusually brave souls like Harry Hay and John Burnside, remained in the closet, even while accompanying freedom riders against segregation in the South, organizing against the war, or fighting for a woman's right to choose. Whether due to the shame and guilt society instilled in homosexuals, or from fear for personal safety, of losing a job, or other persecution, or perhaps just because of the seeming impossibility of queer organizing in the face of fierce hostility from the mainstream, these progressive activists rarely revealed their homosexuality or considered promoting a movement for the civil rights of homosexuals.

Many still believed the dominant paradigm that everyone was heterosexual but that some had a mental illness that caused them to commit homosexual acts.

The shift to understanding that homosexuality was natural and healthy, although unusual like being left handed or having red hair, had begun among growing numbers of homosexuals by the time of Stonewall and the early Gay Liberation Front.

It was believed that sexual liberation and social revolution to effect radical change could only be achieved by eliminating repressive social institutions, including marriage, the nuclear family and the military-industrial complex. One of the chants heard in early gay liberation marches was "2-4-6-8, smash the family, church and state!"

185

By 1979, gay liberation marches had become lesbian and gay pride parades. The movement was turning into a market. The clone look predominated, imitating hetero masculine stereotypes. Leonard Matlovich was a hero, glorifying homosexuals in the military.

Concerned that the essence of who gay men were was being obscured by hetero values and culture, Harry Hay and his partner John Burnside, with cohort Don Kilhefner, facilitated the first Spiritual Conference of Radical Faeries at a Hindu ashram near Benson, Arizona.

The Radical Faeries were founded for gay men. Harry asserted that for gay men to discover who they really are they needed to remove themselves from who and what they were not. The Gatherings were places where gay men could individually recreate themselves, create community, explore faggot essence and create their own culture, free from the dominant all-encompassing hetero viewpoint.

Harry believed, as did the lesbian separatists at the time, that women needed to define themselves for themselves, the way gay male Radical Faeries were doing.

Harry and John and some of the intellectuals in the early Radical Faeries were atheists and anarchists. Others came to the Faeries with backgrounds in paganism, Wicca, Buddhism, Native American spirituality, other practices and no practice at all.

Radical means "to the root." Radical Faeries seek answers to gay men's questions about our essential qualities, such as who we are, why we are here and what our unique gifts are that we can share with the world at large.

These gifts include the ability to achieve ends through cooperation rather than the hetero paradigm of competition. Walking between the worlds, resolving dualism with subject-SUBJECT consciousness in which we view others through the same loving lens with which we view ourselves, may be one of the most powerful gifts we have to offer.

Heart Circles, powerful encounters where a talisman is passed among the circle of gay men and each man speaks profoundly from his heart, became a central feature of Radical Faerie Gatherings.

From the beginning Radical Faeries deconstructed economics by creating a sliding scale for those who could pay little or nothing, and no one was turned away for lack of funds. I have an audio tape of this particular discussion at the 1980 Gathering in Denver, Colorado.

Previously, those who could not pay the fee for a Gathering were asked to do work exchange, such as cooking in the kitchen. On the tape people discuss how a poorly paid childcare worker is probably doing society more good than a $200-an-hour corporate attorney. We create community by taking care of one another. The lawyer and the childcare worker should each be taking turns caring for each other and everyone at the Gathering, cooking or otherwise being of service, as should everyone at the Gathering who is capable of doing so.

Later, when the HIV-AIDS holocaust was decimating gay men, Faeries forced onto a meager disability income due to illness were able to attend Gatherings because of this policy. Many who could afford to do so gave extra money to compensate for those who couldn't afford to pay.

Radical and progressive politics were a common thread among the Radical Faeries. Askance action was a Radical Faerie technique. In Santa Cruz, California, in the late 1980s, a billboard advertising whiskey featured a man holding a "straight" poker hand of cards. The sign said "straight man's drink." Some Santa Cruz Faeries altered the sign to make every card a queen and the lettering to read, "Don't drink, be gay."

There was also direct action. Many Faeries joined ACT UP and Queer Nation, being arrested during civil disobedience on the Supreme Court steps during the 1987 National Lesbian and Gay March on Washington, to protest the Hardwicke decision in which the Supreme Court upheld sodomy laws across the country. (The court later reversed itself in 2002.)

Faeries were also arrested at the offices of pharmaceutical companies for advocating for the availability of retroviral drugs for people with HIV-AIDS, as well as at other related protests. Some Faeries continue to practice political protest, marching against the Iraq wars, protesting the Palestinian occupation by Israel and fighting for healthcare, tenants' rights and other social-justice issues.

In contrast, the mainstream LGBT movement is becoming more conservative. I've recently heard a term which I find descriptive of the direction today's LGBT mainstream culture is moving: "heterowashing." When Harry said gay men need to "shed the ugly green frog skins of hetero conformity," he was illustrating the necessity of transcending the heterowashing of queers, both individually and as a culture.

What exactly does "heterowashing" do to queer communities? There is no such thing as an LGBT or for that matter an LGBTQQIA (lesbian, gay, bisexual, transgender, questioning, queer, intersex, allies) community. Each of those letters consists of multiple communities and movements. While we come together as political and sometimes cultural allies, in truth we lack a vocabulary to accurately describe ourselves either as individual sexual minorities or in the aggregate. Until we can develop a vocabulary to accurately portray ourselves and our communities, we are confined to an annoying mishmash of letters which says little about us. Lacking a better word, I use "queer" as a term for our communities as one.

The upper-middle-class, mostly white male, queer "leadership" (especially the clueless and arrogant Human Rights Campaign) is heterowashing, dumbing down and guiding our queer communities along a conservative path to failure.

Instead of deconstructing the failed patriarchal institution of marriage, we clamor to be included in it. For the sake of argument, if one assumes that queer marriage is worth achieving, let's take a look at the idiotic way our assimilationist queer political leadership—at least in California—has gone about this in a way that ensures failure.

Let's say, for example, that queer marriage advocates want to approach the African-American community for support. Any intelligent or experienced activist knows you would ask African-American community activists what *their* issues are and how they would like our community to support *them* on these issues. Then we can ask for African-American community support for queer marriage in exchange for the queer community supporting African-American issues.

Instead, affluent white queers go into the African-American community to "educate" them to support queer marriage. Why should they without a *quid pro quo*? This arrogant approach has been a recipe for failure, as well it should be. Add to that flushing forty-five million dollars down the toilet with an ad campaign that failed to include the voices of actual queer people and so-called marriage equality may have been set back for years in California.

Queers are being heterowashed with marriage, fighting to join the military-industrial complex, marginalizing or even demonizing the pederast, drag, leather, sex worker, homeless and other non-mainstream queer communities and ignoring our duty to ally with people of color, women and other oppressed minorities. Largely forgotten are the politics from the early gay liberation movement with its roots in socialism and anarchy.

One of the most disgusting things I witnessed in the queer community was gay men with two-million dollar homes in San Francisco's Castro neighborhood successfully organizing to keep a queer youth shelter out of the Castro, as it would lower their property values. For consolation, I have to remind myself that intelligent radical activists in the queer (or any other) community are a small minority and that it takes a long time to educate and win the minds and hearts of what some Radical Faeries sometimes refer to as "the muggles in the mainstream."

We are coming out of an era of extremely conservative politics and culture. It will take time to heal and recover. I hope that eventually the majority of queer people will decide not to try to live like mainstream heteros, adopting all of their dysfunctional and often harmful institutions.

Because I honestly don't believe that queers can live that way.

Today the Radical Faerie movement includes women, transpeople and others who identify as Radical Faeries. Whether this is an evolution of the Radical Faerie movement or a dilution of a radical gay men's movement is a subject of debate, largely across intergenerational lines.

Have Faeries become less radical, focusing on fabulous outfits, amazing performance art and wonderful social Gatherings, but losing their transgressive social and political edge? Will the Radical Faeries continue to be an antidote to assimilationism? I hope so, as now more than ever we need such an antidote to the heterowashing of queer communities in which today's conservative queer political leaders are complicit.

Now more than ever the world needs men who are "not for fighting, not for war." We need queers who have radical askance alternative viewpoints to dominant cultural mores. May the Radical Faerie movement continue to play its role in providing a cauldron of change so needed in this ignorant and repressive world.

Choosing Faerie

by Chris Bartlett (The Lady Bartlett)

IN THE LATE 1990S I used to walk friends over to the 17th Street house in San Francisco where Harry Hay lived. I wanted all my friends to meet Harry Hay—to experience his Gandalfian omniscience and to experience a bit of living gay history. Once, I brought Jeff, who was at the time new to the Faerie scene. As we entered, Harry said, "Bring that young proto-sissy over here where I can talk to him." Jeff giggled nervously and protested that he was not sure that he was a sissy. But of course we all knew that Harry was right.

But why use the term "proto-sissy" or its related term, "proto-Faerie"? What did Harry mean? I think he meant that Jeff was fundamentally, at root, a sissy and Faerie. I think of it as a Faerie or sissy-about-to-be-born, an incipient Faerie. It is a Faerie about to shed the frog skin of hetero imitation. And yet this process of emergence from "proto-Faerie" to full-on Faerie is only minimally theorized or understood. Are we born Radical Faerie, do we choose it, or is it simply declared?

I'm fascinated by the distinction between being born some way and choosing to be that way. I've always felt more empowered to say "I choose" rather than "I was born that way." So I distinguish in my own language between being homosexual (a genetic and behavioral marker) and gay (a cultural choice). I choose to be gay; I may or may not have been born homosexual.

This way of thinking relates to my self-conception of my becoming and being a Faerie. I full-on choose to be a Radical Faerie—choosing the culture, the ethos, the ways of being.

The beauty of Faerie culture, at least in part, is that it restores the power of choice to being a certain type of queer. Radical Faerie did not just happen to us: we fully embraced it; we dove in. (I acknowledge that for some of us the choice may be an ambivalent one.)

I get discouraged when I hear queer brothers and sisters use the language of what I consider to be victimhood. "We were born this way" or "We can't help it" and (implied but unstated) "Full citizenship should accrue to us because we were born this way and did not choose." I am troubled by the self-hatred implicated in statements that "We did not choose to be this way."

In contrast, I like cultures that use rituals to embody choice: the Amish Rumspringa when Amish teens, following a year of exposure to the outside world, choose to join the Amish community (be baptized) or are shunned. Another example is the bar/bat mitzvah when young Jews choose to take on the responsibilities of adulthood. The investiture of a priest in various religions is another moment of powerful choice. When participants in a culture choose to embrace that culture, they become full actors, as opposed to passive recipients.

How can we Faeries create a culture (for it is indeed created, over centuries), how can we create a culture that has a ritual of choice—to say, "I am a Radical Faerie. I have chosen. There is no turning back"?

I picture a scene on the Short Mountain knoll—a Faerie who is ready to choose. She is surrounded on the outside by her elders and ancestors, who watch approvingly as she chooses Radical Faerie. Sitting on the inside are those "proto-Faeries" who have not yet completed the ritual but who are inspired by the courage and certainty of the woman about to choose Radical Faerie.

The ritual begins: all the circles spin around the chooser. She marvels at the colors, the glistening eyes, the deep appreciation all around.

She reads of a text—chosen by her: some Whitman or Hay or Edward Carpenter, a poem by Audre Lorde, some songs by k.d. lang. The texts are symbols of her choice. She chants, "You can not destroy the Master's house with the master's tools."

Three elders who have chosen decades before stand to tell their own stories: a leatherman who chose Faerie in the late 70s, an ACT UP veteran who chose Faerie when she was charging the ramparts, a trans Faerie who transitioned to the Faeries as part of his transition.

The elders share the power of their choice. They surround and initiate the Faerie—the proto-Faeries see in the ritual the possibility of their own future choice and what is at stake.

Paradoxically, communities are stronger when there is an element of inconvenience to participate. Think yourself of the effort required to visit a Faerie Sanctuary: the time commitment, the travel over bumpy roads, the risk of intimacies.

Choosing is part of the inconvenience that binds us together. It is the opposite of accident. Being an accidental Faerie is one possibility (neither better nor worse) but community is strengthened, I would argue, by Faeries of choice.

At a recent Short Mountain gathering I heard our great elder, Be, speak about Harry's theory that we are born Faeries. This hypothesis may or may not be true.

The moment of power comes, I believe, when this Faerie fetus, the incipient Faerie, the proto-Faerie, the accidental Faerie, *chooses* to be Faerie as a distinction, not merely as an accident.

Impressions of an Improbable Faerie

by Artwit

I WAS ACTIVE IN THE FAERIES (1980-1989) in San Francisco; less active, after that, in the Pacific Northwest. I now consider myself more "formerly a Faerie," only going to the occasional coffee or soirée. I don't identify with mixed-gender or mixed-sexuality groups who now claim Faerie identity.

"Improbable" is no exaggeration. I have a Ph.D. in theoretical physics and don't believe in spirits or spooks. On the other hand, my grandmother fingered me as a Highly Sensitive Person when I was still a preschooler and I grew up with the ritual and mysticism of Eastern Christianity.

I was introduced to brain chemistry via LSD the day after I got my Ph.D. for a thesis on the very dense early stages of the physical Universe after the Big Bang. Four years later on my thirtieth birthday, on Gay Day in San Francisco, I got to experience that very same early universe, mystically, courtesy of that very same friendly substance and the guidebook (based on the *Tibetan Book of the Dead*) by Leary, Alpert and Metzner.

Sexually, my first fantasies at age seven were of men connected like pop beads and my first imprints were of longhaired men, possibly from Disney cartoons. I discovered masturbation at age twelve. I came out shortly after the great Stonewall Clash of 1969.

Unfortunately, the gay culture I found myself in was "no fats, no fems," nowadays euphemized HWP ("height and weight proportionate"). The Faeries dealt with the "fems" part. I was a fat baby and since birth the DNA of my starving and freezing ancestors has kept on giving and I usually find myself on the outside looking in where sex is concerned.

Discovery

I first heard about Faeries from reading *RFD* when I was finishing up graduate school and bouncing about the world trying to stay employed. I got the impression of a bunch of silly men whose idea of a good time was wearing women's attire in the woods. That didn't interest me, so I just let it pass by. Eventually I arrived in San Francisco in the fall of 1978 and took a while to assimilate. It was the heyday of the Castro Clone look. All American Boy sells no trousers with waists bigger than thirty-two inches. Still, there were remnants of hippie culture and hints of future Faeriedom. I remember Murray Edelman's workshop "A Different Kind of Night at the Baths," which included some breathwork and bonding instead of the usual games.

In 1980, a group called Bay Area Gays and Lesbians in Science (BAGLIS) emerged, though there never was a critical mass of lesbians. At one of the meetings in early fall of 1980, my friend Bill Hill mentioned that he had been at the Radical Faerie Gathering in Colorado. He said there was more to it than silly guys wearing dresses, so when an article about the Faeries appeared in a local gay paper, I took the train to Berkeley and met some Faeries at a house on Harper Street and was introduced to the Circle.

My impressions were mixed. There was a fellow with a rather crude Southern accent who spoke loudly and introduced himself as Crit. I must have liked the folks enough to come again, as the Circle drifted from house to house, including Sai's place in the Haight, where I attended a few times. The Thursday-night Circle eventually moved to Bound Together Books on Haight Street, where it persisted for decades as the "disreputable" Circle.

My metaphor for the Circle is the Mössbauer effect of recoilless scattering of photons. While a big energetic cosmic ray can dislodge a single atom, if the atoms are connected, then the group can absorb the hit and protect its members. Mentioning that in a Circle would usually get me catcalled for not speaking from the heart. I suppose that meant that I could not think and feel at the same time.

A Perfect Storm of Neurotransmitters

A Gathering was planned for Harbin Hot Springs over the Winter Solstice, which that year was also close to the full moon. Taking time from work at an aerospace contractor and the first public performances of the San Francisco Gay Men's Chorus, I landed at the Gathering and settled into the sleeping area, where I spotted two hippie-looking guys, one in tie-dye. The old fears about attractiveness arose, so I moved along. I also remember a Circle of Loving Kindness after Buddhist *metta* practice that Sequoia led and I wished kindness in ever-expanding circles.

There was grass and kissing and relaxing in the warm water and then a Heart Circle. After the rituals had died down, I encountered John who offered me some acid and told me that he had found his lover on it. Set and setting had become a setup! Five of us partook and the rest is mystery, save that I would remember those five in my *metta* prayers for decades after. One of the five—call him Tadzio—was the one I had seen earlier having oral sex when I moved in.

Now I felt that I had held myself back from love and maybe should express that feeling instead. So as an act of will I told him that I loved him and there followed an embrace, which to me felt like a collective form of enlightenment. He said it was a miracle, but then the trip continued alone. After I bedded, visions of all that sex going on without me appeared and subsided. Then I slept, only to be awakened by James Broughton reciting "This Is It" at breakfast. Then it was back to work in the big city and singing in the chorus.

I had never known romantic love before and over the next two months now it hit me full force. (The ego dissolving serotonin and dopamine of the acid experience having unhinged me with the phenylethylamines of falling in love.) I communicated with Tadzio about it and infatuation grew in his absence.

But now he was no longer sleeping around and settled on somebody who was six feet two and blond. I never fully recovered from the trauma of rejection for looks on my first time at bat. It only gradually decayed like radioactive fallout with a half-life of four to five years. Was it a shaman's wound that enables the healing of others? I still don't know. Perhaps I should have quit with Faeries then and there, but truth be told, there seemed nowhere else to go and no way out but through.

Clear Light Opera

I was lucky enough to give an invited talk in Albuquerque about a month before the third national Gathering at Pecos Wilderness, outside Santa Fe, New Mexico. On that trip I visited with Henri, one of the organizers in Santa Fe. The spare bed was home to more visitors than me. Things were looking up and anticipation was rising for the upcoming event.

This was a huge Gathering, about two hundred and seventy all told, for a week in the woods. When we all circled together we couldn't identify our brothers on the other side. At that Gathering we had consensus to hold smaller, regional Gatherings rather than national Gatherings. Harry and John, who had lived in New Mexico before, were at Pecos, perhaps my first meeting with those who would be patriarchs if we weren't all anarchs. I got lucky sexually three times at the Gathering, so my usual depression at being alone while the slender twinks slept in pairs was less severe. One man, call him Nemesis, was especially good at parading his conquests.

It was cold at night at such an altitude and some men were feeling unwell, at which point someone noted that the kitchen Faeries were not putting salt in the food. We prevailed upon them to at least have salt available. Self-righteous beliefs about food seem to be a hallmark of the Faeries. We used to joke in the kitchen about making "Cream of Vegan" soup for our next meal. Some men caught cold in the chilly weather and from all that hugging and kissing. I slept through the post-nasal drip in Dennis's yurt after the Gathering, having stewed tomatoes for breakfast.

Breitenbush Early Gatherings

Back in San Francisco I noticed a Call for a Northwest Gathering to be held at Breitenbush Hot Springs over Valentine's weekend, 1982. At that time Breitenbush was still a hippie commune, not yet a business, so some of our stay involved a work exchange. I remember how we turned work into play, by singing songs (not the usual Faerie dirges) while we passed logs from one side of the barn to the other.

The only creature discomfort was inadequate food. Hearing "Faeries," they naturally assumed we were all one hundred and ten pounds, ate only tiny helpings of vegetables and had shit that didn't stink. Imagine their surprise when the lumber-jacks showed up. By the time the Gathering was over, we were ready for bacon and eggs in town, pie at Vi's on the road back, and beer and pizza in Eugene that night. My host Bill Blackburn asked what I found of value. I said that although for many men (me not included) sex was easy to come by, intimacy was not. I valued the Faerie intimacy.

I attended the next dozen winter Gatherings. At the 1984 Gathering I had a reprise of the Harbin experience, as we were as many as five to a cabin and one morning I was awakened to the sounds of fucking going on about three feet from my head. Nemesis and his new love were happy to disturb the rest of us and feelings of isolation and loneliness had the better of me once more. Having that roiling inside me at Heart Circle, I burst into tears. The Heart Circle absorbed the shock and I was levitated on the hands of the Circle and given an imaginary ring to kiss whenever I felt lonely and unloved. I'm kissing it now.

In 1985 a group of us from San Francisco decided to charter a Green Tortoise bus to make the trip to Breitenbush. The buses had a communal sleep area which was put to good use. Two of our numbers were going at it orally in the middle of the platform. One Faerie had the inspiration to pass out some carrots so we could munch along. It was like starting the Gathering early, but it led to what I dubbed the Drag Wars Gathering.

The first two Gatherings had that old rustic-northwest-jeans-and-flannel flavor and here come these queens from California doing wigs and make-up. So a small culture war was started at the Gathering, with the hosts deciding not to send the Call to California next year. I was informed later that the whole group had failed to pre-register, creating a crisis in the larder and in their opinion that was the reason we weren't invited back. Over the years, wigs and makeup won and overtook whatever Heart Circles there were.

I did a stint as Queen Registrar in 1991, the same year they started having summer Gatherings. I opposed them because I wanted to see Faeries spending resources on their own land at Wolf Creek, which we had acquired by then. I stopped going after 2002; a little drag and wigs and shrieking goes a long way with me. The "luscious love lounge" to which I wasn't ever invited took over all the space, so I had not even a place to sit down and had to go back to my cabin.

The Unbearable Lateness of Eating

Many Faeries think that the latest time a meal was ever served at a Faerie Gathering was the Moroccan Feast at the First Blossom of Bone Gathering in Napa, California in 1983. That meal was scheduled for 2 p.m. and the food was ready by 2:30. But the serving did not begin until ten at night, as the waitresses had to choose their drag. And then there was the Autumn Equinox Gathering in 1982 at the Mendocino Woodlands, an old WPA camp. Dinner was planned for the usual time. However, at the precise moment of the Equinox, many Faeries, including the cooks, took acid. A tour through the kitchen was vaguely reminiscent of Fellini's *Satyricon* with Eon sitting in a lotus position on one of the counters surrounded by candles and sacrificial offerings of carrots. That meal was prepared for at least six hours and was never served.

A Bone Blossoms in Napa

At the Madre Grande Gathering in 1983, after a stunning group meditation in a big natural bowl, under the full moon, a few of us from San Francisco got the idea that we should have a Gathering in Northern California. So we got together to plan it.

One of the first meetings was at Harper House in Berkeley where I had met the Faeries for the first time. We were mostly in our thirties and our organizational skills were sharp and we were enthusiastic and committed. One of us had a connection to Green Valley Ranch in Napa, so we ventured to hold a Gathering on land with basically no infrastructure. This meant trucking in water, building an outdoor kitchen, procuring the food, buying insurance, renting porta-potties and all those organizational things. It was a labor of love. The fastest-ever consensus: should we have coffee at the Gathering? Sequoia looked up from his espresso and said "Yes!," emphatically ending the discussion.

The Gathering was held over a week and two weekends, so I went to work on the weekdays. I sat at my computer at NASA with a green-painted nail on my middle finger, feeling a spiritual connection while in a government office. It was a successful Gathering and we had a little extra money left over to seed future Gatherings, despite turning no one away for lack of funds. At the recap meeting, I read from Whitman's "Proud Music of the Storm:"

> *And I said, moreover,*
>> *Happily what thou hast heard O soul was not the sound of winds,*
>> *Nor dream of raging storm, nor sea-hawk's flapping wings nor harsh*
>>> *scream…*
> *But to a new rhythmus fitted for thee,*
>> *Poems bridging the way from Life to Death, vaguely waited in night air,*
>>> *uncaught, unwritten,*
>> *Which let us go forth in the bold day and write.*

Shadows at Madre Grande, 1984

The second Madre Grande Gathering I attended became known as the "Shadow Gathering" because of the nimbus of Mitch Walker and his acolyte Chris Kilbourne. Mitch showed up, taking charge—uninvited—at the welcoming Circle, and was in his groove about "you're not looking at *Shadow!*" To which many of us responded, "What the fuck is Shadow?" We asked what he meant and Mitch only reiterated. He had a particularly smarmy delivery at one Circle, passed around some Mother Nature in a pipe and was all about how he was teaching us "to break the rules of the Gathering." Heaven forbid!

As was our wont, we let him go on until he ran out of steam. Perhaps it is a weakness in Faerie culture that Heart Circles can be so easily hijacked by individuals on a rant (or off their meds). The typically Faerie response, however, came at the "No-Talent" show where we were treated to "shadow theater." Remember the old family games of putting up a back-lit sheet and making images of birds and butterflies and the like by moving your hands in front of the light?

"Buy Land, Build Buildings"

At the Napa Gathering I was talking with my friend Mica about the future. We were quite burned out by the process of schlepping everything, from wood, to stoves, to water, to the land, having to set it up and take it down. My response was: "Buy land; build buildings."

There had already been a search for land for the Faeries by Will Roscoe and others, in which I was not involved. The rumor I heard concerned a lost Faerie fetish, a Rubbermaid bowl of fruit salad, which Chris Kilbourne tossed at Harry Hay for not acknowledging his uninvited (except by Mitch) presence on a land search.

A group of us decided toparking keep on looking for land for Gatherings and form a legal entity for acquiring and managing the land. We picked a name for our non-profit on the evening of Tuesday, September 12, 1984, at Touchstone, the home of Mica, William Stewart and Lin Mazlo. For me this was my break night in the San Francisco Symphony Chorus' four performances of Mahler's "Symphony of a Thousand" with the San Francisco Symphony. We lay down on the floor and did some free chanting, letting names arise into consciousness. One candidate was the Greek *Omphallos* from *Omphalos* (the center of the world at Delphi) and *Phallos* (guess). Eventually the name Nomenus settled upon us with echoes of the *numinous* (divine presence), of *nomen* ("name" in Latin), "no menus," and "no men us." In no way were we ever invoking or including women. We were fags loving other fags.

A few years later I had a dream. In the parking lot at Wolf Creek, a great theater with a marquee had been constructed, bearing the legend: "Nomenus, Not Just Another State Theater." Maybe so, but tons of drama were set in motion, continuing into the foreseeable future.

Gatherings Come Thick and Fast

At the California Men's Gathering in 1985 (eventually these developed a Faerie flavor, to the consternation of some of the hetero men there), I took on the Faerie name "Marvelous Persimmon" from two sources. The first was the Zen fable of the Ripening Persimmon as the ripening of Wisdom into Compassion.

The second was the character "Marx Marvelous" in Tom Robbins' *Another Roadside Attraction,* who wanted a name that was both commie and fag. At this Gathering, Nemesis asked me to move because I was blocking the sun for his tan. We Morlocks are just supposed to remove ourselves when Eloi demand. In H.G. Wells' *The Time Machine* the bearish Morlocks eat the twinkish Eloi. I can see why.

A bumpersticker seen at the Gold Creek Gathering in Southern California in 1985: "Expect a Miracle!" Steviekins comes up to me and wants to spend the night. Well, of course! Miracles already! At a circle I called "Giving Looksism the Evil Eye," Beautiful Day calls me on my own looksism. Guilty as charged…and that's the problem. I find it difficult to argue with who or what gets me hard, self-defeating though it may be.

A New-Ager ignites me by blaming the victims: The poor "choose their poverty," not the capitalists who exploit them, he said. And the Jews stepped willingly into the gas chambers? By this reasoning if I wanted sex I should have chosen to incarnate into a slender body. Faeries gathered round, helped me breathe more consciously and calm down. I got some good feedback and support and some attitude like I just described. An irritating thing about the Faeries is making social problems into personal ones: e.g. "Artwit's problem" rather than "looks prejudice."

Later in the Gathering, Joey gives instructions for a Full Moon ritual that he and others have mapped out. There will be directions invoked about and in the pond, chanting of the Tallis canon with my "Moon Goddess" words, a Labyrinth and a Birth Canal. The Moon Herself fails to show through the clouds during the ritual. Ida, the black dog who travels with Al, leads some of the howling and chanting.

A giant size pentagram is a bit tough to handle and hands are stretched to the breaking point to circumscribe the pond, but the ritual is carried on with a surprising amount of respect (i.e., I restrain my usual commentary). I do several turns of a jig as we follow each other through the Labyrinth and then use my silky rainbow scarf to drape over the newly born Faeries who are passed under pairs of hands to be reborn into the Circle standing by the fire.

I first spied the land at Wolf Creek during the West Coast Symposium that Marvin from Portland put on. He could have warned us about Assunta, he says now. It was hot and dry and water was trucked in.

While continuing the search for land, after Will Roscoe parted company with us, we set about cranking up the miracle machine once more: Blossom of Bone II in Napa, 1986. For this one, I channeled my forebear "Stara Baba Kapusta Zaprashka" or "Old Lady Cabbage Brown Butter Sauce." Any drag I do makes me look like my peasant ancestors, even without the babushka. After three days of supervising veggie-stuffed cabbage and borsht, I flamed out the afternoon of the banquet and was bailed out by William Stewart, who later showed us how Russians suffer so beautifully. Miss Mylar debuted his outfit that revealed and barely concealed a monster cock, leading to the now ubiquitous "Show us your dick!" shout out at Faerie No-Talent shows.

During the Gathering, Glennda, a good friend from BAGLIS and newly back from Anchorage, asked about forming a household in San Francisco. Soon I was a junior partner in the house at 1502 Golden Gate, the top-floor flat of a Victorian, with eleven-foot ceilings, lots of book room, shared with techno-faerie Harry Ugol and David (Leo) Ayers. I was still mostly living and working on the Peninsula, but it was a nice *pied-à-terre* for weekends. Before long we became a party venue for the Faeries, given the spaciousness. I remember a "potluck and orgy" that we hosted and

Leo spraying semen on seven Faeries. I also remember the legendary Bennett leaving our house for a naked stroll of San Francisco, then showing up at our door at 4 a.m. "Don't say you know us," I said.

In December the fate of the land search was sealed when the last surviving owner of Wolf Creek wanted out and we stepped up. Assunta disingenuously said she'd watch over the place, but instead plotted to sow dissent and drive us away. Eventually Oskrr volunteered to move to the land to represent our interests as the first Nomenite monk. Assunta's gambit was used more successfully a decade later by the women and pan-genderists who sowed dissension in their successful hostile takeover of the land.

Stuart Timmons from Los Angeles reads my palms at Gold Creek in 1987: "I have never seen someone so sensitive. Take comfort in inanimate objects. Be aesthetic like Oscar Wilde. Play a stringed instrument and play chamber music. A lover would have similar aesthetic patterns. I have friends who I don't value enough. Buy a Victorian and fill it with treasures."

Stuart was uncannily on the mark. Like many single gay men, I have had to make up for the lack of a lover by creating a comfortable and beautiful home and filling it with objects that recall positive associations, and creating a garden with plants that reward me with their beauty. While I don't know if I'll be fit as a fiddle at ninety-five, the other readings turned out to be true.

Taking Leave

HIV-AIDS was making its ghastly presence felt, though at first a few foolish Faeries thought being spiritual would somehow protect them. Over the next few years, many of our natural leaders were taken down and we who survived had to cope. I was present in 1988 when our brother Myles took his leave, holding hands with him in a Heart Circle as he expired. I hope my end will be that way

In the fall of 1989 a lot happened at once. I got a job offer in Portland, there was an earthquake, I sang in Russia and then Glennda passed from us, dissolving the Golden Gate household. Mother Nature was telling me it was time to move on. I threw the I Ching and got all sevens: "This is the best fortune you'll ever have. Go!" I drove north, carrying Gary's ashes to Wolf Creek, leaving them with Oskrr until next summer when we would scatter him under Grandmother Oak.

In Portland I connected with Faeries, spent some time in Scotty Dog's harem (a mistake for someone with abandonment issues) and got laid off six months after being hired. Seattle was next in line and I still kept up some Faerie work, registering for Breitenbush in 1991 and being Nomenus treasurer in 1992. I still went to a few Gatherings, like SexMagick in 1993 and the Nomenus Great Circles.

Disenchantment

At the Nomenus Great Circle in Portland in 1997 I was blindsided by events and soon severed my relationship with them. Without consulting the Great Circle, a group had invited a heterosexual woman to take up residence on the land for five months, calling it "a visit." A week is a visit, not five months. It was a *fait accompli*, not communicated in advance. I felt railroaded and disrespected by the subsequent decision, which I should have blocked, which essentially precluded gay male sacred space unless it was specifically asked for.

The land became a heterosexualized, desexualized generic residential hippie commune. Women living on the land, however well intentioned, undermined and cut off at the root the sacred gay male space for which we had bought and developed the land—where we could do the hard work of integrating sex and spirit.

I imagine what Glennda of the Grannies would say as he planned phallic shrines to contain the ashes of our departed brothers, with benches to facilitate fucking: "If I'm not getting my ass pounded, it's not my religion."

The author Stanislaw Lem wrote in one of his books about how a biological agent escaped from an Army lab and removed the pleasure from sexual intercourse. Thereafter, the only people who engaged in sex were the Mormons, out of a sense of duty. For me, going to Gatherings has now become a duty rather than a joy, having once been told by a young twink in Thailand "not everybody should expect to have sex at Gatherings." I have no desire to be a Faerie Mormon and make breakfast while the pretty ones sleep in and fuck.

At sixty I have returned to the philosophical materialism with which I began, like Einstein following Spinoza. I have no need for nonmaterial entities: "Oh, I don't want 'em, you can have 'em, No more spooks for me" (tune: "She's Too Fat" polka).

The sexual impulses in my body are failing, the self-defeating erections in response to skinny men having seldom brought physical contact, relationship even more rarely; the rarefied atmosphere of high culture and intellect making it all the harder to connect physically.

For the Faeries and me, it was a love affair that ended badly and now I'm grateful it's over.

A Realm of Freedom?

by David Finkelstein

IT IS OBVIOUS TO MOST people entering a Gathering for the first time that they are entering a realm of relative freedom. A place where the rules and customs which stifle and distort our true natures in this post-capitalist, sexist-homophobic-racist, earth-raping culture are suspended or altered for an agreed upon and limited duration. And that a space, an opportunity, has opened up, which can be filled by less destructive, more congenial ways of interacting. But there is danger in this freedom.

Increasingly people with HIV/AIDS and others who are especially vulnerable because of psychic, spiritual or physical battles in their lives have expressed shock and outrage that the Gathering is no longer a place where they feel safe and cared about, but that the freedom of the Gathering has taken on a callous and frightening edge.

Is there a conflict between the creation of these weekend or week-long zones of freedom where "anything goes" and our need to build a permanent, supportive community? What metaphors do we choose to guide us in our creation of these realms of freedom?

Is the Gathering an especially good weekend party, with plenty of sex, drugs and if not exactly rock-and-roll, at least passable drumming? Is it a vacation, not just from work or from the city, or from the isolation of country life, but from the responsibilities and attitudes of our regular lives? For those of us who are doctors, social workers, nurses, teachers, professional caregivers, is the Gathering a place to let go of the carefully controlled compassion we use in our professional lives and indiscriminately let out all the viciousness and mayhem we usually suppress?

Or is the Gathering a laboratory to test personalities and attitudes we might later want to adopt at home? Is it an ongoing dress rehearsal for utopia? For the revolution? Is it an improvised theater piece where all inner thoughts and feelings, rational or not, may be acted out? A leaderless cooperative group therapy marathon? A sneak preview fashion show of styles which will be seen on the runways of Paris and Milan in two or three years? A playground where you can disrupt as many games as you want and probably no one will say anything? A cooperative church in which we all take turns preaching sermons at each other? A conference where people living outside the corporate economy can trade notes and network with each other?

Is the Gathering a dance, alternately sad and joyful, in which the dancers move freely from solos to duets, trios and larger ensembles? Is it an opium den that provides pleasure to wipe out the repetitive pain of loss? Is it a cooperative school where we come to teach each other survival skills? Or a doorway through which an entire community propels itself into ever-higher spiritual realms? A family reunion? A cruising strip for fats, femmes and druggies? A sacred moment of overlap, where gods, goddesses, the dead, elders and novices all intermingle? A periodically reappearing small gay town, where everything is noticed and everything is immediately dished? Are Gatherings the feasts and council meetings of a tribe, which has miraculously reappeared after thousands of years of suppression so severe that it nearly rendered us invisible?

I have sensed all these metaphors and many others operating underneath the way different people approach the Gathering. Each emphasizes a different use of freedom and suits different tastes and agendas. (I myself am partial to the ongoing-theater-improvisation model.)

It seems to me that those metaphors of the Gathering as a place for what I call "negative freedom," i.e., as a place where you are free to *not* be as responsible, caring, thoughtful or sensitive as you usually are—and are free to act on any nasty or vicious impulse—are metaphors that make the Gathering an unsafe, unfree place for others.

The metaphors that I call "positive freedom"—the Gathering as a place to realize a vision, share a creative impulse, make something happen which is not possible in ordinary life—are metaphors which make the Gathering come alive in a way which everyone can share.

One more metaphor: how about the Gathering as a bridge, which over the years connects isolated individuals to the ongoing supportive community we hope to create?

Into the Woods

by Henry Holmes

I AM A RADICAL FAERIE OF color.

Radical Faeries are often criticized as being "hippie, idealist, pagan, gay libera-tionists." Critics discount the questions and values of Radical Faeries as naïve rem-nants of the 1960s, gay New Age romanticism that ignores the hard political realities of contemporary society.

Such critics fail to understand a fundamental point of what we are about and what effective political and social change is about. A radical revolution in conscious-ness is fundamental to true and meaningful change. For if the majority of people in society still think that being gay is morally wrong, merely gaining "rights" is not going to make gay any safer than those who would use us as scapegoats in the future. What "rights" we have today can be taken away tomorrow. It happens all the time. It is extremely ironic that we even have to fight for civil rights in the first place, though that struggle is an important one.

But the fight for "rights" alone has done nothing to change the majority of people's moral attitude toward our fundamental integrity as gay people. It is one thing to say that people should not be discriminated against. It is quite another to recognize and accept the inherent and immanent value of gay people as they are without moral condemnation or mere social tolerance. Our communities, gay and straight, have not successfully addressed this issue.

True change comes first from personal evolution. There is a very real connec-tion between individual action and the well being of the greater collective whole. Consciousness, the state of being aware, especially of something within oneself, is the fundamental building block for broader collective change.

And so the real challenge is to liberate ourselves and not depend upon others to give us what is ours in the first place. It is not for the dominant straight society to give us the right to be gay and to define who we should be as gay people. We ourselves, as gay people, as Radical Faeries, will redefine and reinvent ourselves as a step toward self-direction and as part of the dynamic ebb and flow of the energy of all life on earth.

But where do Radical Faeries of color go from here and what do gay men of color have to say about the Radical Faerie experience?

For many, Radical Faerie Gatherings have become wonderlands in the woods, a vacation oasis away from day-to-day activities in the predominantly straight world. Many express the feeling of having reached a plateau. Recognizing that many people come to Faerie Gatherings at different stages of continually evolving consciousness, as a whole, the Radical Faerie movement has enabled a basic sense of identity, consciousness and perspective of Radical Faeries as unique people different from traditional societal notions of "gay," "straight" and "bisexual" to evolve.

But this evolution has taken place predominantly within a white, Euro-Anglo ethnocentric context. While the issues with which Radical Faeries are involved also concern many gay men of color, most of the participants up to now have been white. For that reason, the Radical Faerie is ethnocentric to a degree, reflecting the life experience of mostly white gay men in America.

Why more "Faeries" of other cultures, colors and heritage have not heard or responded to the Radical Faerie call perhaps has to do, in part, with the language with which Radical Faeries speak. Images, symbols, words and concepts embodied in calls to Gatherings that are predominantly white ethnocentric in origin cannot be assumed to strike responsive chords in people of other cultures and heritages. The "Faerie-like" consciousness of people of other cultures and colors needs to be discovered and explored. New languages of spirituality and gayness that incorporate images, symbols, words and concepts that are multi-cultural and multi-racial must be created. This, quite simply, cannot happen without people of color. The Radical Faerie Call and vision cannot become truly universal in reality without the "Faerie" consciousness of African Americans, Native Americans, Latinos, Asians and other gay peoples of the world.

Radical Faeries have a broader cultural role to play in society. We are in a unique position to facilitate a broader multi-racial, cross-cultural and cross-gender awareness and to bring awareness of spiritual immanence or immanent value—what we call subject-SUBJECT consciousness—to a broader segment of society.

This recognition of immanent value, or subject-SUBJECT consciousness, is not, of course, unique to gay people. The black civil-rights and feminist movements, for example, have at times raised issues of human relationships based on inner qualities of individual persons that have nothing to do with race or gender. Martin Luther King, Jr., spoke of a time when people would not be judged by the color of their skin, but by their character and spirit. On the issues of sex roles and power relationships based on gender some women have been speaking of inherent value, self-worth and individual uniqueness for some time.

However, gay people by their nature and varied experiences throughout human history are particularly well suited to facilitate and mediate the reemergence of spiritual immanence and subject-SUBJECT consciousness on a broad multi-racial, cross-cultural and cross-gender scale.

Radical Faeries must renew their awareness of the political within the realm of the spiritual. Spirituality must be incorporated into the politics of the present day to end economic oppression, ecological destruction, prejudice and fear of all that is different from "mainstream" culture. Here is a gentle way, a life-affirming, life-celebrating way. Radical Faerie Gatherings should not become political conventions where social justice and political issues are debated in the abstract. But our consciousness must include political and social awareness, for it is nothing short of the survival of humankind with which we are involved.

The path of truth and light, wherever it may lead us and no matter what the issues, is one we cannot avoid if we are to be true to ourselves and our lives as Radical Faeries. We have shared our unique gifts among ourselves and grown in our capacity to love and be vulnerable. Radical Faeries, black, brown, red, yellow and white must now share them with the rest of the world.

Gay people of color must go beyond the general group or collective racial history experiences in America to look at the history of our own people. Who were the gay people in our own cultures in other parts of the world from whence we came? What do we feel now, as gay people of color that the assimilationist, straight-identified-faggot culture leaves us thirsty for? What of our yearning for more than the bars and businesses run by our "own kind" for us? What of the ache in our gay psyches that stems from our beginning from times past?

We can share with our white Faerie brothers explorations of our own consciousness from our life experiences and needs as gay men of color. Knowing where, what and who we have been can enable us to better know who and what we are now and where we are going.

Radical Faerie Gatherings can be a place to explore these ties with diverse gay histories and to celebrate the spiritual immanence that unites us as gay spirits in the world today. We cannot truly be healed and the world cannot truly regain its health and make itself whole until we share, understand and respect each other for our unique differences and also recognize the common bonds that unite and strengthen all of us.

Editors' Note: Despite every effort to locate and contact Henry Holmes to obtain his permission to include this essay here, all attempts have been unsuccessful. Nevertheless, the issue of racial inclusiveness in gay communities has long been a vexing problem and no less so than for the Radical Faeries. Writer Henry Holmes, a black-identified Faerie, was among the few men of color who attended early Gatherings. His frustrations and deeper questionings about the lack of a wider racial representation in the Radical Faerie movement was voiced in a major article that first appeared in the June 1990 issue of BLK, a now defunct magazine for African-American GLBT people. Holmes later reprinted the lengthy essay in a widely distributed pamphlet by the same title. It is a critical on-going concern, shared by many in the community, regardless of race. Holmes' concluding thoughts are presented here as part of that discussion—as well as including excerpts from an important historic document. Holmes' insightful and candid words are republished here in the spirit of prophetic witnessing we feel he would wish to further.

Chants of Silence:
Notes of a Deaf Radical Faerie-in-Spirit

by Raymond Luczak

Come worship the kisses of sun and satyrs Gathering around in this circle.
Some of us are naked; most of us wouldn't survive the first cut of potential
 centerfolds for pornographic magazines.
Some of us don dresses and halter bras, while our long goatees are braided.
We dab our eyelids with glitter and we celebrate the complete absurdity of gen-
 der expectations with our fashion felonies, with prances and laughs.
We are satyrs of the sun.

I'VE DESCRIBED WHAT I IMAGINE such a Gathering is like and I've never attended a Radical Faerie Circle. It's just too hard to lip-read if people are always moving their heads or arms, or want to chant in the flickers of a fire. So I've never gone. But then again, I've never felt like the type of person to join other people's chants.

Once, in the magazine racks in the back of Lambda Rising Bookstore in Washington, D.C., I came across a copy of *RFD*. I was completely taken with it because as someone who grew up in Michigan's Upper Peninsula, a land of small towns, I found the idea of gay people *choosing* to live out in the country, as opposed to feeling the need to congregate with their own kind in large numbers in cities, to be quite thrilling. I'd understood that being gay meant being unconventional so *RFD's* unconventionality in layout and tone thrilled me no end.

The first picture I saw of a Radical Faerie Circle was in a book back in the mid-1980s; a small group of men, mostly strange looking and unattractive by the A-list gay men's standards, all gaudied up, holding hands up in the air somewhere in a sunny woods. It was as if they were the *anti*-drag queens of drag. But their looks of exuberance were undeniable.

I'd come out as a freshman at Gallaudet University in August 1984, and I had mixed feelings about the Catholic Church. The more I read on the history of homophobia, the more I realized that I had to denounce my involvement with the Church for their ongoing role in it.

I became more aware of Deaf history. I use the capitalized "D" in the word "deaf" to indicate a cultural and linguistic—as in American Sign Language [ASL]— perspective on deafness, as opposed to the medical and educational establishment's view of deafness as a medical condition that must be corrected.

And as I also learned stories that had been passed down orally without much of it written down, I had to question the role of religion in society. I attended Mass given to the members of Dignity, a gay Catholic group, at Georgetown University. Even though it was sign-interpreted, I came away vastly disappointed. How could any gay man attend Mass and *not* feel rage at an institution that hadn't hesitated to use its power against lesbians and gay men? I found the whole spectacle incredible.

I dabbled in Zen Buddhism, but being a twenty-something filled with hormones, I found it tough to sit still. I gave up.

Two years later, I decided to study the history of witchcraft and paganism in America. I used Margot Adler's *Drawing Down the Moon: Witches, Druids, Goddess-Worshippers and Other Pagans in America Today*, which I found to be gripping. I even contemplated the idea of becoming a pagan of sorts. But as a college student I had to deal more with the reality of getting through school.

After I turned in my report, I was delighted to see a pair of Radical Faeries walking up Connecticut Avenue from Dupont Circle. I'd read some about them, but had never seen one in person. The taller man wore dark turquoise lipstick, a necklace of ordinary stones, glittery nail polish, a reedy moustache and a t-shirt that stated "ain't i a drag?" His wispy friend sported a full beard, with dabs of rouge on his cheeks, a pair of denim cut-offs and a pair of cowboy boots.

My Deaf friend said in ASL [transliterated here in English] "These-two weird!"

"Not think s-o."

"What? Why?"

"Them force people stop expect-expect everyone look same. If everyone *require* look behave same year-round, same hearing people, then no room Deaf people finish."

He said nothing.

Did I try to shock with my *own* clothes? Only a little, as I didn't feel strong enough. It's tough enough to be Deaf, having to educate people so that you can lipread them. Many hearing people never realize the amount of effort that goes into speaking clearly enough and what a damning art lip-reading truly is. So much depends on context and acoustics. Furthermore, many hearing people feel intimidated by the idea of approaching a Deaf person in the first place. If I tried to drag up as a Radical Faerie in appearance I'd have alienated even more people.

When I was eighteen years old I read Quentin Crisp's autobiography *The Naked Civil Servant*. I was stunned. I had never read anything like it, certainly not with that keen voice of his. I scoured pictures of him with his fedora hat, ascot, cane and suit.

Some years later I had dinners with him and his best friend, who was my partner. I was filled with admiration. He had stood his ground and never changed one bit even though the world around him accelerated and left him behind.

I consider him the first Radical Faerie I got to know, even though I'm sure he'd have thought the notion of men strangely dressed and prancing about and paying worship to all sorts of goddesses and gods to be an absolute mistake, much like sex and music. If a Radical Faerie means being a non-heterosexual man completely independent in mode of dress and attitude, among other things, Quentin certainly was one.

Years later, at a reading held at A Different Light Bookstore in New York, I saw Harry Hay himself. Faeries of all sorts, often strangely costumed without trying to hide the fact that they were still men, gathered around him. That he had a balding pate and stringy white long hair along with his dangling feather earrings didn't seem to faze him in the least. He was what he was; the rest of the world be damned as he sat there with his wood carved cane. I knew of his involvement with the Mattachine Society, but I hadn't quite realized that he was equally influential in the Radical Faerie movement in America.

I try to live my life without regrets. That I never got to say hello to him is one of mine.

Then Walt Whitman came ambling into my life. I don't remember the first time I'd heard of him, but I suppose he'd been everywhere like shadows that no one notices until they look up at the sun. It was in the late 1980s that I picked up a used paperback of the 1855 edition of *Leaves of Grass*.

In those days I was lonely in New York, often wondering whether anyone would want to be with a Deaf gay man who'd just graduated from college. Younger readers may be surprised to learn that in the 1980s we gay men had to find each other the hard way: *in person*. Gay bookstores and bars did very brisk business back then. But out there in person, I couldn't Photoshop out the reality of my hearing aids tucked behind my ears.

Once Whitman started his nonstop word-train of sensation and emotion, he deliberately sabotaged his own brakes. It was sheer madness to see him enumerate one sensation after another. Each line was like a stroke in an extended masturbatory session, each quiver of body adding to the symphony of body and love in sweet tension.

Then my mind flashed back to a book written about Walt Whitman. In its opening chapter, the writer described the man in very sensual terms. The sea and shore mingled with his entire being and was dripping with his sex, as he waded into the waters off Brooklyn, sometime in the 1840s. I no longer remember the book title or the writer's name, but the imagery of a man attributed with Christ-like features, with full carnal knowledge of homosexuality, has never left me. There, in a corner at the Lambda Rising Bookstore in Washington, D.C., I felt shaken. I was only nineteen.

It would be years before I could articulate just *what* had shaken me.

One Halloween I donned a huge black Afro wig and a hot pink dress in the privacy of the apartment I shared with my partner. He too wore drag; that year he wanted to convey Julia Child in all her vocal idiosyncrasies. "Why, hel-*lo!*" he greeted all our visitors.

The evening was nothing but a bunch of gay men trying on a bewildering array of truly bad thrift-shop dresses, usually made of skin-irritating polyester, and trading wigs and adding on yet another layer of pancake makeup in the bathroom before trooping out onto the runway of our living room for another round of flashbulbs going off. By the evening's end we were all walking trainwrecks.

Even though we all wore women's clothing, I still felt very much an outsider. Perhaps it was because everyone talked and laughed all at the same time, so it was tough for me to lip-read or follow what people were saying. Dressing up in drag was fun, but it was all about posing for the camera more than anything else. I eventually became the chronicler of their various poses. At least I knew what went on because I was busy directing them and angling my camera for what I hoped would be memorable shots to be enjoyed a few months later at a Christmas.

In the middle of writing a sequence of poems inspired by my unrequited feelings for a gardener fifteen years later, the ghost of Whitman appeared unbidden before me. It had been so long since I'd even thought about him. Why now? I felt his firm hand grip my shoulder as I tried not to look up into his face while focusing on the computer screen as I typed. He was all about the Earth in all its moods, from lust to decay. Had I wanted to bury my heart in this rotting and rank Earth, too?

I ferreted out a used paperback edition of Gary Schmidgall's *Walt Whitman: A Gay Life*. Schmidgall explored Whitman's life from an unabashedly gay perspective and it was then I felt a stronger kinship with the man. Flush with the revelations of lust, love and the male body in the few years leading up to the self-publication of *Leaves of Grass*, Whitman understood even back then that not everyone could be pigeonholed so simply. I have no doubt that if he were alive today and not afraid of what society thought of him, as he was in his later years, he'd have been cavorting with the young men he so craved, much as the poet Allen Ginsberg had done so freely.

I was disappointed to see that as Whitman grew older, he kept expanding and revising *Leaves of Grass*, so much that he drained his masterpiece of its initial exulting homoeroticism, which had been like a shock of scarlet in the mid-1850s. The deathbed edition of *Leaves of Grass* had become a mind-numbing doorstop. So many pages and for what? Money and respectability? How could he possibly have lost his verve? Too many of his poems were sloppy misses; his watered-down revisions, more insulting when compared to the originals.[1]

Did I truly want to grow old and play it safe as he had?

By the time I finished my gardener poems, I felt as if I'd slept with Whitman himself, having beseeched him to teach me never to forget what he'd forgotten in his quest for respectability. I awoke with my beard wet from morning loam and my fingernails black from digging up the most beautiful weeds.

Growing up as the only one deaf in a family of nine children, I often sought sanctuary in both the printed word—usually books borrowed from the public library—and the unkempt woods across the street from my house. I loved exploring the woods and I had my own favorite places. I felt safe, because the woods, just like books, never judged me. It didn't matter that I was deaf or that I was starting to find myself attracted to men. In those moments I never felt like an outsider. I was just me.

Velvet Goldmine, the Todd Haynes film about the rise and fall of a glam rock star, always captures my undivided attention whenever I play the DVD. It is a nonlinear love letter to what it means to be a *fan* of a pop star, at best a feverish dream. Ostensibly inspired by David Bowie's "Ziggy Stardust" character and the British glam rock scene in the early-1970s, the movie follows Christian Bale's character who, among many other things, comes out and dresses up differently.

There's a terrific moment of liberation when Bale's character, disguising himself in a winter jacket, slips out of his parent's house and chucks his jacket inside the shrubbery outside his house. In tight pants and a skimpy shirt, he hurries along the street even though it isn't warm. Then he tries to walk nonchalantly past a group of people his age who are obviously into dressing differently. His look of longing to fit in with them is memorable.

Each time I watch *Velvet Goldmine* I am reminded of how Radical Faeries have had to find each other not just in appearance but also in temperament. Outsider-hood is a frame of mind that only those who live it *get* about other people and simply accept that about them, as opposed to treating them as weirdoes and novelties.

Does a man need to dress up differently to be a Radical Faerie? I should hope not. Because to be *expected* to dress weirdly to conform with other Radical Faeries would be no better than those men who buff up and wear the right designer clothes to score a hot trick at the swankiest club in town. Appearances cannot be everything in life, can they?

Even though I have yet to hang out with Radical Faeries and sprinkle glitter all over my beard, I'd like to believe that I am one in spirit.

Does that make me less of a Faerie?

I should hope not.

---

[1] I recommend tracking down Schmidgall's *Walt Whitman: Selected Poems 1855-1892* for a good overview of Whitman's best work.

Stewarding the Future: A Call for Sacred Witness

by William Stewart

At the core of Harry Hay's vision was the belief that we—the people he variously called *third-gender men, non-assimilationist gays, two-spirits*—and finally Radical Faeries—have a calling and responsibility to be of service in our communities, in keeping with our experience and inclinations.

Among our typical traits, in his view, are the skills of artists, healers, tricksters, ritual makers, shamans and intermediaries between the worlds. The offering of these skills for the benefit of society as a whole, he maintained, is central to our purpose, our reason for being here.

Harry's assertion that social function rather than sexual preference should be seen as the defining characteristic of our kind is as radical now as when he first conceived of it in the dark days of McCarthyism. Bruised by the collapse of the original Mattachine Society and deeply troubled by the direction of postwar society, he had immersed himself in anthropological studies and moved to the Southwest to connect more deeply with the indigenous cultures there. Out of these investigations, cross-pollinating with his intuition and Marxist education, there emerged his pivotal insight that we queer folk have an essential role to play in maintaining and enhancing the common good.

Based on his research, Harry believed this was implicitly accepted in traditional societies across the world, as manifest in the frequent existence of classes of individuals with special status and obligations as ritualists, medicine persons and the like. If this is the anthropological norm, then Western culture's stigmatization of nonstandard gender identities is actually an aberration, of a piece with all the other ways in which our society has deviated from healthy, sustainable practices to pursue exploitation on an unprecedented scale.

Indeed, in this analysis the persecution of homosexuals and other people of "deviant" tendencies is intimately linked with the rapacious capitalism and spiritual fragmentation of modern life. In its greed to plunder the Earth and its peoples, our expansionist global society has dangerously upset the balance of things and has

215

ostracized the very folk most attuned to what's actually happening—the shamans, the visionaries and the walkers-between-worlds, who are proportionally, more often than not, also the queers.

Harry died in 2002 with many hopes and many fears for the future of our tribe. Now, as we go deeper into the twenty-first century, I believe that we have an obligation to take this line of thinking to an entirely new level, in this era when resource depletion, climate change and environmental degradation loom ever larger on the horizon.

The sacred stewardship identified by Harry as our archetypal vocation, which the dominant culture desperately needs but pathologically rejects, will be tested and tempered in ways we can scarcely imagine as the planet faces collapse on an unprecedented scale.

For we are confronted by nothing less. Perhaps if these imminent crises were independent of each other, the high-tech quick-fix approach might be adequate to address them individually—but even though the prevailing paradigm insists on seeing such phenomena in isolation, ignoring their overarching context, in fact they're all manifestations of the same self-amplifying system of beliefs and behaviors that threatens the very foundations of planetary life.

It's no accident that climate change is beginning to spiral out of control just as fossil-fuel scarcities approach a tipping point; or that languages, species and entire ecosystems are disappearing at similarly accelerating rates. These and an endless list of other meltdowns—environmental, economic, social, spiritual—are all ultimately the result of human ingenuity run amok, acting on the disastrous misapprehension that the world's natural resources can be exploited without negative consequences and essentially without end.

It's not hard to see how this error arose. Until recently, all the evidence suggested it was true. Beginning with the development of agriculture some ten millennia ago, we as a species have been manipulating our environment with ever-increasing effectiveness, enabling a trajectory of exponential growth.

It's only in this unique historical moment, when for the first time we are able to view the entire human experiment as a single episode in the context of planetary time, that the inherent unsustainability of the growth model has become apparent. From this perspective, "civilization" is an anomaly of breathtaking proportions: never before has one species so completely dominated the planet, capitalizing on the evolutionary edge of its large brain size and taking advantage of an unusual interval of climate stability to drastically increase its numbers and power through plant and animal husbandry, resource extraction and social control.

It is an open question whether this pattern of human development would have been sustainable without the additional factor of fossil fuels. But once humankind discovered the secret of concentrated energy, the genie was out of the bottle. Expansion on a previously unimaginable scale became possible and naturally, as a species determined to maximize control over everything around us, we took advantage of the available opportunities.

This one-time unrepeatable raid on the strongbox of petrochemicals has fueled a binge of mind-boggling proportions. Burning up eons of stored sunlight, we have exhausted most of the readily accessible sources of these substances within just a couple of centuries, enabling us to briefly, grossly exceed our planet's carrying capacity, with unheeded environmental consequences accruing all the while.

Even those aspects of petroleum-driven growth which may seem the most benign—I am thinking of things like modern agriculture and medicine, which have made possible massive global population growth and, for some, a better quality of life—can now be seen as deeply problematic, because they have increased the burden on global sustainability.

Immersed as we are in this era of overextended, carbon-leveraged growth, our natural inclination is to experience it as "normal" and a significant effort of consciousness is required to discern just how far removed from any previous reality our current situation is.

But in truth, we are in dangerously uncharted territory. And this is precisely where we queer folk come in—for who better than we, with our outsider status and our multi-focal vision, to see beyond the insidious trance that holds society transfixed? While the "well-adjusted" sleepwalk through a world of material glut and anomie, we walkers-on-the-edge are already ahead of the curve in our ability to comprehend the spiritual bankruptcy and potentially catastrophic consequences of the Western way of life.

I don't mean to suggest that this take on our global predicament is uniquely ours. Many provocative thinkers unconcerned with sexual identity have argued that we're heading for collapse and their conclusions are no less valid just because a queer perspective isn't part of their analyses.

But even though it's not necessary to look through Harry's "gay window" to see the peril we face, I believe that we two-spirits have an important insight to bring to the table. As mediators between the multiple dimensions of reality we have a predisposition to see the essential *spiritual* nature of the coming global crisis. Our window reveals how it's the *psyche* of the modern world that is fundamentally out of balance.

All the other imbalances are tied to this disease of the soul and nothing short of a revolution of consciousness will be enough to turn the tide.

Like addicts generally, our culture is hugely invested in denial. We grasp at the delusion that solar panels and clean coal and carbon-trading protocols will allow us to continue on our current path with only minimal sacrifice, as if the whole super-structure of modern life were not built on the myth that we can always spend our way out of trouble.

Like medieval sinners buying indulgences, we imagine that we can trade up to an ever grander fantasy while ignoring our ever larger debt—fiscal, environmental, psychological and spiritual. Hooked on the rush made possible by fossil fuels, we insist that we can maintain increasing population and resource extraction without courting disaster; and we eagerly devour the media blandishments proffered endless-ly for our consumption by commercial and political power-holders who pander to those beliefs out of venal self-interest, since that's where their short-term profits lie.

I do not claim for us queer visionaries a messianic calling to turn the world from the error of its ways. We may have some insight into what's happening, but even in conjunction with our many allies in awareness, I believe that we are power-less to stop it. The momentum of uncontrolled growth and its destructive impact is simply too great to be reversed, no matter how many of us in the vigilant minority put our shoulders to the wheel.

No, only collapse will break the cycle. We could, perhaps, use our Trickster ways to marginally hasten it along—but destructive energy most often backfires and in any case, the process will follow its own trajectory, so intervention would serve no meaningful end. Just as the addict must hit some sort of bottom before recovery can begin, so the requisite shift in consciousness will become possible only when global expansionism collapses under the weight of its own overreach.

It's unproductive to speculate about how, exactly, the coming crisis will play out. The points of vulnerability are virtually endless and chaos in any one of them could trigger a domino effect among the others. We can only hope that the process will begin sooner rather than later, since the longer current patterns prevail, the more brutal the ultimate debacle will be. Even a high bottom will create enormous suf-fering for our own and our kindred species, while a few more centuries of heedless consumption could condemn all life on Earth.

This is why I put my faith in collapse. The sooner the growth model crumbles, the greater our chance of salvaging some measure of human culture, some fragments of viable ecosystems, some potential of spirit from the wreckage. In breakdown lies our last, best hope of redemption.

And then, my fellow Faerie shamans-in-waiting, the world will need us as never before. In those dark days, if I read the omens right, a mighty and solemn task will be ours, provided that we can accept it. In short, I believe that our calling as queer spirit folk will be to midwife the death of the world.

For who knows better than we how to face the dark? Throughout history we have embraced The Shadow, challenged denial, flirted with death. We dance close to the fire; many of us have gotten our wings burned and not a few have gone up in smoke. Unlike the bulk of humanity, stupefied by falsity and averse to any psychic travail, our queer tribe knows how to meet the demons—our own and also those of the dominant culture, which cannot see that it is about to be consumed by the unacknowledged Shadow within.

And thus are we tempered. Because, while the collective psyche of modern society will have no bulwark against disintegration when its material scaffold crumbles, *we* have the tools to hold the Sacred Circle, even as everything around us falls apart.

We have done it before. We kept the flame alive during the HIV-AIDS plague years, when our own gay world was turned upside down and shaken to the core. And perhaps our experience with HIV-AIDS was just a foretaste of the work that lies ahead. Perhaps what we did for our own immediate kin—tending them, bearing ritual witness, calling on the ancestors to ease their passage onward—is what we will be summoned to do for the planet itself in its hour of mortal need.

Our strength lies in our heart-energy. The essential truth we know is this: in a world of endangered resources the one inexhaustible resource is love. With mineral and bio-wealth exploited and abused to the point of near-terminal depletion, with oceans dying and a suffocating shroud of toxins enveloping the globe, where else to turn but deep inside, to the pure well of our hearts?

Compassion, insight, imagination—these are assets which are *not* depleted by use and should be squandered lavishly because they're actually self-renewing. We're creators of magic and ritual and we don't need tinsel and Christmas lights to do it.

The key ingredient is spirit and we have it in abundance: sacred keening, ceremonial rites and intercessions with the gods, sexual trance and boundless tenderness, Heart Circles, wild play and daredevil laughter in the dark night of catastrophe. These are some of the skills we've assembled that will allow us to undertake the shaman's journey on behalf of our imperiled Mother Earth.

So gaze into the fire with me now, let it take us far into the future, a thousand years hence. See a time when all current social and technological infrastructure is gone, when the biosphere has been convulsed by loss and countless humans and other species have died in the fight for what remains. Find some little resilient band of queer-spirit men, determined despite everything to bring an element of grace to a desecrated world.

And what are they doing? Holding a dying child perhaps, or telling tales of songbirds gone extinct; stretching the soup a little further, invoking rain for the growing season, ritually carrying nature's grief, welling up with the heartache and joy that love, play and magic still live on.

Yes, wind farms must be built, wetlands restored, patterns of living reinvented. None of these efforts are wasted. What better way to spend a lifetime, in the shadow of incipient doom? Regardless of the outcome it makes karmic sense for us to do what we can, here and now, to minimize the damage we have done.

But material remediation alone will never turn the tide. Like the addict, we as a species need to recognize the extremity of our sickness and surrender our ego-driven will to the deeper wisdom of animals and plants, of stones and seas and stars. Of course we resist this reckoning, because we instinctively know how painful it will be. But face it we must, since cataclysm will confront us with the results of our hubris and the suffering will be great.

In anticipation of that moment, to my fellow beings I say this: we, your two-spirits and intermediaries, will hold you in your anguish. We will not flinch from our responsibility to witness the planet's despair. Indeed, in the coming epoch of collapse you will see us emerge into the fullness of our being, in strength and humility and heart.

This, I believe, is the sacred task awaiting us queer-spirit folk: to steward the end of the world and to hold space for its rebirth.

THE FAE WAY

The Power of the Heart Circle

by Mountaine Mort Jonas

I WAS LUCKY. THE FIRST TIME I went to a Radical Faerie Gathering, in Autumn of 1992 at Short Mountain, my orientation included where to eat, where to sleep, where to pee and poop and where to assemble for Heart Circle.

I understood the Heart Circle to be "the heart of the Gathering," the place where we paid attention to each other in a deep way. I knew I could have fun socializing, hanging out for hours over coffee and conversation, giving lots of focus to dress up and drag and theater and ritualizing and partying together. But when I got to a Heart Circle, I knew immediately that it was different. Here I could be very, very real.

Since then, I've experienced many glorious hours of listening deeply to my fellow Faeries and then having the talisman passed to me, enticing me to dig deeply into myself, so as to find something to say that mattered. Because I love this format so much I want to share that love, dear reader, with you. Note that these comments and views are my own except when others are quoted.

History

Most Faeries think of the origins of the Heart Circle as Native American. Many articles can be found on the Internet which refer to an old tradition of bringing a decorated "talking stick" or an eagle feather to council meetings or other gatherings and using it as a sacred object to indicate who has the floor in discussions. But this seems to have varied greatly depending on the tribe.

In recent years, Clyde Hall has become well known among many Faeries through his attendance at Breitenbush Gatherings in Oregon and also through his sharing the ancient ceremony of healing and renewal known as "The Naraya: A Dance for All People" at the Wolf Creek and Short Mountain Faerie Sanctuaries. Clyde is a Shoshone/Metis elder—an acknowledged authority on Native American culture. I asked him about the talking stick he said it wasn't part of his tribe's traditions.

223

"Growing up on the reservation and attending all kinds of meetings and 'doings' as a child and young adult," Clyde said, "a stick was never used. When men got together to have a discussion of importance the pipe was smoked. When that ceremony was done and the pipe was taken apart, then the matter at hand was discussed again.

"It was just a simple courtesy that the person speaking was not interrupted and given due respect. It is part of our unwritten teachings on social conduct called the *tennewyppe*. I do think it's funny that here on the reservation, the people use a stick now, in talking circles and at certain other times. So it has become a 'tradition' amongst the Shoshone people, but a new one!"

It is clear that the tribes of the Iroquois used an object called a "roll call cane" or "condolence cane" to focus their sharing. Charlie Patton, a Mohawk elder who attends some of the Naraya ceremonies, spoke of this with Clyde, who recalls: "Apparently the cane was passed at the beginning of Long House ceremonies or other meetings to the various 'bands' or clan chiefs to identify who was in attendance at the meeting.

"It was a kind of check-in, and speeches were said. It was called a condolence cane because when the cane was first presented to the clan chief by the women, who chose the leader. It gave him his authority and recognition. The women felt sorry for him because of the heavy burden of leadership that was now his. So it was called 'condolence cane' for that reason," Charlie told me.

In other tribes, if a person wanted to bring up a potentially contentious issue, they would bring their own stick to a meeting and hold it while speaking. Sometimes there was an "answering feather" which was passed to others who wanted to respond. It was traditional, elsewhere, to hang a talking stick on the west wall of the home. Any family member was empowered to take it down when they felt the need for a serious discussion. As soon as someone held the stick, all other work stopped, the family sat in a circle and the person who had retrieved the stick expressed their concerns. Then the stick was passed and others shared their feelings about the topic, until some kind of resolution was achieved.

There are also reports that the use of a talking stick is found in cultures around the world. In modern times it began to be used widely in the 1970s, as the human potential movement gained momentum and people saw the value of listening deeply to one another.

Heart Circles were adopted at the first Faerie Gatherings and the word "talisman" began to be used for the ritual object that was passed. I haven't been able to discover when or why this happened, but I have a guess. Faeries feel free to pass *any* object and that object need not be a stick. At the first Radical Faerie Gathering a talisman was used to ensure that every Faerie voice could be heard.

Mechanics

The essence of a Heart Circle is the creation of a safe container in which participants feel free to speak from their hearts without concern for being judged, criticized, or given unwanted advice.

There are a variety of ways of creating the safety of the container. In general, the more consciousness and care is brought to the process, the more likely it is to be meaningful. In many cases, especially when there are people in the Circle who are new to Heart Circles, a facilitator is selected to help provide structure. Depending on the local tradition and style of the facilitator, there may be an opening ritual to help focus the container.

At a large Gathering it is common to call for announcements first. This allows the Heart Circle to be focused more on feelings than on upcoming events. A Tarot card may be drawn to give a theme to the circle, or the facilitator may suggest a theme (with the caveat that sharing outside the theme is welcome too). A guided visualization for grounding may be offered before the talisman is passed.

Typical guidelines given by the facilitator might include:

- Listen deeply and well. For each person in the Circle, far more time is spent listening than talking. Stay focused—no "cross-talk" or side conversations. Avoid using your listening time to think about what you are going to say when the talisman comes to you. The deepest sharing is often unplanned and spontaneous.

- Don't interrupt the person speaking—only the person holding the talisman is empowered to speak. And when it comes your turn to share, avoid commenting on something another person shared, other than what it brought up in your own heart.

- When the talisman is passed to you, before you speak, you might want to study it for a moment, to see if it brings up any images in your mind that might inspire your first words. This is one way to start sharing from the moment, spontaneously.

- Say your name before you begin to speak. This is not only so
  people get to know your name—it's also a way of bringing
  your complete self into the moment.

- Speak from the heart. This is difficult to define, but it probably
  includes an emphasis on feelings over thoughts and beliefs. Use
  "I" statements whenever possible, not sentences with "we" or
  "you." You have full authority to speak of your own experience,
  but don't assume that others feel the same way.

- If you choose not to speak, that's okay.

- Pass the talisman in a consistent direction (clockwise or counterclockwise), so it moves from you to the person. This contributes to the ritual feel of weaving a web among the participants.

- Once the talisman has been around the Circle once, it is up to
  the facilitator to ask the group whether it wants another round.
  One option is that a second round is for those who didn't speak
  the first time. After that, the Circle may end, or the talisman
  may be put in the center for anyone who would like to pick it
  up and speak again. Or it may be passed around multiple times
  until everyone feels complete.

- What is spoken in the Circle stays in the Circle. This means that
  it is inappropriate to repeat someone's Heart Circle sharing in
  a social or gossipy setting. If you want to discuss what a participant said with them later, ask for permission first. Sometimes
  everyone is asked to commit to this confidentiality before the
  Circle begins.

In smaller Circles or Circles in which the participants are experienced with the
format, the role of the facilitator can end once the guidelines are established. At the
end, participants may join hands and sing a closing song together, or choose some
other way of completing their work together.

"Silence during a Heart Circle is a blessing," says Mohabee, a longtime California Faerie. "This is one of the few times many in the Circle get to really witness silence, which may not occur very often in our lives. Those who attend Heart Circles regularly know it's best to treat silence reverently and to practice patience. Rarely does anyone break the silence that might occur in a Circle."

Pitfalls

Sometimes a Heart Circle becomes very unpleasant for one or more participants if they feel disempowered by the structure or facilitation style. Here are some suggestions for minimizing this:

- Don't apply the guidelines too strictly. Don't interrupt someone's sharing in order to enforce the guidelines. One of my most painful moments in Heart Circle was a time when guidelines had been stated clearly, but as often happens, several people (including me) made the mistake of using the word "we" rather than "I" a few times. After being interrupted and corrected harshly, it was very difficult for me to find a way back to feeling safe in that Circle.

- Don't hijack the Circle for a personal agenda. Heart Circle is not a place for announcements, or gossip, or badmouthing someone who's offended you. If people start sharing in these ways, the feeling of safety can be seriously compromised.

- At the outset it is best to decide whether people are allowed to come and go. Allowing persons to join who weren't present for the opening can cause difficulty if the new person isn't familiar with the guidelines. Usually, among Faeries, that is a risk that is taken, to allow for as much openness as possible. But it can backfire if a strong container has been created and someone joins the Circle without the sensitivity to pay close attention.

- Some Faerie traditions make a distinction between a check-in (a quick round, intended to share names and maybe a sentence or two) and a more open-ended Circle. A check-in is especially valuable when there are many people in the Circle and some would like a quick taste before moving on to another activity. If the distinction between these is unclear and people enter a check-in Circle without understanding that the sharing must be kept very short (or if they don't want to restrict themselves to that), uncomfortable chaos can ensue. Often, if a check-in format is used, those who want a longer Circle may reconvene once the check-in is completed.

Glories

I asked some Faeries for their comments on the power of Heart Circles, so this article wouldn't be entirely in my voice. In response, Teddy Bare said it's all about connection. He broke this down into three aspects:

Connection with one's self: you are speaking of your feelings and your life situations. You do this sharing in a safe and supportive environment, where you are free to look at parts of yourself that you may have been avoiding.

Connection with others: you are revealing information about yourself that you may not have revealed to the general public. You do this so as to be more genuinely known by those who are present in the Circle.

Connection as community: while each person is sharing, the others are listening. Listening with their ears, minds and hearts—empathizing with the speaker, providing a space for them to reveal that which they keep protected. Witnessing. Because people in the Heart Circle really care about what is being said and really care about the people who are saying it, a communal bond is created.

Len sent an evocative email beginning with the words "The trick or not the trick is…" and then went on to describe his experience:

"The person across the Circle from you says something that stirs your heart and you *want to* respond. But you hold, let go and listen. And as others let go and add new heart to the Circle, what you are holding will be let go by someone else. So pretty soon your heart is exploding with love!

"Now comes the hard part: the talisman finally reaches you and you are so welled up with love that you want to dance, sing, chant, cheer, cry and/or scream. Instead, what you do is let go further and let the silence speak. Sort of like a *bardo thodol* experience, a *satori*, a snap into cosmic awareness.

"So the reward for paying attention with your heart is peace. Self-discipline in the fine tuning of the heart is what Heart Circles are all about. Listening from the heart blasts the I-centric of me-I-mine into a group-centered consciousness of the unlimited."

As for me, a fond memory is sitting in a little pavilion on a gorgeous beach in Thailand, the last day of an AsianFaerie Gathering. I was surrounded by about ten guys from almost as many countries, listening to their very diverse experiences of love life, work life, queer life, Faerie life—whatever truly mattered to them. I don't remember what I said—I just remember how much pleasure I got from listening. A note from my journal emphasized "standing in a Circle, losing the perception of separate beings around me, feeling the all-that-is oneness within while connected to others' hands."

Another time, I was in the midst of a decision about whether or not to travel to Europe. The talisman came to me and it took a few minutes for my words to meander to this issue. I realized as I spoke about it that I had been thinking—assuming—the decision was a monetary one. That led to clarity: the choice didn't need to be based on funds. It was more a matter of whether I needed to go or not, whether it fit with my ongoing interest in uplifting the planet and me. I made a commitment (Faeries and talisman as witnesses) to explore the choice from this new perspective. Within a day, I had decided to go. Within days the money fell into place with little effort.

Harry Hay felt his last gift to the world was the Daisy Chain SexMagick Workshop, an eight-day intensive experience, based on the group discovering itself through Heart Circles. I attended one of these events with twelve men and was once again amazed at the self-awareness and the awareness of others that emerged. In particular, one person shared something personal that was very difficult for the group to deal with and it took two or three days of full day-long Heart Circles to come to resolution. For me, the process of digging more and more deeply for what was real, beyond opinion or belief, was a revelation.

Dozens of times I have been present in Circle when someone has announced the taking of a new Faerie name. It's always marvelous to respond in the traditional Faerie way, saying that person's new name three times, and it feels particularly strong when witnessed in a Heart Circle.

Not all Radical Faeries appreciate Heart Circles. I am often shocked and saddened when someone expresses this. The excuse is usually an aversion to being forced to listen to negative people ranting and venting and complaining. But in a Circle with clear guidelines, when negativity is expressed, it's a huge gift. In our world, safe space to express the Shadow—the darker sides of our lives—is difficult to come by. And how else can we deal with fear and pain, integrating them into our larger life experience, than by speaking of them and being heard? Often I feel that avoiding Heart Circles is a way of avoiding both the Shadow and the potential for bliss that can result from embracing all of who we are.

It takes courage and discipline to set aside an hour or two or more to be devotedly real. When a Heart Circle is available, it's often up to each individual to choose to be there or not.

May these words provide inspiration for more Radical Faeries to allow the sweetness of Heart Circles into our lives.

Growing Up with the Faeries

by Pete Sturman (Mockingbird/Pistol Pete)

For a freaky little queer boy like me the Radical Faeries were the family I hardly dared to dream might exist. I was twenty-one and I'd only come out a year earlier, a revelation that had not gone over well with my mom.

The gay scene in Durham-Chapel Hill, North Carolina, where I was at school, seemed cliquish and unwelcoming. I had long hair and was into the Grateful Dead. While I'd played around with a few hippie girls, I really wanted a guy. At concert after concert, I burned with desire for gorgeous hippie boys dancing around shirtless with Indian-print skirts, all of them straight. Something had to give.

Then some friends set me up with a gay Deadhead boy they knew. We hit it off initially but when I went to Tucson to visit him he dumped me. I was crushed but, traveling on, I met two gay dudes at a Rainbow Gathering in California. They suggested that if I was heading up to Oregon, I ought to check out the Faerie Sanctuary there.

Though there was no event happening at Wolf Creek when I visited, I got to skinny dip in the creek and managed to have my first threesome. I'd never seen so many butterflies and my broken heart began to heal.

I caught up with the Faeries *en masse* later that summer in northern Minnesota. Just as at Rainbow, they said "Welcome home" (or the more Faerie-like "Welcome homo"). It was such a relief to find a group that embraced me and encouraged me to be as weird as I wanted to be. I made friends there that I have kept to this day.

Since then I have gathered with the Faeries at Kawashaway, Blue Heron, Faerie Camp Destiny, Wolf Creek and Zuni and have made regular and extended visits to both Short Mountain and IDA. Now forty, I feel as if I have grown up with the Faeries and am grateful to have found them at such a young age.

The Faeries provided me with a safe environment to try all sorts of different things. I could split wood in high heels, bake bread in my underwear or run around covered in mud. I could laugh like a hyena or take a day of silence. They helped inspire me to become a musician and songwriter, a loud and proud queer troubadour.

At first I couldn't sing or play very well but people clapped and cheered and told me to keep it up. Listening to tapes of myself from those early days I know now just how kind they were to me. I got the same patient encouragement as I learned how to keep a beat in Drum Circles.

I also was exposed to an unconventional approach to sex, love and intimacy. I might share kisses, hugs, massages or sexual contact with someone, but that didn't mean we were boyfriends, nor did it mean we'd only "tricked." The platonic, romantic and sexual blended into each other in a way that I'd never seen before and that I've not seen anywhere else. People who expect a perpetual orgy are often sorely disappointed because it's really something else that's going on. Any touch given with love and respect might be spiritual. Expanding our sexual landscape need not be incompatible with the search for spiritual connection.

At one of my first Gatherings I had a fling with a Faerie named Salamander who led me around in leather and bondage gear, something I'd never experienced before. He later invited me to come visit him in New Orleans. A week before I was to arrive he told me he'd met someone else.

Confused, I asked if he still wanted me to come.

He said yes and so began our triad experiment. It didn't last, but I fell in love with New Orleans and Salamander and Gregorian went on to have an over-the-top, performance-art wedding ceremony a few years later.

The Faeries taught me that not only was it wonderful to be a freaky queer boy, but that we had a unique point of view and a special gift to bring to the world at large. At Gatherings, for instance, we step outside of conventional society and explore what we *want* to be. We exchange ideas and energy and try to heal ourselves and each other.

But this withdrawal from society (or "dropping out") is temporary and when we come back we bring Faerie energy to share with the world, each in our own way. I met many Faeries who were involved in staging urban events and performances with style, a sense of humor and often a political message. I was impressed and really wanted to form my own Faerie music group.

In New Orleans I became buddies with a singer and pianist named Paul. He'd been a little intimidated by my spandex outfits and raucous songs about masturbation but I wooed him with my softer side. One of our first performances together, as The Tennessee Lounge Lizards, was singing country songs at Short Mountain. We later took the name *Pistol Pete & Popgun Paul* and always felt that our partnership had been baptized by the Faeries.

Working almost as hard on our costumes as on the music, we went on to other, sometimes bigger gigs singing songs like "Superfag" and "What If God Was a Homo" in bars and coffeehouses across the country. We would stay in spare bedrooms and on couches, usually those of folks we'd met at Gatherings. They'd help us find venues to perform in, call their friends and pass out flyers, cook us dinner and sometimes get cozy with one or both of us. When funds got too tight to keep an apartment the Faeries offered us the opportunity to live with them at IDA for a spell.

We got to realize a rock-and-roll dream and though we never achieved any kind of sustained financial success, the excitement we encountered led us to believe that there was value to what we were doing. We came to see ourselves as ambassadors from Faerieland, traveling from town to town with a message: *Be yourself, try to live joyfully and in harmony with nature and your fellow humans*. This sort of idealism is, at least for me, at the very core of what the Faeries are about.

It is easy to criticize Faeries for inevitably failing to live up to such a vision. And, besides, a Faerie vision is not intrinsically superior to that of the uninitiated. We haven't come up with the answers to all the world's problems. Not all GLBT folks find our approach appealing, especially across lines of race and economic background—like the hippies, the Radical Faeries are largely the product of white middle-to-upper-middle-class privilege: one must first be "in" before one can "drop out."

We haven't eliminated looksism, ageism or bitchiness and we're still not sure how to handle substance use and addiction in our community. Like everyone else, we have problems and disagreements. While a Gathering is a staged festival, year-round communities face all the hassles and politics of people trying to live with each other.

Sometimes I've gotten disenchanted, such as a few years ago, when circumstances dictated that I clean up my act with regard to lots of things, including my heavy pot-smoking. I anticipated it would be my phasing-out of the Faeries, but instead I was surprised to find a great deal of support for sobriety there. Since then, I've felt an increased ability to participate in and be present for the Gatherings and events I've attended.

I've also heard it suggested that the Faeries have lost touch with the radical politics of founders such as Harry Hay. There may be something to this, but Faeries are a ragtag bunch that tend to defy blanket statements. Moreover, while the mainstream gay world fights tooth-and-nail for Marriage Equality, many Faeries are manifesting their own visions of polyamory, community living and other sorts of non-nuclear families. I daresay in this, at least, Harry would approve.

Still, with all due respect to Harry, he was never our leader. We don't have leaders. And increasingly, today's Faeries seem to be reaching beyond Harry's original vision by welcoming any that wish to gather, including women, transgendered folks and even heterosexuals. Faeries didn't kick me out when I became romantically involved with a woman. The world has changed; perhaps we're more comfortable with our status as gay men and feel we can be more inclusive.

We go to great lengths to explore frivolity and delight, but we also try to take care of each other. Faeries have reached out to me when I was feeling isolated and been willing to confront me when I was out of line. Through the Faeries, I've had all the perks of family life—lovers, friends, siblings and parental figures. Our New Orleans contingent, holding weekly potluck dinners and a great big Mardi Gras Ball each year, is particularly cohesive, providing social support and serving as a viable alternative to the bar scene.

And, sensitive to the plight of our community, Short Mountain became a true sanctuary for dozens of evacuees after Hurricane Katrina. This was particularly notable for me because during that time I got very sick with Hepatitis C. In desperate need, I fell into the care of my old friend and former lover Salamander, who stepped in to be my nurse while at Short Mountain, even invited me to stay at his Baton Rouge apartment to recuperate as autumn began to grow chilly.

Things have gotten better. I underwent treatment, cleared the virus and now do what I can to help others dealing with that disease. Through my difficulties, my mom and I have gotten a lot closer, like old pals. I recently attended my first Dead show in eighteen years with two gay Deadhead buddies of mine and I ran into Faeries there. I'm part of a number of overlapping communities and whatever zigzagging path my life takes, my Faerie family still cheers me along.

In 2006, Popgun Paul and I spearheaded the first post-Katrina Faerie Ball as a fundraiser to help rebuild a local HIV-AIDS hospice in New Orleans. We still sing together when we're in the same city, which is not often enough. He's still down there, now studying to become a nurse, and I live in New York City, still hoping to find love around the next bend, singing my songs wherever I can, going to Drum Circles and dancing like a freak.

Faerie and a Father

by Tyler Tone (Stitch)

THE SEWING MACHINE BUZZED OVER material I was pushing past the needle. Iridescent dragonflies adorned the fabric that comprised the bodice and green sleeves descended from the armholes. The full skirt was a pale sage fabric, with the hem finished in box-pleating and trimmed in a thin rainbow ribbon. I was making a dress for my son.

We were off to an event in Seattle called Ravenna Ravine; a Faerie May Day celebration. My son had carefully chosen the fabrics for the new dress which wasn't the first one I'd made for him. Oh no, this was the third.

The first dress was made out of colorful neckties that he wore marching in the Vancouver Pride Parade in the summer of 2005. The next dress, for his first Ravenna event, was a beautiful collage of green and blue fabrics. My son had a growing spurt during the previous year which necessitated the construction of this new creation.

As I was bent over the sewing machine I stated to my son, who was visiting me for the weekend, that this wasn't a typical event—a father making a dress for his son.

"A father could most likely make a dress for his daughter, if he even knew how to sew," he said. Then he revised his observation. "But maybe he'd make a dress for his son if it was Halloween?"

"But you don't need to wait until Halloween to wear a dress," I said.

"No, I wouldn't wear a dress even then. I like blood and guts and scary things."

"I think Halloween is a time for people to look pretty," I stated.

"Nope, I like to scare the crap out of people!"

We had a laugh and I focused on the task of securing a zipper in the back of his bodice.

My son was eight when the Faeries fluttered into my life, smacked me with Faerie-dust and altered the course of my life. The Faeries gave me a focus I was lacking. They supplied me with a continually inspiring tribe of men who accept my son with open arms and wings.

The Faeries have given me many memories to hold and examine as a father. I stand these next to the memories of my dad and it's glaringly evident that my son and I have lived very different lives. My childhood was filled with years growing up begrudgingly on cattle ranches; endless hours circling hayfields on the tractor, helping my dad brand baby calves, having my insides turn to liquid while being bounced around in the cab of the large truck taking cows to the range for summer grazing. The closest I got to fairies was Tinker Bell in *Peter Pan* or the chubby ones from *Sleeping Beauty*.

I've witnessed how freeing it's been for my son to frolic with the Faeries. He was so joyful and buoyant the first year at Ravenna when he donned his dress with sneakers. The blue polka-dot skirt fluttered on the breeze as he dashed to join the Circle ready to call to the Goddess, waking her from her winter slumber. When the procession followed the newly aspected Goddess into the ravine, my son was at the head of the line walking in step with the Faerie Divine. The next year he was chosen to carry a flag and marched proudly waving the colorful pennant for all to follow.

My son and I marched side by side in the Pride Parade within the first year of my immersion with the Faeries. It had been a couple years or more since the Faeries had blessed the Vancouver parade and it was time we made a splash again. I built a large sweeping dress for myself and my son donned the necktie-dress.

We joined the other Faeries, waiting to take our place in line to march down Denman and Pacific streets. But then a curious incident happened. This handsome young fellow painted green, as one of the six parts of the rainbow flag, came up to me and told me that putting my son in a dress was "indoctrination."

I looked at this green man (green with envy perhaps?) and asked him what it would have been like for him, when he was a little boy, to be able to wear anything his heart desired. He was dumbfounded, sputtered out some sounds and stumbled off to join the other five colors.

Another area of my life that blossomed due to the Faeries ruffling into my consciousness was the concept of spirituality. This was a heavily shrouded topic and one to which I hadn't frankly given much thought. Conversations swirled around me at Gatherings and Faerie coffees where words like *Wicca, pagan* and *first-nations' beliefs* were commonplace. My curiosity burst into bloom and I eagerly took in all the information.

This curiosity led me to a sweat lodge ceremony predominately supported by Faeries. These were powerful moments for me, nestled in the dark with the steam penetrating the small space with its healing vapors.

It was even more profound when my son joined me. He was mesmerized by the fire that heated the stones. He wasn't entirely sure he could handle coming into the sweat lodge. For the first round he sat with the Faerie firekeeper, but his curiosity got the best of him and he joined us for the second round.

His skinny little body was bent over on, concealed under a towel and nestled safely behind the bulk of my frame. The sweat lodge leader asked for songs during the round and requested one from my son. His muffled voice said he didn't know any. The sweat lodge leader was persistent and said that even "Twinkle Twinkle Little Star" would suffice. My son started us off with the familiar jingle. I think he'd stuck his face out from under the towel, so his singing wouldn't be muffled.

My son also gave his time to the intimate sweat lodge community. Every year there was the cleaning and sprucing up of the land. We tore down and rebuilt the lodge. This required a huge fire and my son was definitely interested in watching the old blankets burn, releasing the prayers from the previous year into the atmosphere. He also took up a rake and cleared old leaves and twigs from around the fire pit area. He was helping a community that had embraced him and at times guided him.

I'm proud that I've given my son these opportunities. I've been humbled witnessing him at sweat lodge, marching beside him in a parade and making colorful dresses that have been adored by people he's felt comfortable with and who've accepted him in all his glory.

My son is at the beginning of his teenage years and I'm curious to see how much of being with the Faeries he'll bring into his adulthood. I'd love it if my young adult son paraded with me through the Ravine again. Then as the years passed he brought along whoever he was dating. Then the grandchildren can come and see grandpa all done up in some fabulous costume as well...

I'm getting ahead of myself.

Worlds of Wonder

by Wow

*"It is only with the heart that one can see rightly, what is
essential is invisible to the eye."*
—Antoine de Saint-Exupéry

A Faerie Tail:

That which wiggles and wags
and draws attention
from the mundane to the magical

ONCE UPON A TIME, IN a small village far, far from the sea, a child was born. Born on
a winter's dawn as both the sun and the moon rose on the horizon. A boy child with
golden hair and eyes the color of a clear summer sky. He was full of the light of love.

This child's light shone so brightly, all who saw him were drawn in to get a
closer view. Peering into his luminous blue eyes, ringed with heavy lashes, set in an
angelic face, haloed with sunlit hair, they would exclaim: "What a lovely child. What
do you call her?"

Upon hearing that the child was not a girl, but a boy, they protested. "Oh, no.
Look at those eyes, those golden curls. He's too pretty to be a boy."

Too pretty to be a boy? Too pretty to be a boy...too pretty to be a boy...is what
the child heard again and again and so, he was not a boy, though his body clearly
gave evidence of his sex and still he clearly was not a girl. This child of the sun and
the moon was something distinct. Something fine and bright and full of gentle joy.

As this creature grew he naturally loved the things of both genders. Depending
upon his mood he would entertain himself for many hours with toy trucks and cars
that he moved through the sand and dirt, as well as play with his sister's dolls which
he dressed carefully and sat with, pouring imaginary tea and eating invisible cakes.

Sometimes the cakes were mud cakes and the dolls would drive the trucks and he would dress in his sister's clothes, causing some confusion in the village.

As the years passed he too passed—as a boy—and sometimes was mistaken for a girl and he/she was both and she/he was neither.

Gifted in the arts, the child drew and painted pictures of his own imagining and wrote stories filled with fantastic possibilities. In this way he created worlds of his own making: worlds where mythical creatures flew through deep sea waters and swam in brilliant summer skies; worlds of wonder and delight where he could be whomever, whatever and wherever he imagined himself to be.

And so he became the voluminous shape-shifting clouds he longed to touch, drifting high above old oak trees. Or he became the gnarled trees themselves with great arching limbs held wide over the first winter snow, still and quiet as the frozen crystals. S/he might just as easily become a beautiful woman with raven wings whose songs could make the leaves tremble with joy or sorrow.

In this way the child found he/she could be the things that the world told him she/he was not and in these worlds of imagining this creature was always safe and never lonely though he was often alone.

Years went by and the boy who was not just a boy, grew into a man who was not exactly a man, but something else, something in between; in between the two genders that the world offered as the only choices: this or that, one or the other, male or female. Yet somehow he knew, in a deep secret place, that there was something more. Something genderless that held space for all the numerous nuances of being in a human form. Not exclusively female or male nor even exclusively human for that matter.

More time passed and he tried to be the man the world saw him to be. He grew a beard and worked hard to be a good son and brother. He even took on the responsibility of raising a child, also a biological boy and also filled with the brilliant light of both the sun and the moon.

But there was something essential missing from this existence and little by little the life force began to ebb from his body. The soul of the creature who was neither a man nor a woman grew restless and dissatisfied and the creature grew weaker and weaker for his heart was troubled and his thoughts full of anger and sorrow.

Discouraged, he took himself to visit friends in a city in which a great carnival was being celebrated, a wondrous, whirling dance of love and lunacy. There he met others who were neither one thing nor another, but were shape-shifters who could change their appearance in a flash and enchant you in a moment with their mesmerizing eyes and seductive ways. Absurdists, mystics, playful sprites and much, much more, they called themselves fairies and some called themselves Radical Faeries. In this new world of enchantments this in-between creature found joy and delight with other oddities of All Creation.

The Year: 2000. The Place: New Orleans.

The magical ritual of Mardis Gras is alive and in full bloom. Wending my way through rooms of a house where a Mad Hatter's party is hitting overdrive, my senses are hyper-activated. Everywhere my eyes scan there's something more fantastic to see. Buff queens with skyscraper wigs, chorus girl eyes, five o'clock shadows and nosebleed high-heels. Shape-shifters whose appearances defy gender and species and even gravity with girlish garments over hairy chests and hair ascending to the heavens like the flames of a bonfire. Hybrid humans with feathered wings, goat hooves and horns, or faces with three sets of eyes in two-point perspective.

"Have I died and landed in some surreal heaven or hell?" I wondered. "Whatever this is, I love it."

This occasion marked the beginning of a journey which, at the age of forty-six, changed my life forever, for I am the girlieboy/man with the sky in his eyes. And this is a tale of Radical Faeries and my reclaiming of the magic that dwells in the world and comes to life whenever we direct our gaze towards it.

Upon leaving New Orleans, I traveled to Short Mountain Sanctuary and into the swirling vortices of this Radical Faerie Sanctuary in which the living force of magic has revealed itself to me these past nine years. Years of pleasure branded by pain made bearable by the rituals of healing I have come to know.

Radical Faeries in the Woods and How Wow Got His Name

The time was late April, 2001. The occasion was Beltane at Short Mountain Sanctuary. Beltane is one of eight annual primary pagan rituals. By celebrating the purification by fire and fertility rites, Beltane assures future growth and renewal. After attending Beltane in 2000, I returned the following year with a bag of drag and a few tricks up my sleeve, under my hat and down my pants.

Arriving on Short Mountain, I choose a campsite beneath a young tulip poplar in the forest just beyond the perennial gardens, which bursts with irresistible masses of blue flag iris and florid pink peonies. I begin to settle in.

Saging myself, the area and my belongings to dispel any unwanted negative energies and to assure a positive ambient energy, I take in the vitality of this young forest rooted in ancient land. Centered and clear, I begin the creation of my altar, an assemblage of the elements of Air, Fire, Water, Earth and Spirit.

This complete, I pray to honor the five directions and call in my spirit guides and ancestors, spelling my intention for the Gathering. This is a playful and reverent devotion to being in loving grace, and fully present to my highest being in each and every moment.

Shedding my clothes and turning to my drag bag, I am intuitively drawn to a long sleeveless dress, colored in fiery hues of red, orange and yellow that clings seductively to my chest, waist and hips. The skirt, flaring to a full circle around my limbs, moves in the wind like the dancing flames of a fire. On my head, a broad brimmed straw hat adorned with long trailing veils of hot pink, red and orange netting enhances the illusion of dancing flames. Golden mica dust lightly powders my face and beard. Transformation complete.

Meet Blaze. Blaze is the embodiment of a modern southern belle on fire. She loves to laugh and dance and see that everyone is having a fine time while she herself has a blast. Gracious, loving and just a touch naughty, Blaze makes her way through the Gathering dispensing doses of good humor, vitality and wit. A most auspicious beginning this Blaze turns out to be.

The next morning dawns, shedding different light on a different face. Brownie emerges from the early mists of this magical spring morning wrapped in folds of dark brown embroidered with fine threads of gold. A cloche hat of palm bark adorned with a tin bumblebee brooch wraps around his head. Brownie is a breath of warm air, a whisper in the wind. Whereas Blaze's light burned strong and bright, Brownie stays in the shadows and moves silently, observing the marvelous world of the Faeries in the deep woods of this most magical forest.

Sparkle spouts whole on day three of this journey of discovery. Iridescent blue and violet veils adorn her from top to bottom and her bare bottom does appear from time to time. Silly, salacious and sympathetic, Sparkle never appears to be still. Even while resting, the sunlight dances across her mercurial veils shimmering in the slightest stirring of the wind.

This was the day a fellow Faerie turned a wicked face upon me and shrieked, "You can't change your name every day!" Sparkle laughed in pure delight, consoling the befuddled fae for a moment, before spinning her luminescent self up the knoll, disappearing in a patch of sunlight beneath the trees.

Now all this silliness is leading up to some serious fun. Radical Faeries in the woods celebrating the Beltane Fire of All Life need a pole to plant in the hole symbolizing the male energies being received by the female body. This comingling synergizes a potent growth surge, thus assuring greater fertility and an abundant future harvest. This surge is both physical and metaphysical in nature.

Beltane arrived on day four and the tree was needed. I dressed in jeans and boots, a light flannel shirt and a new friend "topped" me with my first wide-brimmed leather hat. Sounds butch? Good enough for me. I like to keep it simple. And so Butch I am.

Butch circles with the Faeries gathered on the knoll ready to enter into the woods in search of this year's Maypole. Forty-three Faeries set off through the orchard into the forest and down a ravine covered in spring greens and blossoms, in search of the one tree that will call to us, offering itself up for this seasonal ritual of fertility and renewal.

A kaleidoscopic kinship of cross-gendered and genderless Faeries, soulful bards and truck-driving bears with hairy chests and randy ways entered a forest on a warm clear morning in May: all for one and one for all.

The youngest among us were two children, a biogirl and a bioboy, Kaya and Rowan. Faerie kids in the forest. Children familiar with the magical ways of their world. The eldest among us was Weeder, a longhaired, Faerie-butch sissyman who knows how to properly handle an ax; a creature of few words. And the rest were gender shape-shifters and Faerie-queer in-betweens.

We frolicked and danced. We sang, grew quiet and listened. And then the call of the tree came. The tree we would cut and carry to the knoll to be anointed, painted with prayers and prepared to enter the sacred hole. Circling this arboreal entity we join hands in a spiraling embrace of gratitude as we honor the life of this living creature soon to be cut and transformed into a mystical antennae. For each year the new Maypole becomes a transformer and transmitter of dreams and prayers for the unfolding twelve suns and thirteen moons of the yearly cycle. And so here, in the young forest of an ancient land a circle of humans honors a tree.

Breathing in the musty richness of the forest air, I feel our anticipation as I join hands with one of the bears to my right and an elfin being to my left. A few moments pass. I am in a calm and loving state of reverence when quite suddenly my heart is gripped with panic.

Startled by this sudden emotional shift, I take a deep breath feeling as though I am about to release a river of tears, tears of grief, tears of deep sorrow. And in the moment of that breath I turn my head to the right and the great burly bear of a man holding my hand sobs, releasing his tears, his sorrow, his grief, now expressed for us all.

Exhaling, I am returned to my place of loving grace. My calm is restored as I now know this emotional outpouring is his not mine. Eyes open, I take in the scene before me as I send waves of warm compassion through my heart and hands into this circle of entwined hearts and souls.

This empathic relay reminds me of the deep interconnectedness of all life in this mad mysterious dance of love and learning. This is a strong lesson for all empaths as we hold space for ourselves in this vast sea of others' emotions.

Silently we continue our prayers of thanks to the tree spirit and indeed to the great Goddess Gaia. An Om is toned and our voices join together, clear and full, and we bless the tree. We thank it and we bless one another as we feel the pulse of life's mighty web of connection.

Now the time has come. Who will make the first cut? The ax is sharp and ready. Its wooden handle is an offering from yet another tree. The iron forged into the blade yet another extension of Earth and Fire. It is decided that the youngest will make the first cut. So Kaya is handed the ax, which is about as long as she is tall. Here I say I saw what I saw and so did we all. Kaya, a sapling of seven years, raises the ax and readies it as if she has just lifted a long feather. She swings sure and strong and the first cut into the tree-flesh goes neatly and cleanly. This Faerie child moves like a dancer and swings again and again as the tree yields itself to the blade, opening itself to its new destiny.

Now Rowan, perhaps a head taller, follows with equal confidence and soon there is a buttery notch of exposed wood, clean and satiny smooth gleaming in the afternoon light. We each follow in turn, playfully, tearfully, reverently, notching both sides of the trunk until there comes a great creaking as the tree teeters and falls, stretching its forty-plus feet onto the forest floor.

Some Hours Later...

Laid in the center of a grassy knoll beneath a spring sky, this sacred tree is ceremoniously stripped of its bark, bathed and anointed with sacred water and painted with prayers in a myriad of hues from base to crown. Then a brilliant assortment of hand-cut ribbons is attached, forming a multi-colored cascade of threads, ready to be woven into a criss-crossing of our hopes and dreams.

We circle, for the time has come to raise the pole. But a tremendous gust of wind sweeps down upon us and the sky darkens. A crackle of lightning splits the darkness as electricity fills the air. Thunder bursts the brief silence that follows the lightening as pellets of cold rain descend, stinging our faces as we scurry and take cover. The ceremony is abruptly curtailed. Many minutes pass, as does the storm, leaving the air power cleansed and highly charged. A call goes out to begin again.

We circle once more, make the count of three and pull. Scores of hands tug in unison on three ropes. We are not enough and the tree rises only a few feet from the ground before it drops. More hands are needed. Another call goes out and others join in. But we fail to work as a team and the tree stalls midway and drops once again to the rain-slicked earth.

Now a heartfelt prayer goes out to join our hands and our hearts with our breath to unite as one. We grow quiet. Our silence determines our will to raise this tree. On the count of three and for the third time, hand over hand we pull with our intention strong and this time the tree rises up as if a master puppeteer is pulling invisible strings.

The base of the poplar slides over the rocks that circle the hole. The Maypole is now topped with hundreds of free-flowing ribbons in a rainbow of prayers. Every ribbon is a magical conduit for the energy of renewal. A great shout of hurrah goes up into the sky as the hole is filled with earth and bigger rocks are shoved into place to steady the Maypole.

Then the dance begins. The pole in the hole reunites three worlds: the lower world of soul, the middle world in which we live and the upper world of spirit. The veils between these worlds are at their thinnest in this "time out of all time."

Wild and sure, the drummers weave a beat and the dancers, each with one of the hundreds of ribbons held in their hands, begin to circle the pole. Twisting and twining in both clockwise and counterclockwise motion, each dancer moves closer and closer, touching every ribbon over and under, under and over. It is the devotion to the ritual and to our dreams that grows more magic in this weary world and we help to heal Gaia, as we heal one another and ourselves.

This magical day of revelry flows fluidly into dusk and the Beltane fire grows as last year's Maypole is fed to fuel the flames that leap higher into the darkening sky. The drummers pound out an ecstatic rhythm as the dancers twirl and spin and rise and fall in this heartbeat of love and joy.

I dance quietly by the edge of the quickening fire. Watching the embers glow and feeling my heart grow fuller and stronger I am mesmerized by the flickering firelight. I enter a trance and am held in the arms of Spirit in this community of Faeries and freaks and genderless queers deep in the forest of this ancestral land.

I dance to know the depths of my soul and in this dance suddenly and clearly and in a voice both delightful and amused, I hear the crackle of the fire cry out. "You be Wow! You be Wow! You be Wow!"

Laughing out loud I shout back as I shake, "I be Wow! I be Wow! I be Wow!"

In this instant between the worlds I am reborn. I am born anew with this gift from the fire. Smiling, I turn to the one standing next to me. It is Weeder, who led us through the forest earlier this day.

I look into his face enlivened by the firelight and exclaim, "Weeder! I got my Faerie name!"

"Great!" he replies. "What is it?"

"Wow!" I proclaim.

"You're very excited," he says. "But what is your Faerie name?"

"Wow is my Faerie name!" I explain. He pauses and then looking me in the eyes, he nods. Drolly he replies, "Wow? Yesssss, that's available."

Laughing, I return to the fire and dance and sing and pray through the night and into the dawn, a creature of light and shadow, of laughter and tears. I am a genderless in-between with the power of joy coursing through me. Laughing once again, I proclaim, knowing three times be the charm, "I be Wow! I be Wow! I be Wow!"

And so, with Blaze and Brownie, Sparkle, Butch and many more all merged into one body, my body, Wow is born and borne again in this mystery of magic, in this muddle of the mundane. A creature of many hats and many cloaks all embroidered with Spirits' threads. Trusting the invisible, that which the heart knows yet the eyes do not see. Dancing in a whirlwind of willingness. Alight in a spinning world. Ever-changing. Mischievous. Miraculous.

Truly, a magical world of wonders.

No Authority But Our Heart

by Yusef Leo Schuman

In a lodge, in a forest, off a glacier-plated mountain, we'd wrapped my first No-Talent show and I could still feel laughter pealing through my head. The North Wing had cleared, though you could still feel the heat. I stood there, soaking in it. To my right, a flutter couldn't let the music go, so they sang around the old upright. To my left, some sweaty puppies fucked and giggled in the glow. Ahead, a chatting cluster spanning twenty up to sixty and beyond, wove sex, love, death and metaphysics in a Pan/Socratic tapestry. Snow was falling. Someone saw my face, whispered "Welcome Home" and I felt my heart explode.

Men? Not like any man I'd known growing in Montana. Some could have slid down from a freight cab (to my face), yet held forth with eloquence not much found in eighteen-wheelers. Others cross the wires in any reference I'd ever registered. These men were *supple*. Unwilling to fit any molds in my mind. Unable, really. Too big for my too-small thoughts of manhood.

Beard in a skirt. Shotgun pansy. Three piece princess. *Rock on boys, it's party-time.*

Dancing through this playground. watching man-loving men step through makeup, shawls, condoms, chaps, skirts, jocks and other skins in search of self in others' eyes and deep within their own, left me breathless. Panting. Feeling my own skin peeling back. Wanting more of this...spaciousness, so very not like the world I'd left outside.

Thunder and it's done. We pledged, promised, swore we'd take it to the world. This raw freedom couldn't be locked up in so small a box as a *Gathering*. We'd surge forth smearing rebel love juice through the galaxy, spurting seeds to watch them root, bloom, die and compost. Pump holes full of love. Then with our bond deeply felt we slipped back from the pile. Stood tall, one last time in Circle. Unbroken—but open—then walked back through our gates.

Pop the bubble. Smell the diesel. Hear them barking in the lakeside store. Look at him, handsome lug, standing past an acre of counter-top, ringing the register, sullen, hot and hard. How does *your* laugh sound, man? Guarded eyes say *that don't happen much. Not for you, bud, you look sorta queer.*

Instinct knows wrong moves are dangerous. So I smile big anyhow, open eyes well practiced in recent days. It passes through some chink and echoes back a shy grin. Surprise! Nothing more. Plenty. Hope someone loves him good. It's sweet in there.

A few dozen Gatherings and a decade or so later, that moment still bears symbol of my hopes in this tribe called "Radical Faerie." Men opening our baggage without spilling the contents.

Such contents. The word *manhood* earns cynical projections these days. So much wrong done in its name; and right, for those who see it. War, destruction, endless oppression. Art, construction, boundless compassion. Siddhartha was a man. Jesus was a man. Arjuna was a man. Oscar Wilde was a man. Harvey Milk was a man.

So, are Radical Faeries *men*? We rush to the shelter of *we're all self-defining*, rejecting hard conceptions from the bad men in our lives. Then my gaze falls over the shapes, sizes and colors scattered through my stack of *RFD*, the chronicle of our tribe, and they look like men to me. Are looks deceiving? Am I just projecting? Is *man* a word we Faeries cannot own?

It's easy to forget we walk down different paths to Circle. To me, men are gravity. To me, men are nutrition. To me, men are passion. To me, Gatherings are forest rolls, stretching roots in the soil and weaving branches across the sun- and moonlit mountains of our lives. Pan, Cernunnos, Odin, Zeus, Apollo. Raven, Hermes, Thoth. Father of us all. To me.

Time has also taught me the measure of this path I walk to find my view by watching others stroll different landscapes, each unique if sometimes similarly bent (not always). Good hard lessons rise when, mistaking mine for another's, I *should* all over the scenery. Such a mess.

My men. Full house in the hand. Shelby, the gold-hearted rocker dude who taught me to love The Scorpions—*there's no one like you.* John, the well-traveled bookseller who delighted in dropping *dharma* through an altar boy's mind. Dad, the immigrant vintner's son who plowed wit, love and laughter into a business big enough to pay the bills, yet send him home to dinner every night at five. Brad, who taught me to suck cock, jack and probe the mystery of ass. His brothers, hippie cowboy archetypes which still get my zipper stiff. Mr. Robinson, renegade Catholic high school teacher who knew boys could use some Zappa. Darren, who argued the meaning of art until burning the book was a better choice than watching it rot.

Ryan, who…too bad these men are (mostly) dead. We all compost eventually. And, eventually that's okay.

All this walks into my Gatherings and is stitched deep in my skirt. I love men. And this love for men who love men and the many ways we do it keeps me Gathering with the Faeriemen, all while knowing there are many different paths around this mountain. As many as our wings, at least two each. Mine is mine and I'm grateful for those I stroll with.

We Faeries are self-defining. There's no authority but our heart.

Faerie Phallos Ceremony

by Ian MacKinnon

[*To be performed live with music, candles, confetti, dildos and naked gay male Faerie dancers.*]

THIS RITUAL SALUTE ASKS THE question:
> What Work Of Gayness Makes Me Wanna Fucking Cum?
> Is it a love poem
> by Percy Shelly, or by Rumi, or Rimbaud?
> Is it the smooth white curve
> of a statue by Michelangelo?
> Is it a painting
> of Zeus and Ganymede?
> Or is it a cock
> sliding up a delicious asshole?
> Is it the tireless work
> of countless gay leaders from our past
> who rose out from the homophobic
> shit-mire of toxic hatred
> to erect the pillars and the framework
> upon which we all stand today?
> Is it Baldwin's *Giovanni's Room*
> or Ginsburg's *Howl*?
> Is it the trail of Gay Semen Consciousness
> that burns a flaming rope of cum from this
> moment through Harry Hay
> to Edward Carpenter
> to Karl Heinrich Ulrichs
> to Plato
> to the dawn of humankind?

Is it *The Symposium*
or *The Riddle of Man-Manly Love*?
Is it the gilded sequined eyelids
of Jack Smith or
The Angels of Light
or The Cockettes?
Is it Whitman's *Calamus* poems
or water splashing over a naked man's buttocks?
Is it Divine?
Is it Walker's archetype of The Double?
Is it the thought of how many
millions of men are making love to each other
right this very second?
Is it cum dripping from cocks
standing in a circle out under the sun?
Is it tears like cum running down
the face of a brokenhearted gay boy
just yearning to be loved?
AAAAAAAAAAHHHHHHHHHHHHHHHHHHHHHHHHHH!!!!!
Is it pubic hair?
Is it the promise of self-love through
Radical Faerie brotherhood?
Or is it the shadow that haunts,
sabotages, freezes, and teaches?
Is it the enraged Gay child that lives inside,
demanding the love he never got?
Is it the strong hairy arms of a muscled masculine
dominant sweaty musky throbbing jock
strap clad daddy who knows
exactly how to treat a man's body right?
Is it the scream of abandoned gay infants in the night?
Is it the rainbow flag unfurled like fire,
or the subtle pink pucker of a nubile quivering
boy-hole yearning for penetration?
Is it my own cock?
Or all of your cocks?

Or The God Cock of The Universe!?
Is it two rose-lipped
      faerie-boys in the bloom of youth
      dancing naked in a field while
      mountains swell like ocean waves?
Or is it a lover, leading me,
      through love, to know myself deeper?
Is it my growing relationship
      to my own Gay Soul?
Is it my Faerie Soul-Buddy?
All yes
      All Yes
      Oh yes yes yes.
And for this gay inspiration
      we give thanks to thee
      Phallos Protos,
      Father of Gay Psyche!

[*Lights and music change, candles are lit, dildos are employed, and the ritual begins.*]

Generative force of nature
Meat of the universe
Fill us and feed us
Tonight of all nights
Here where so many cocks
      parade your glory…
      Give us this night the cum of enlightenment.
Erupt for us a geyser of jizz.
Wash us clean with your cream.
You are all that is, and then some.
      Phallos Protos, God Cock in the sky.
Penis master, please don't pass me by.
Phallos Protos steady as the tide.
Swing down your chariot lube it up and let me…
      OH! Stretch us wide with your girth.
Penetrate our souls,

and our butt holes too please.
God Cock save us from our
    venomous internalized homophobia
And bless us with your holy sticky load.
       Phallos Protos, God Cock in the sky.
Penis master, please don't pass me by.
Phallos Protos steady as the tide.
Swing down your chariot
    lube it up and let me ride.
Let me ride, let me ride,
Lube it up and stick it inside.
God Cock,
    endow our lives with meaty purpose.
Phallos, imbue this sacred space
    and the people in it with
    your spermy consciousness.
Wiener Lord, we thank you
    for ejaculating us into existence.
And we know that soon
    there will come a day
    when you will
Oh baby,
    when you will
Cum on our faces!

REMEMBRANCE

Inventory

by Dennis Miles

I am not a man nor do I want to be
I don't have to rule to feel accepted
Don't have to possess in order to exist
War is a heinous crime to me
I'm not obsessed by my being right
When in anger I rage
I am not my penis and my penis isn't
    me
I can be friends with women
When in ambivalence I admit to it
I rely on intuition
On occasion I am struck with grief
I'm given to enjoy bouts of self-pity
When dancing my body moves like
    wind tossed by a leaf
I don't patronize children
My courage lies in my passivity
I have the freedom to be other than
    society's
Conscription of what I should be
I have no need to subjugate sexually
When in joy I soar with glee
I stay away from violence
My touch can be as light as a
    caterpillar's fleece

When in doubt I don't look severe
I don't pretend not to be terrified
In my loneliness I am accompanied by a
    love for me
I can be childlike
Swing on a swing
Countries have nothing to do with my
    identity
I don't diffuse my pain by humor
I don't disguise my power behind levity
Nor do I dissolve my vulnerability in
    laughter
I am not self-sufficient
Nor am I some resigned provider
I can hold on to the memory of
    someone's skin
I'm not stern in my sorrow
My weakness is a joy in my knees
I don't expect to succeed
I'm not necessarily what others think I am
Or think that I should be
I can love other men who aren't men
But who are gentle
I am often powerless thus sometimes free
I am not a man nor do I want to be

Memory, Trees, Children and Queens

by Robert Croonquist (Covelo)

At this year's Walt Whitman Gathering at Faerie Camp Destiny, Daisy Shaver called us to gather at the Memorial Grove.

It had been a while since I had been to Destiny. I was expecting the grove to be like the memorial at the Short Mountain Sanctuary that has stones carved with names, or like Wolf Creek's altar with names written on ceramic plaques.

Instead there were just trees. Nobody would even know it was a memorial.

"Well, this isn't right," I thought, "We have to do something about this."

Daisy led us through a ritual of remembrance. My beloved Martin Worman, who died in November 1993 at the height of The Great Catastrophe, after many friends had already gone to the other side, talked often of Remembrance Responsibility.

Remembrance became so important to us that the Faeries had a remembrance ritual at the Lincoln Memorial as part of the 1993 March on Washington. Our heads were adorned with garlands of rosemary for remembrance as we recited the names of the dead.

So Daisy gives us a perfect ritual with a beginning, a middle and an end. Concise, precise. A ritual a New Yorker could love.

We circle the grove and call out names. I begin slowly—Michael Herthneck Bumblebee, Jada Joyous, Soula, Jamal.

Tede Matthews, Harmodious, Crit, Hiya.

Bobo. Don Carufo, David Summers, Vito Russo.

Sal Licata. Timo Butters. Harvey.

Others called out Marilyn Monroe, Allen Ginsberg, Judy Garland, Walt Whitman, Oscar Wilde. The young Faeries, it dawned on me, didn't know anybody who had died. I kind of felt sorry for them and kind of felt better than them. And kind of, but not really, felt they were lucky.

Hibiscus George Harris, Martin Worman, Brent Jensen, John Flowers, Rodney Price, Kreemah Darryl Simmons Ritz, Magdalena Joe Vigil Montezuma, Pristine

Keith Blanton Condition, John Rothermel, Dusty Dawn, Reggie, Donny Ward, Sylvester, Divine, Goldie Glitters, Ken Dickmann, Ralph Sauer.

Marshall Rheiner, Justin Stowe, Mavis, Michael Gebe.

Stephen Keats.

I started choking up. Oh my God there are so many more and I'm not remembering them.

Mountain Bear Thomas Moore, the love of my life. Light Eagle David Stewart, the love of my life. My mountain family, Jasmine Frances Parker, Kozmeaux Parker, Glenwood Bear.

Who else? Who am I forgetting? Doran Mollin, pure child if ever there was. "Bobby, I want to be a hairdresser when I grow up," he told me as he looked me in the eyes and groomed me for a party at his parents' house one night.

Moon Maher. Doris Reid.

All of these people created us. Those who were older and those who were much, much younger.

I come from the San Francisco branch of the Faeries, conceived by the Diggers and Alan Watts and Esalen and Anna Halprin and the Merry Pranksters and Timothy Leary and Ram Dass and the Free Land Ahimsa Church and Morningstar Ranch and Irving Rosenthal and the Kaliflower Commune and the San Francisco Mime Troupe and Joan Baez and Ira Sandperl and Kepler's Bookstore and Non Violent Direct Action and People's Park and The Cockettes and the Angels of Light and the Hula Palace and Arthur Evans and the Faery Circle. Land's End and Devil's Slide.

I come from the Faeries who were conceived in the cauldron of the Civil Rights Movement and Martin Luther King, Jr. and the Kennedy brothers and Lyndon Johnson's Great Society and our collective revulsion to napalm being sprayed indiscriminately on the people of Vietnam and the bombing of Laos and Cambodia and the complicity of Stanford Research Institute.

I come from Small is Beautiful and Right Livelihood and Wendell and Thomas Berry and Helen Caldicott and sit-ins and boycotts and the Abalone Alliance and the Diablo Canyon Blockade and the Big Old Mushroom Cloud looming over us.

I come from Buddhist monks immolating themselves.

I come from LSD and marijuana.

I come from the Women's Movement and Lesbian Separatism and Gay Liberation and Liberation Theology.

Shulamith Firestone, Betty Dodson, Bluestockings.

Gay Solidarity with the Chilean Resistance.

Salvador Allende and Archbishop Romero and Faggots and Class Struggle.

And I remember.

I remember Robert Kramer who gave us San Francisco Newsreel and who tweaked us in full paragraphs and chapters with his brave footage from North Vietnam.

I remember Harry Hay, John Burnside, Gryphon Blackswan, Wessie and Assunta.

Tommy Pace. Leonce. Redwing. Ana Roy.

Forgive me, Ana, it took this long to speak your name, my Faerie Godmother and most badass *compañera* of them all.

Fran Macy.

We Faeries are in very good company indeed.

These seeds of the 1960s and 1970s created a vast forest of free land Sanctuaries around the country. We called them communes where proto-Faeries could sprout branches and blossoms and leaves. From The Farm in Tennessee to Libre in the Huerfano Valley to Black Bear Ranch in the Salmon Trinity Alps—they sheltered us and nourished us and provided oxygen for us to breathe and come to life.

My Sanctuary days preceded Wolf Creek and Short Mountain. They were in the mountains of Covelo, California, in a Digger commune started in 1969. When I moved there in 1975 the men had left their barefoot and pregnant women and taken to the road with their guns and horses and saxophones and guitars, leaving Mountain Bear behind to fill the void.

He was a big, handsome, burly young sissy from Queens who came to Covelo via the Red Paint Children's Commune in Putney, Vermont. In his patchwork cape and crocheted, goat-horned cap, he lured us up to The Land, as it was called, from the Faerie Circle and from our commune at 529 Castro. And some of us stayed. And we raised goats and gardens and children.

And after six years it was time to leave the mountain with all the accumulated knowledge of consensus decision making, circle process and cooperation as the highest form of anarchy. I left knowing one can survive without electricity, knowing how to chop wood and haul water and dig wells and store food and repair engines and handle men with guns.

Hiding in the woods is good. I left thinking globally and acting locally and with a deep abiding love for the Earth that gives us life, the storms that bring us wonder and the droughts that give us an appreciation for every drop of water we drink.

I left knowing the potential of personal strength and collective power. And when I got my calling that it was over, I became a New York City public school teacher. Inspired by a book I did not read but judged by its cover, Neil Postman and Charles Weingartner's *Teaching as a Subversive Activity*, I came down from the mountaintop to teach teenagers—the people who terrorized me as a young, popular, secret desirer of men.

Harry taught us that the struggle we face is epochal and that we must fight it askance. We must not face our adversaries head on. They will always win.

Remember that a mere thirty years ago the Women's Movement overthrew 4,000 years of patriarchal oppression in a brief ten years. The male, supremacist monotheists are panicked and would rather kill their children than lose ownership of the means of reproduction. They mean it. And they will fight to the death because their lives aren't so hot to begin with. So we must have a little patience and we must be clever.

It falls upon us to restore some balance. We Faeries come from Earth-centric, pagan traditions that honor the female principle, the male principle and the in-between principle.

We are the principle that makes the yin/yang line a wavy one.

If we are clever, one day the world will look back and see that balance has been restored and the patriarchs have found themselves alone, screaming to the wind and we will then welcome them back into a new world.

We Faeries are perfectly situated to make this profound clandestine mischief because we are invisible. We come out in full glory as Faeries when in Sanctuary or in public celebration, but when we are alone out in the world, which is most of the time, our fae spirit is invisible.

A friend of mine said, "I really believe in Faeries, the mystical beings people can't see." From what I gathered she meant some glowing creatures that appear in gardens at night, fluttering their wings. I agree with her that Faeries are mystical beings that people can't see. I depart from her in that I see us not just as ether and air but also as flesh and blood, semen and shit.

Look at us at a Gay Pride March—at least in New York City—and we are a small, motley crew with some very large puppets. What's up with that? To most we are either cute or embarrassing. People can't see us!

In true Faerie fashion, we can only be seen by those who have eyes to see. But in our Sanctuaries and our Heart Circles, our Gatherings and our rituals, we have had the wisdom and the luxury to take the time to look into each other deeply. And wow. We are humbled by the depth, breadth and splendor we see in one another. Harry Hay saw it and was perpetually amazed and delighted by it.

And so I brought my Faerie spirit to the world by teaching. Askance. I taught a global, interdisciplinary, multicultural survey of literature in the most ethnically diverse county in the world, Queens County, New York and in my twenty-five years of teaching, none of my students really knew what hit them.

But they knew they were turned on and their lives were forever changed. They knew that they loved this man and they loved what he revealed within them that they had never seen before. From the captain of the football team, to the immigrant geek, to the girl in hijab who was as clever as Scheherazade, to the girl from Jamaica who was as self-possessed as a beauty queen, to the children of postal workers and corrections officers, cops and the chronically underemployed.

They loved this man who, by the miracle of public education, honored each and every one of them and showed them the love and harmony and dignity and respect that might be hidden, but is also firmly embedded in the roots of the traditions from which they came.

Maybe it's our woundedness. Maybe it's our complexity. Maybe it's our otherness. Maybe it's that we truly carry magick. Whatever it is, Faeries in the world make a difference. A Radical difference.

And so I remember the passions of the idealistic young man I was several lifetimes ago, and in remembering my work takes root.

I remember where I come from. I remember my father Neil Clarence Croonquist and my ever-so-much with us mother Betty Ross Ryland Croonquist and feisty Aunt Jeanette Croonquist Edwards. I remember my grandparents Cora Belle Garvin Croonquist, Otto Clarence Croonquist, Harris Steiger Ryland and Sara Louella Ostrander Ryland.

Memory. It's just trees. May it forever be so.

Let our spirits rest where only those who have eyes to see will know where our ashes lie. Give the young Faeries the gift that we who survived The Great Catastrophe were given. The gift of Remembrance Responsibility.

So listen to our stories and tell us yours.

They are our trees.

They thrive in our secret forests.

Pass it on and remember me.

The Star Seed

by Mati Livinit

THERE WAS A TIME WHEN the humans could fly.

They had long beautiful multicolored wings. They would spend their days soaring through the clouds, making love. There was a myth that if you could fly to the sun, pick a sun seed and feed it to your lover, it would be the ultimate in bliss.

This became their favorite game. Higher and higher they would fly toward the sun until the power of the sun would repel them back to earth. Free falling, they would dive back to Earth so fast that their wings would leave a trail of color behind them.

And these trails became known as rainbows. Day after day the humans spent finding new ways to play and soar in the sky. And when they were tired they lay down under a tree or rock and slept. And when they were hungry they ate nuts and berries. This lifestyle left them sometimes cold and wet and sometimes hungry.

Some humans got tired of sometimes being cold and wet and sometimes being hungry. They realized that if they stayed on the ground they could build their own shelters and grow their own food.

Over time they slowly lost their wings and even forgot they ever flew. They learned to build elaborate shelters so big that they never had to leave them. If they were too hot or too cold all they had to do was push a button and the temperature changed. And their food, all they had to do was ask for anything they wanted to eat and it was delivered to them without them even having to cook. Now the humans spend most of their time making sure they had everything they wanted and they always wanted a little more.

There were some humans who remember flying. Remember not in their heads, maybe, but in their hearts or spirits. These humans dressed in bright and weird colors, painted their bodies and mainly wandered around and were sometimes cold and sometimes hungry. They would spend their time developing elaborate rituals out in fields and under trees to help them remember.

261

One day the buttons stopped working for the humans and when they ordered their food it didn't come. The humans panicked and didn't know what to do. It was then that they turned to the weird ones to help them remember.

Crooked Faerie Tales:
Remembrances of a Middle-Class Fae

by Giuseppe

MAGDALEN FARM, 1976: THIS OREGON commune is contained in a beautiful bowl of green hills. First night, there's a circle of men blessing our meal. How I've dreamed of this moment. The barn holds a grand Victorian bed. My host, lacking candor, expects sex. I respectfully decline.

Second day, the communards are off to confront the Grants Pass branch of the Forest Service in full Radical Faerie sissy garb. Only kind Len is left behind. We wander the land together, talk late until we fall asleep, no sex needed.

Last day, there's a parting lecture on proper (class-conscious) drag and by the way, that rash you have is scabies. At home, the doctor says, "No, it's poison oak."

I learn through the grapevine that I'm considered a cocktease back at the farm.

San Diego Gathering, 1983: Wow, these are the Radical Faeries. I'm a Faerie, too! I help in the kitchen, naked. I'm a satyr in the play, *Midas Well*. With Harry Hay moderating (*who's he?* I wonder) I learn to do Heart Circle, waiting hours to hold the talisman, taking in every word. Full moon ritual? I don't have to believe in every incantation, it's theater, therapy.

Okay, maybe there is some magic to it. At a quiet moment an owl calls and, un-noticed, a tarantula walks in and out of our circle past my folded legs. All others only have eyes for the dancer taking his python out of its basket, for real. We are exquisite, we would heal the planet.

Nomenus Homecoming Gathering, Wolf Creek 1987: We have saved old Magdalen Farm. The land is our temple. It says so in the document Faerie lawyers sent the IRS claiming religious non-profit status. We have a Madame Treasurer, her badge of office—a big red purse. All of us are on the board.

As months pass, gardens grow, repairs are made, a bridge is built. Our Great Circle could put Quakers to shame with its consensus successes.

Hold on though, because garbage and ennui pile up, devoted faes burn out, some residents tune out. I find another season's marijuana plot, a mini clear-cut on the azalea-lined creek, piles of plastic irrigation tubing, abandoned, cracking in the sun. Faeries respond with silence to my fears of federal agents dispossessing us of our land.

The March on Washington, 1987: We circle beneath the big phallic monument. Queers of all stripes take over the nation's capital. On "E" Street, one marcher in our contingent sucks off another under his camouflage skirt. Reverend Phelps doesn't see this.

We join thousands of people for the largest-ever civil disobedience on the steps of the Supreme Court. Police in Darth Vader drag and white latex gloves take hours to process all those arrested. Faeries chant, "Your gloves don't match your shoes!"

Winter Solstice, Wolf Creek, 1990: There's a Faerie survey in the Gathering registration form, "Which deities do you follow?" A non-believer, I find no box to check.

Our Sanctuary is transformed by record cold. All are inside the farm crocheting. I'm feeling left out. Oskrr gives me lessons in knit and purl. As we clack away, he explains the central dogma of his one monk order: Playbor (play + labor = fun).

Playbor with Oskrr. It's true.

Every time a bell gets rung it's the holy obligation to smoke another joint. Am I the only one feeling queasy from days of secondary smoke? All the while great effort is made to honor each fae's dietary needs. "Ironic," I say and another Faerie giggles and reveals we're in the designated drug-free space.

A week later: Heartwood, Mendocino County. The Billys' Blue Moon Gathering. I hear Billys are Faerie-lite. Don't believe it—their Heart Circles are the real thing. Women and straight men sit with us. All are moved.

Nineteen ninety-one arrives on a frosty, clear night, high above the Eel River. A Billy appears in full moon mask and blue gown. We waltz around the bonfire, humming the Blue Danube *en masse*.

Short Mountain, 1997: It's been one kind of intentional community or another for decades. Under dogwoods, Faeries build the Maypole. I see my first fireflies. The barn houses the Goat Boutique, anything from ball gowns to rubber boots can be found here. At the crowded evening dance I ask another dancer to put out his lit cigarette.

"Fuck off," he responds.

He will one day advertise as a teacher of etiquette.

Terschelling, The Netherlands, 1998: A new subspecies of the tribe emerges: the EuroFaerie. We struggle with language but not with drag. We wander the dunes and frolic on the edge of the Wadden Zee. Dutch vacationers walk through our space and ask, "Where's the loo?" Only us American privacy-conscious faes seem miffed. On the last day a windowsill altar almost sets our barn on fire. Clever German Faeries repair curtain and trim. The owner never knows.

Tropical Paradise Gathering, Koh Yao Yai, Thailand, 2004: It's the first Asian-Faerie Gathering. Lekker Ding is the mastermind. Our mission: to bring Radical Faerie ways to the East. It's an island of Muslim farmer and fisher folk. I worry about colliding cultures. There are Muslim separatist incidents two provinces to the south. A EuroFaerie builds a mock altar, a demented, wave-tossed doll's head is its focus. Muslim or Buddhist, I'm convinced the Thai family that runs our resort will only see "black magic." In the morning the doll head is gone, I blame whatever passes for raccoons in the local eco-system.

Two experienced California Fairies show our recruits how to conduct a Heart Circle by screaming bloody murder at each other, one dashing the talisman to the sand. Brand new Asian faes dust it off and calmly continue. Few have ever had safe space to tell their truths. A Faerie impresario from Madrid plans a talent extravaganza, asking five dollars from every attendee to rent a cabana and buy up all the hot pink fabric in the island's only store. Western faes are aghast. All that dough will ruin the culture and economy of the locals. Faerie colonialism?

We invite the neighbors. Grandmas make local delicacies. Palm fronds, borrowed orchids, little lights and all that hot pink fabric hang from the rafters. One quiet Thai Faerie opens in a pastel gingham mini skirt and belts out "The hills are alive with the sound of music!"

Post-show, the locals are mystified but happy for the rent. Young Thai men (some foot boxers?) rush to try on wigs and pearls. Are they compensating when they flex biceps for our cameras? No matter, our hearts beat faster. The last two Faeries to leave Koh Yao Yai , including one with a London-punk, electric-blue Mohawk, present the show's two hundred dollars profits to the local high school to pay for Internet access. Students and teachers tell the Faeries they look like rock stars.

Home, Northern California, 2009: It's been thirty-plus years and I still don't know the correct spelling for "Faerie." I've felt every emotion concerning my tribe, joy competing with exasperation for First Place. I don't see the old tribe often. On this plane or not, there are so many I miss. We still reject the selfish, materialistic culture we were raised to partake in, right? We Faeries are special—and yet, are we really all that different from any other subset of humanity? I have to remind myself that the Faeries will continue their meandering path whether I'm around to kvetch or not, amazing themselves and startling the world.

And I was a Faerie before I could talk. I always will be—even if it means being a Circle of one.

Ripples

by Pat Gourley

NOVEMBER 17, 2010—IT'S 10 P.M. and I have just returned from attending a Heart Circle. This is one of several programs offered by a group in Denver called Element. Their central mission is to build and foster a healthy gay male community in the local area. The following quote is from their e-newsletter that advertised tonight's Circle: "Heart Circle is one of the central traditions created by the Radical Faerie community. Faeries come together in a Circle to speak from the heart and to listen to one another through our hearts."

There were eleven men present at tonight's Circle. None of the participants had much in the way of Radical Faerie connections, past or present. The two facilitators would both have been less than ten years old when the first Gathering happened in 1979. I view this as an amazingly positive ripple effect emanating from those early Faerie efforts.

My personal connections with the approach to LGBT people—and specifically gay men—as being a distinct cultural minority ("a separate people whose time has come") was through Harry Hay and John Burnside. From the mid-1970s on I was immersed in Denver gay politics through our Gay Community Center and enjoyed the sexual delights of those days with great relish. But this sexual enthusiasm was sometimes tempered by thoughts like… is this all there is to being gay? So, it was with considerable interest that I happened across the movie *Word is Out*.

I saw the documentary film one night in 1978 and the next morning raced into the Community Center to rave about it. I had been particularly impressed with the segment featuring two "older" gay men—Harry and John. A woman named Katherine, who said she knew the couple and had done activist work with them in New Mexico, overheard my ramblings. She offered to put me in contact. A subsequent visit to Denver was arranged and the rest is history—only slightly and occasionally revised.

Harry and John were involved with several other gay men, notably Don Kilhefner and Mitch Walker in Los Angeles, where the seeds for the first Spiritual Conference for Radical Fairies had already been sprouted. At least a dozen gay men from Denver and I attended that first Gathering in Arizona. It was an amazing event. Yet, I can honestly say that it was not life changing. Impactful? Yes. Life changing? Not so much.

The success of the first Gathering quickly led to discussions of "Let's do it again!" There was a lot of dialogue, in the form of endless correspondence, actually written by hand and sent by mail in those days. Many interminable meetings in Denver with our collective occurred to facilitate the planning for the second event. It was to be called *A Spiritual Gathering for Radical Faeries*. The Denver collective, myself included, were really Faerie neophytes and took significant direction from Kilhefner, Hay, Burnside and Walker.

This Gathering occurred in August 1980 at a National Forest campground in the foothills west of Denver, Colorado. Over 300 Fairies were in attendance and it was hailed as a great success. A movement to take over the queer world seemed imminent. But I don't think that happened. If it did, I missed it.

My involvement with things Faerie continued in one form or another through the 1980s, although I never did attend another large Gathering. But ongoing local Faerie events regularly happened through the decade.

There were two significant distractions that steered me away from any further national Faerie activism. The first was the rather intense personal conflicts among key players in the movement. I allowed myself at times to be pushed and pulled by various factions. Finally, rather than assign any individual blame through some sort of "Faerie litmus test," I decided to slowly withdraw.

The real clincher in my decreased involvement was the fact that I tested HIV positive in 1985 and was already very locally involved in HIV-AIDS education efforts. Yet I have to say my considerable efforts in the HIV-AIDS arena were then—and continue to be—strongly informed by Radical Faerie philosophy. We really are so much more than what we do in bed!

I am recently retired from a thirty-eight year nursing career, with the last twenty-one as a nurse clinician in Denver's public HIV-AIDS clinic. Daily contact through my work with thousands of gay men of all ages, class backgrounds and races continually reinforced for me the disheartening, un-actualized potential we have. At the same time there were endless glimmers and often frank displays of our true gay, male natures. It was that "gay window" that provided the juice for me to keep at it for over two decades.

I actually have great hope for the future of continued Radical Faerie influence on the larger LGBT world that is currently consumed with marriage and military service. A couple of specific validations for this optimism come to mind.

One relates to the amazing, loving, persistently dedicated and compassionate San Francisco Faerie collective who cared for both Harry Hay and John Burnside in the last years of their lives. They were the essence of loving companions. [Harry died on October 24, 2002, at age 90. John passed away on September 14, 2008, at 91.]

The second validation is the Heart Circle I attended last evening. That sort of honest and open communication between gay men in America in 2010 is quite astounding. Ongoing ripples from stones tossed way back when.

Am I a Radical Faerie?

by Don Perryman (Dawn)

Over a decade ago, my good friend Doug explained to me, partly by way of introduction, that he was one. Or at least he tried to explain. I really think this may be a case of must-be-one-to-understand. I don't recall exactly what he said at the time, all about gender-bending and nature worship and over-the-top antics, but it convinced me that I definitely was not one of *those*, open as I might have been to others who were.

Ha!

Some years later, after I'd mellowed into a happy retirement and loosened up a bit, he helped me satisfy a lingering curiosity about what I might have been missing all those years by suggesting I go with him to Short Mountain for the May Day celebration.

I packed my gear and a few other things I never would have taken on any ordinary camping trip and we headed north from Atlanta to Liberty, Tennessee. One of the first surprises on my arrival in the Sanctuary was a repeated greeting from folk I'd never met, "Welcome home." And it soon was home.

Oh, my! In my ancient Latin Club toga and tunic held over from high school, I took to it all, as one elder up there commented, "like a duck to water." That sunny, warm first day of May dawned like a rainbow miracle after a week of drizzle and mud. I was ready to shout to the blue heavens above, "Yes, yes. I am indeed a Radical Faerie."

And oh what a frolic and oh what an education it was and is. I haven't missed a Beltane or a Fall Gathering since. I've even been up there when it wasn't such a circus and I was able to enjoy quiet, equally satisfying experiences with a much smaller, laid-back group of residents.

Which is not to say I'm all that much of a Radical Faerie. It's more like the way I became a belated hippie. Or maybe the way National Guardsmen in the Reserves are Weekend Warriors. I dipped voraciously into that sensuous smorgasbord of carnival costuming and countercultural mind set, embracing everything from vegetarianism to visits to the communal privy to skepticism of all major political affiliations.

I luxuriated in the hedonism of free love that was more sincere and satisfying—and less rote—than the trickery I'd gotten used to in the big city, and the Heart Circles, where the most intimate details were shared and supported. There was mesmerizing drumming and dancing at the Fire Circle every night and the openness of joint tokes and random hugs and gropes in front of God and everybody.

There were invitations to explore and practice every spiritual pursuit known to humankind and some that were unheard of until dreamed up on the spot. The option of unselfconscious nakedness was daunting at first until I finally realized that mine would be blithely ignored. And supporting it all, the simple rule: Be nice or leave.

Then, nice as it was, there came the time I would have to collect my gear, my memories and my countless photos and leave. I would go back to my more-or-less comfortable suburban life, which isn't all that bad really. But, well, to be quite honest, less authentic in a crowded world of locked doors, traffic, fast food, cell phones, computers and countless lost souls who have no idea what it would be like to be radical or to be gay in the broadest, most fabulous sense of the word.

I would not leave happily, though, satisfying as the experience was. If anyone said to me, "So, back to the real world, huh?" I was quick to correct them, "No, I'm going back to the *un*-real world!" And as my car made its way along the winding dirt road down off the north slope of Short Mountain there were tears of regret for all I'd miss until I returned.

But when I did return and approached that amazing place where no one is turned away for lack of funds, or for lack of anything else except common decency, tears would begin to well in my eyes for a very different reason. And I was never disappointed, no matter how many unexpected personal issues popped up in that quaint haven, as some certainly did in its safety, prompted by the question: "What is your intention here?"

But, no—one does not become a Radical Faerie by making faithful trips up to Short Mountain, or to any of the other Sanctuaries around the country and the planet where such Gatherings occur.

Or maybe one does. Maybe the designation of Radical Faerie is amorphous and broad enough to encompass in theory every human beneath the sun and the moon. Whether they ever get it and Gather or not, far too many of those poor, lost bastards out there in that grayer world have no real idea that such a potential exists within them. After all, I didn't for decades. Sadly, our gay brother Thoreau was right: "The mass of men lead lives of quiet desperation."

The first night when I watched naked folk gyrating to those hypnotic drums and other musical instruments in the golden glow of the firelight, I thought of a phrase of poetry that had rattled around in my head for years: "The pure dance of a person becoming himself." And when we dare to celebrate that way and make the most of the precious time we have here on Earth to become our truest, freest selves, I think we *are* being radical. Simply because that fundamental commitment to life's possibilities strips away so much that's superfluous and false and opens up a space within for countless new and better experiences.

Experiences like knowing I couldn't make a fashion blunder up there if I tried, sporting the gaudiest garb that had been waiting in my closet for years, somehow escaping the Goodwill donation bin, or maybe like throwing together something fabulous or foolish from the colorful, musty resources of the Goat Boutique.

Like walking up to an absolute stranger on the knoll and speaking candidly to her or him assuming it really was a friend I just hadn't met yet—and finding out it was indeed. Like washing an endless barrage of dishes after a meal at the cabin and getting hugs and thanks for doing them. Like helping to make new benches and tables for the deck there or joining a wood detail to keep the home fires burning and feeling like a valued contributor. Like watching a No-Talent show of performances that ranged wildly from the beautifully sublime to the delightfully ridiculous—and even beginning to wonder what I myself might get up to say or do.

Finally, after a couple years of shy watching, I did get up to read three poems I picked from my huge bale of unpublished stuff after endless agonizing over what might conceivably appeal to such a conglomeration of diverse spirits. Only to discover that it did. Or I did. And I'm pretty sure my appeal had much less to do with being some eloquent poet and more to do with being a flawed, still-somewhat-closeted gay man. I was willing to take the chance of being naked in that precise verbal, emotional way before an audience of fellow humans I thought I could trust. So I did and that trust was rewarded beyond my expectations.

There is, of course, more to being a part of all this than the sharing and celebrating. For instance, the solitary strolls I always take out to Memorial Ridge, where roughly inscribed stones and boards remember Faeries who've gone beyond but stayed right here in spirit. As I gaze at the trinkets and mementos, battered photos and loving words in that silent space, I realize what a close-knit tribe this is, and how sweet it would be to belong and be remembered so sincerely, so unpretentiously.

In a colder world where ageism often seals us older gents off from the youthful banquet that passes for gay life, this love and respect for elders is a blessing I appreciate more and more as the years advance.

On one visit to the Sanctuary I watched a small plane fly overhead, scattering the ashes of one who'd lived and loved here and been loved to his dying day and would be from then on. His clothing, his poems and more of his ashes were offered to those who wanted some tangible remembrance. I still think of him each time I put on the sweater I took—even though we never met.

Among those still very much alive in body, mind and heart, I continue to develop deeper friendships, truer intimacies, fresher insights and a better understanding of a unique realm that most of the world ignores and is ignorant of. I ponder how it is that so many things matter in the outside world that don't matter here—clothes, secrecy, cars, conformity, fear, conspicuous consumption, rape of the land. And how it is so many things are valued here that hardly are anywhere else—candor, kookiness, homegrown vegetables, courage, diversity, vulnerability, community, paganism. Who knows what's next?

I still marvel at one unpredictable incident during an early visit down to the communal bathhouse. As I opened the sauna where naked Faeries and open-minded friends of Faeries gather to stoke the wood stove, pour dippers of water on the hot rocks, steam, sweat, converse—and sometimes play—I saw a beautiful young woman sitting on a high bench, obviously very pregnant.

As I stepped in she gave a little "Oh!" and I asked, "Did the baby kick?"

"Yes," she said, "Want to feel?" And without reservation I put my hand on her slick belly and felt the lively poke, thanking her for an experience I hadn't had since decades ago in a former life when my own were on the way. I think about that baby's eventual coming out and the liberal, loving, nurturing world she or he was likely to have come out into. And what if more children could be born to all this?

So, am I one of these amazing folk? Yes, I surely am. After all, a Radical Faerie is not so much something you are, but someone you continue to become.

A Day and a Night in the Desert

by Mark Thompson

THE EARTH WAS AS RED in places as dried blood on parchment skin and every step was marked like a bruise in the sand. When the wind came spurting across the desert from far canyon walls, it tinted everything a dusty rose. The land was stark in every direction; the only distinguishable point on the map for miles around was our cloistered sanctuary of low trees, a few adobe buildings and a pool. Never has a body of water seemed more purifying. But cleanliness alone was never the point: quite the contrary that day.

By the second morning of the Gathering, we were exhausted from talk. The previous day was a gushing torrent of words and images and pent-up feelings, a heady brew of near feverish intensity. Now it was time for silence. Leaving all clothes behind, a group of men awoke early and left the walls of the confine, trailing one by one to a special recess in the desert. Each man carried a bucket of water, careful not to spill a drop. Soon, we arrived at the nearby dry riverbed and a big puddle of mud was made.

Cries for "more mud" rang across the fields of cactus and sagebrush as we took turns anointing one another with the reddish ooze. Twigs and blades of dry grass were woven through hair, adhesive hands linked and a group of almost forty newly-minted Faeriemen formed a circle.

Then we came close together and lifted a brother high above our earth-caked tribe. Arms held high, we silently swayed in the clear morning light, bound as one. The scene was as atavistic as it was enlightening, a harmonious act of personal erasure and rebirth. Many of us kept our mud suit on for the rest of the day.

But by the next day we were clean again as we festively dressed and painted ourselves with bright designs for another ritual to be held that night. At dusk, a deep-toned bell chimed and we once again walked single file into the desert, Darkness swiftly fell and our costumes caught on sharp branches. Low candles, dimly flickering, lit the path and now and then someone stumbled against an unseen stone.

Nervous apprehension soon melded into contemplative appreciation, however, and our unfamiliar surroundings ceased to be an obstacle.

After about twenty minutes we arrived at the designated site. More candles had been set around to form a glowing ring and musicians serenaded our arrival. Our band of two hundred made a circle—a grand convocation of Faeries.

The music ebbed and, quietly at first, a litany of friends and guiding spirits were called forth. "I evoke Walt Whitman," said one man. "Marilyn Monroe," the next. "The shadow of my former self," declaimed another. Other names came more boldly now. "Peter Pan." "Kali, our creator and destroyer." And so on until everyone was heard. Then a gut-wrenching sigh collectively arose up from the Circle like an offering to the starry sky. We began to chant, each note rumbling deep in our throats.

Then the Circle split itself into two concentric rings. Facing one another, we greeted each man in front of us with a tender embrace and kiss. The rings moved forward and intertwined while declarations of "Faerie Spirit, Faerie Love" reverberated across the desert floor.

Music was played again and each man made an offering to a basket that was passed around; a feather from Woolworth's, a stone from the Ganges River, a lock of hair, a handwritten poem. We began to dance with the music and in a few moments noticed we were being joined in our merriment by a large horned bull. Naturally shy, the animal was drawn close in. The bull stood and watched motionless, like some ancient hieroglyphic painted on a cave wall, then he just as inexplicably vanished.

Soon, we too began to drift away into the dark chill air. None of us would ever find again this particular place of red earth that had nourished us so. But even to attempt a return would be missing the point. Our journeys as a new kind of men, having been thusly inaugurated, meant that we would have many destinations, far and wide, still to attend.

An Afterword:
The Radical Power of Roots

by Bo Young

AFTER READING THIS ANTHOLOGY CAN the reader answer this question: What is a Radical Faerie?

Perhaps there is still confusion? The Radical Faerie experiment—the movement—has long grounded itself in what has been called "gay spirituality." Having published and edited *White Crane Journal*, a journal that addressed the subject, I can attest that there are as many highly subjective, deeply spiritual answers to that existential question as there are reporters on the subject.

And like opinions, everyone has a right to their own gods but not to their own facts. Perhaps we might turn to "gay anthropology" or "gay sociology"—rational sciences, specifically evolutionary science and, as elders before us have suggested, find empirical answers there, too.

Harry Hay, like others before and since, built theories on a foundation of science. Sometimes it was political science and the idea that gay people were an oppressed minority. But behind that revolutionary idea—indeed supporting it—Hay posed the idea, in the words of Charles Darwin that, "Natural Selection acts on the observable characteristics of an organism...the genetic (heritable) basis of any organism that gives a reproductive advantage will become more common in a population..."[1] This cast a new, clear light on the idea that same-sex-loving people persist across time and cultures for a natural reason.

In plainer words that means nothing persists in Nature that doesn't *serve* Nature in some way. And by "serve" we mean "supports survival." Which begs the question: Reproductive sex would seem to be the most obvious survival trait, but what possible reproductive advantage does *non*-reproductive sexual behavior offer?

Dave Nimmons, in his *Manifest Love* work, offers the lovely suggestion that the purpose of homosexuality—or at least *one* of the purposes of homosexuality—was what is sometimes referred to as "the altruism gene" and touts the GLBT community as having, "…pioneered social experiments involving ethics of love and nurturance, non-violence and sexuality, intimacy, friendship, bliss and community…"[2]

He points to the altruistic, loving care demonstrated in the GLBT community—among men *and* women—in the face of the HIV-AIDS epidemic as a prime example. We invented institutions that would care not only for our own sick and dying, but any and all comers, when the dominant culture was content to let us all die. Nimmons goes on to remind us of how many of us are the supportive "super uncles,"[3] caretakers for aging parents, the go-to babysitter.

For my own part, I've suggested that if the putative purpose of heterosexuality was the survival and continuation of the gene pool, then the purpose of homosexuality was to make sure it was Olympic-sized, with nice wide lanes and good towels. If heterosexuality is about *quantity* of life, we are indisputably about *quality* of life.

The Radical Faeries have deepened this and over time have imagined—rediscovered?—a culture of consensus and cooperation, gentleness and play. In a profound way we have moved beyond questions of mere sex and sexuality—which really comes down to plumbing and inserting Part A in Part B—and revealed another vantage point of worldview; a view that, for starters, doesn't treat women like chattel and in which men become something more than archetypal Hunter-Killer-Warriors. We offer the world the altruistic archetypes of cooperation, collaboration, conciliation and culture.

Gay men like Harry Hay, John Addington Symonds, Edward Carpenter and Gerald Heard spent lifetimes researching other cultures, specifically cultures in which same-sex love wasn't marginalized, but, in fact, embraced. We all know about Greek intergenerational love. Still more are now rediscovering Native American culture and the two-spirit traditions. Anyone caring to look will find repeated, demonstrable instances where same-sex lovers were simply not condemned in the way that patriarchal, western religionists wrongly insist "it has always been."

News Flash! It has not always been that way. Film at Eleven.

If we accept Natural Selection as the jumping off place for discussion, then the question isn't about "sex and sexuality" at all, but rather about archetypal roles in culture (and acceptable sex roles) and contributions to the well-being of that culture. Simply trying to convince the dominant culture that "we're just like you except for what we do in bed" (as assimilationist thought has it) is a losing argument inevitably; we would always be pale imitations of their norms in their eyes. Hay would, in fact, insist that the bedroom was the only place where gay people and non-gay people were alike and that we needed to find the ineluctably necessary gift we brought to the table that the larger society needed and could not have without us before we would ever be embraced as peers.

Throughout *The Fire in Moonlight* we see the weft and warp of the definition of "Faerie." The pattern that rises clearly to the surface is how many definitions there seem to be. "The Radical Faeries" are a movement…an *odd* movement, admittedly, even zealously so…queer, one might say; and more so because to be one is to be part of a group that is, in fact, a society of outsiders.

But if we learn to read between the subtle (and not so subtle) lines of history (and between the sexes, we might add) as writers like Randy Connor, Will Roscoe, Mark Thompson and John Boswell have done, encountering recurring archetypal themes of the mediator (Native American), the shaman/priest (European, Native American, African and Asian tribal cultures), teachers (Western European, Native American), culture carriers and ceremonialists (Native American), as well as the jester and the fool (Western Europe/Native American), the clown and the contrary, it becomes abundantly clear that there are roles that have been filled—and *continue* to be filled—by same-sex-loving people.

Queer folk—often as a matter of *tradition*—have done these things for a very long time and across cultures. Is there a connection between their sexuality and their social role? It would be safe to say, in some cases, it flows directly from it, arising and emanating from the paradoxical "mediating-outsider" vantage point. The necessary gift is the gift of perspective of each sex that the heterosexual cannot have.

Thirty years after Don Kilhefner's vision to organize a gathering of gay men away from hetero-noise, the Radical Faerie experience of Sanctuaries has begun to bear fruit. In spending time out of time, in retreat, in reflection, in re-membering, we've done more than semantically redefine who we are. We've recollected our past, recalled and learned from our history and reconnected with our roots.

In a society like ours, which values conformity over individuality, it grows increasingly difficult to stand up and say, "I'm different. I'm not like you." As often as I have personally brought this subject up in conversations, I am as often greeted with the question, "Are you suggesting that gay people are somehow special?" (As if that would be a bridge too far!)

To which I would respond: Not any more so than male or female are "special" and every bit as "special," "unique" and *necessary* to healthy life as those divisions. We have watched as social science has questioned "essentialist *vs.* constructionist" and attempted to count "how many Faeries can fit on the head of a pin."

By any measure, the archetypal social roles historically filled by gay people, same sex people, homosexual people, Faerie people—call us what you may—are essential to life.

[1] Darwin C., (1859) *On the Origin of Species by Means of Natural Selection, or the Preservation of Favoured Races in the Struggle for Life,* John Murray, London; modern reprint Charles Darwin, Julian Huxley (2003). *On The Origin of Species.* Signet Classics. ISBN 0-451-52906-5. Published online at The complete work of Charles Darwin online: On the origin of species by means of natural selection, or the preservation of favoured races in the struggle for life.

[2] Nimmons, D., (2002) *The Soul Beneath the Skin,* St. Martin's Press, NY ISBN-10: 0312269196

[3] Association for Psychological Science (2010, February 4). Potential evolutionary role for same-sex attraction. *ScienceDaily.* Retrieved August 11, 2010, from http://www.science-daily.com/releases/2010/02/100204144551.htm

Contributors

Franklin Abbott is a poet, anthologist, psychotherapist and activist living in Atlanta. A frequent contributor to *RFD*, he is chairperson of the Atlanta Queer Literary Festival. The poem included in *The Fire in Moonlight* was written after the first Faerie Gathering at Running Water Farm in June, 1978 and is published in Abbott's first collection, *Mortal Love*. His most recent book of poems and stories, *Pink Zinnia* (Authorhouse) was published in 2009.

Artwit earned a Ph.D. in Physics (Relativity and Cosmology) from Princeton in 1975 and worked in theoretical and computational physics and computer graphics until retirement in Seattle in 2004. Today, he travels the world and sings with choirs. Involved with the Faeries since 1980, Artwit was known as Marvelous Persimmon from 1985 to 1996. He was active in San Francisco, Portland and Seattle, where he organized Gatherings, participated in Faerie households, help found the Church of Nomenus, developed the land at Wolf Creek, Oregon, and started the national Faerie mailing list. He states that he wrote his essay as a way to come to terms "with maturity as a solid philosophical materialist among ethereal Faeries."

Gregory Barnes (Pan) lives in Canberra, Australia, where he works as a Natural Therapist and teacher of Hatha Yoga, including nude classes for men. "My days are often a continuum of enjoyable experiences," he says. "I wrote my essay in the spirit of sharing my impressions of the Radical Faeries and with the hope it might inspire and inform."

Chris Bartlett (The Lady Bartlett) is a longtime gay community organizer and Radical Faerie from the Philadelphia Radical Faerie Circle. He is currently the Executive Director of the William Way Gay Community Center in Philadelphia. You can follow him on Twitter at http://twitter.com/harveymilk. His article is dedicated to Walter Lear, patri/matriarch of the Philadelphia Faeries.

Jerry Berbiar (Jerry the Faerie) is a longtime Radical Faerie who lives in San Francisco. He is a member of the Circle of Loving Companions, the group that brought Harry Hay and John Burnside to the Bay Area to care for them in their old age. A local activist on social-justice issues such as healthcare, HIV funding, tenants' rights and other issues, Jerry no longer works due to disability but is "always workin' it," as he says. His essay reflects disillusionment with the betrayal of gay liberation by the assimilationist trend of the LGBT community around issues such as marriage and the military.

James Broughton was a legendary poet and an award-winning filmmaker who for many years lived in the San Francisco Bay Area with his life partner Joel Singer, also an artist and filmmaker. In the early 1990s they relocated to the arts community of Port Townsend, Washington, where they lived until James' death at age eighty-five. A documentary film, *Big Joy*, about Broughton's life and work (twenty-three films and twenty-five volumes of poetry and prose) is in production.

Joey Cain is a longtime community activist in San Francisco. He was active in the creation of Nomenus and its Radical Faerie Sanctuary in Wolf Creek, Oregon. He served on the Board of the San Francisco LGBT Pride Celebration Committee, including four years as President, and co-chaired the committee that placed a memorial statue of Harvey Milk in San Francisco City Hall. A thirty-year member of the Bound Together Anarchist Book Store Collective, he co-produces the annual Bay Area Anarchist Book Fair and is a founder of the Edward Carpenter Forum for which he currently co-edits their web site at edwardcarpenterforum.org.

David Cawley lives in Park Slope, Brooklyn, New York, with his Tuxedo tomcat, Bandit. He's a longterm survivor of HIV-AIDS, coping with the subsequent issues of Type-2 Diabetes and end-stage renal failure. He paints, photographs and writes on occasion and still entertains the fantasy of performing a cabaret act. He also hopes for a kidney transplant and the freedom afterward to travel more extensively. His essay "The Faeries Gather" was previously published in *RFD* magazine in 1980. Cawley wrote it as his way of mythologizing the first national Gathering and to place it in Faerie lore.

Vyvyan Chatterjie (Notre Dame des Arbres) is an Interfaith Minister who works mostly as a community builder with the Eurofaeries of Folleterre, France, and with the Edward Carpenter Community in Great Britain. He has a base in London's oldest housing cooperative, Sanford, but lives a nomadic existence between there, southwest England, India and Zurich, Switzerland, where he is a student of Jungian psychology. Chatterjie says the motivation for writing his essay comes from the need to "uncover what lies beneath surfaces, offering a fresh view of often familiar material."

David S. Cohen (Cheiron) acts, writes and teaches English in San Diego, California. His essay, "Re-Membering," first appeared in *RFD* magazine not long after the first national Gathering and was reprinted in the *White Crane Journal* on a later anniversary date. His writing seeks to find the crossroads of the mythic and the personal.

Robert Croonquist (Covelo) lives in New York City where he is Founder and Program Director of Youth Arts New York. In addition to bringing visiting artists to the city's schools, Youth Arts organizes school visits by the survivors of the atomic bombing of the Japanese cities of Hiroshima and Nagasaki. Croonquist wrote his essay "because I have a Remembrance Responsibility to do so. We [gay men] all felt at the time that we were changing the world and it turns out we were. We were a liberation movement, in solidarity with other liberation movements. This root has been lost in much of the contemporary gay rights movement and needs to be honored and remembered. Many of that earlier generation are gone, so it is up to those of us who are left to tell their stories."

Mac Del Ray (Maria) is a Faerie who hails from the north of Ontario, Canada, but has lived most of his adult life in Ottawa. Having worked as a social worker all his life, he is now retired and free to pursue other interests, such as doing healing work in various parts of the world such as Mexico and India. His story in *The Fire in Moonlight* is a true one, he says, "so beware of starry nights during hot summer Gatherings."

Tim Doody (Query) has seen his short stories published in many places, including *Brevity, Alternet, Word Riot, Best Gay Erotica 2003* and elsewhere online and in print. ABC-TV's "Nightline" included Doody in a national list of "particularly troublesome, even dangerous, anarchists" and Rush Limbaugh made fun of Doody and his last name on the air. His website is www.timdoody.me.

Donald Engstrom-Reese is an artist, gardener, Heathen and Witch. He has been consciously involved with Mystery and the Spirit Peoples for over thirty years. Donald's roots spring from the changing balance between the wild, the domestic, art, gardening, Queer Spirit, Hedge Witchery, deep dreaming, shamanic visioning, cooking, clan-hold magics and the exploration of the sacred realms of sex and pleasure. Donald begins each day with this prayer: "I dare to dwell in beauty, balance and delight. I dare to see with clear eyes and an open heart." And then he makes his bed as a devotional act to life. Donald, was a co-founder of *RFD* Magazine, and has taught for over twenty-five years, rooted in a living blend of Queer Spirit, Heathenry, Witchcraft, Nordic and shamanic styles. His husband Mark and their current home/gardens (it names itself Hector) are in Minneapolis, Minnesota, nestled in the arms of the Upper Mississippi Valley.

David Finkelstein is a video artist whose work has been featured in numerous film festivals and has won awards at nine of them. He is the Artistic Director of Lake Ivan Performance Group. He has been attending Faerie Gatherings since 1983 and was one of the first board members of Faerie Camp Destiny. More information is available at www.lakeivan.org.

Patrick James Geise (Wow) was born on an early winter morning in the mid-20th century and raised by loving parents, Joan and Jim, in a small rural community. Encouraged by his father, Wow pursued his love of the arts, earning a BFA from the Art Institute in Chicago. In 2000, he joined the Radical Faerie clan at Short Mountain Sanctuary, where "I reclaimed my connection with the magical realms of life." A self-proclaimed practical mystic and world wanderer, Wow currently lives in the San Francisco Bay Area where he is working on two books of poetry and a first novel, *The Dance of the Dancer*.

Giuseppe tries to keep his Faerie name for at least a year out of concern for people, like himself, with an unreliable memory for names. He resides with his loved one and a Senegal parrot in a cozy little home half way between Thailand and the Netherlands, "within thirty-five years of Magdalen Farm, just a short hop to Saratoga Springs, California, and Short Mountain, Tennessee," he says. When he's not whining about stuff he works to protect tree frogs, meadow foam and other endangered species. On occasion he's allowed to create gardens for nice people who are willing to pay. His remembrances were motivated by a petty need to insert himself into Faerie history and to tell his truths as best he can.

Pat Gourley lives in Denver, Colorado, and is recently retired from nearly four decades of nursing. The past twenty-one years were spent as a nurse clinician/manager in the local public HIV clinic. Pat's nursing practice has been significantly impacted over the years by his own HIV infection as well as Radical Faerie philosophy. He dates his Faerie roots back to 1979 and was an active participant in the planning collective responsible for the second Spiritual Gathering for Radical Faeries held in the foothills west of Denver in August of 1980.

Trebor Healy is the author of the Ferro-Grumley and Violet Quill award-winning novel *Through It Came Bright Colors*, as well as a collection of poems, *Sweet*

Son of Pan, being reissued by Queer Mojo (2010) and a short story collection, *Perfect Scar & Other Stories.* Trebor lives in Los Angeles and his website is www.treborhealey. com.

Henry Holmes was one of the few men of color who attended early Faerie Gatherings. His experiences are reflected in his essay "Into the Woods," originally published in *BLK* magazine in 1990 and later in a self-published pamphlet form.

Mountaine Mort Jonas is the longtime president of RFD Press, publisher of *RFD,* now entering its fourth decade. A facilitator of Breathwork Medicine and a performer-trainer in Playback Theatre, Mountaine lives in the mountains of North Carolina and spends lots of quality time around the Short Mountain Sanctuary. His website is www.mountaine.info.

Jonas (Peterpansy) is a writer, an explorer, an activist performer—on the streets, on the radio, in your face and occasionally on stage. He currently lives in New York's West Village and works as an intensive care nurse. And in case readers think he's not gay enough, he says, he does aerobics (in spandex) at the gym.

Efthimios Kalos was born in Ethiopia, raised in Greece, studied in the United States and has lived in France the past fifteen years. He has written about gay self-expression in the medium of photography, worked as a translator and is now a self-defined "Parisian housewife and occasional Radical Faerie priestess."

Carol Kleinmaier is a longtime gender, HIV and radical sexuality activist-educator living in Oakland, California. "Playing with Black Leather Wings at Wolf Creek, Oregon, in 1991," she says, "is where I discovered my own queer family with roots deep in Radical Faerie tradition." Carol's essay explores the flowing of one self-generating culture into another. The article first appeared in *RFD.*

Leopard has lived at Short Mountain Sanctuary since finding the Faeries by magical chance in 1993. He has involved himself with most aspects of Sanctuary life over the years and has also made a point of spending time at sister Sanctuaries and connecting with urban Faerie Circles throughout the United States. After many years residing in the ancient yurt in the heart of the Sanctuary, he built a log and earth hobbit house with his friend Ha! that he now calls home.

Eric Lichtman (Toozy) has lived in Miami, Florida, since 1986. Raised in the Bay Area, he attended El Cerrito High and UC Berkeley, earning a Masters in Teaching English/Education. After teaching in the secondary schools of the Richmond, Oakland and Santa Monica school systems, he branched out to form a creative arts and consulting business, Transonics. For the past twenty-four years he has been a professor at Miami Dade College, teaching classes in writing, literature and speech. In 2002, he received an Endowed Teaching Chair in Earth Ethics and specializes in studies that focus on creative expression, voice, minority issues and East-West Psychology. He treasures meditation, studies Buddhism and Judaism and enjoys married life with his partner, Beco.

Mati Livinit moved to Daffodil Meadow on Short Mountain, Tennessee, two years ago to begin homesteading after living all his life in the city. "My path led me to a community and a land where I make my life exploring what is possible with love through the healing of our disconnections. We invite others into our community to hold space for life's most beautiful and bold expressions," states Mati, adding, "The badger says 'sometimes we need a story more than we need food.' My stories are my medicine."

Jan/Nathan Falling Long first attended a Radical Faerie Gathering at Blue Heron in 1989. He soon left his graduate studies in Pittsburgh to move to Short Mountain Sanctuary, Tennessee, where he lived for four and a half years, baking bread, milking goats and working on *RFD*. He eventually left the commune to pursue love and then an MFA in creative writing. He now lives in Philadelphia, "Where there's a lovely Faerie community," he reports, writes short stories and essays and teaches at Richard Stockton College of New Jersey. His essay was first published in *Tin House* (Issue #35).

Marco Shokti Lovestar is a London-based Eurofaerie, part of the United Kingdom's Queer Spirit Circle. A performer, priest and prophet, Marco also says he's a "healer, hooker and harmonizer." He is a steward of the Folleterre Faerie Sanctuary. Marco contributed to *The Fire in Moonlight* "because of the great excitement of moving the gay story forward, uniting the sexual with the spiritual through the heart."

Raymond Luczak, a recovering Catholic, is the author and editor of eleven books, including the award-winning novel *Men with Their Hands*. A playwright and filmmaker as well, Luczak lives in Minneapolis, Minnesota. He says he often writes to discover what he didn't know about what he *thought* he knew. Luczak's most recent book is *Mute: Poems* (A Midsummer Night's Press). His website is www.raymondluczak.com.

Sequoia Thom Lundy, MA, has been exploring the interplay between Eros and Spirit and men loving men since the 1970s. He is the founder of MenInTouch. org and offers Transformational Life Coaching by phone. He lives in Vancouver, Canada. Sequoia's website is at www.T-L-C.ca.

Ian MacKinnon is a gay-centered performance artist and curator of queer theater events in Los Angeles. He performs both nationally and locally, creating solo and group pieces for theaters, clubs, performance spaces, art galleries, rooftops and classrooms. In his solo work, Ian combines spoken text, psychological theory, digital video collage, ritual and music to evoke issues central to the queer community and to gay liberation.

Dennis Miles was born in 1952 in Santiago, Cuba, and has lived in the United States since 1967. For the last twenty-five years he has worked for an AIDS research project at the University of California, Los Angeles. He has written a novel, *The Companion*. His book of poetry, *Born in the Negative Tense,* was published by San Francisco's Vortex Press. Miles is an accomplished playwright and many of his plays have been produced for the stage. Miles' poem in *The Fire in Moonlight* was written around the time of the first Gathering and was published in the 1979 anthology, *Fairy Poems* and also in the tenth-anniversary issue of *Gay Sunshine*.

Mykdeva is a belly dancer and an architect—he's practiced both professionally. A Radical Faerie since the first Gathering in 1979, he's grown from that rootstock. He is a founding member of the Gay Elder Council for the Los Angeles gay community. This California native often roams the hills above Santa Barbara as well as teaches raw food diet techniques and how to reach states of ecstasy. He looks forward to another thirty years living in Faerie community. Mykdeva can be reached at mykdeva@verizon.net.

Richard Neely (Osiris), Associate Editor, took his Faerie name in 1998 and has been an active member of the community ever since. A documentary filmmaker, community activist and great cook, Osiris is now focusing his energies on reigniting and nurturing the flame that is the Los Angeles Radical Faerie Circle. He lives with his husband Tim and their two dogs.

Orlando is a writer, journalist and occasional filmmaker. He went to his first Radical Faerie Gathering at Breitenbush Hot Springs in 1995 and still adores that semi-annual retreat in the Cascades of Oregon. Orlando has been writing most of his life and is currently collaborating with an award-winning artist on her memoir.

He went to Humboldt State University in the redwoods of northern California and lives in the Bay Area.

Allen Page was awakened to the sacred history, power and purpose of male-male love and brotherhood by his experiences and interactions at the 1979 Radical Faerie Gathering. Today he is an intuitive spiritual counselor, channeler, teacher and gay elder residing in Los Angeles. He writes to explore the meaning of his experiences and to share them with others. His essay "Army of Lovers" complements the multimedia show he co-created with Mykdeva from their combined color slides of the 1979 event. His article was previously published by *RFD* in 1979 and in 2009. Allen can be contacted at allen-page@sbcglobal.net.

Don Perryman (Dawn) is a retired English teacher, poet and late-life Faerie who wishes someone could have told him how fulfilling his sixties would be. He lives north of Atlanta, Georgia, with his beloved life partner, Gilson. Dawn works as a local community organizer and enjoys growing tomatoes in his backyard, backpacking along beaches and mountain trails and celebrating with other Faeries at Short Mountain Sanctuary. His essay was written, like his other work, to pursue "my lifelong goal of understanding who we truly are and what this world can be at its very best."

Will Roscoe received his Ph.D. in Historical Consciousness (Anthropology) from the University of California, Santa Cruz. He is the author of *The Zuni Man-Woman,* which received the Margaret Mead Award of the American Anthropological Association and a Lambda Literary Award, *Queer Spirits: A Gay Men's Myth Book, Changing Ones: Third and Fourth Genders in Native North America,* and *Jesus and the Shamanic Traditions of Same-Sex Love.* He edited *Living the Spirit: A Gay American Indian Anthology* and *Radically Gay: Gay Liberation in the Words of its Founder* by Harry Hay. He is co-editor of *Islamic Homosexualities* and *Boy-Wives and Female Husbands: Studies of African Homosexualities.* He is a recipient of a Monette-Horowitz Award for lifetime achievement in combating homophobia. His beloved life-partner of many years, Bradley Rose, who designed the "Faerie Tongues" illustration used as the Frontispiece of this book, died of complications of HIV-AIDS in 1996.

Michael Rumaker (Marvel) writes novels, memoirs, poetry and essays in Nyack, New York. He joined one of the first urban Faerie Circles in Manhattan in the late 1970s. His novel *My First Satyrnalia* (Grey Fox Press,1981) narrates his experiences during a night of ritual, music and dance in a loft in the East Village. The segments excerpted in *The Fire in Moonlight* are from that work, which focuses itself on the celebration of two-bodied, two-spirit, male-on-male love and sexuality—a continuing focus of much of Rumaker's writing.

Yusuf Leo Schuman (a Faerie formerly known as "Damien") first met the Radical Faeries in 1991 for an operatically moonlit circle in a Portland storefront home and still connects with them most deeply through the Breitenbush Gathering community. He co-founded Cascadia Radical Faerie Resource and has served for many years as a steward and co-maintainer of the QueerNet Faerie Email List, radfae.org and other online resources. He lives in Portland, Oregon, with his beloved husband, Michael "Peppermint" Henry.

William Stewart, compiler of the *The Fire in Moonlight* Resource Guide, attended his first Faerie event in 1979 and has treasured a sense of being part of a queer-spirit tribe ever since. Over the last couple of decades other karmic loyalties have claimed much of his energy, but he has recently decided to pursue his long-held dream of living in intentional community with fellow radical-visionary queers. He has embarked on a quest to connect with other gay men who share an aspiration to live together in collective commitment and consciousness.

Pete Sturman (Mockingbird) is fairly well known in Faerie (and other) Circles as half of the New Orleans music duo Pistol Pete & Popgun Paul. After Hurricane Katrina, Pete moved to New York City where he reports he has "my fingers in many pies." His essay was written specifically for *The Fire in Moonlight*.

Mark Thompson is a writer, editor and photographer. The author of seven books, Thompson is best known for his internationally acclaimed trilogy *Gay Spirit, Gay Soul* and *Gay Body*. A gay activist for nearly forty years, Thompson has also worked as a clinical psychologist with gay youth and people living with HIV-AIDS. In 2007, he was presented a Lifetime Achievement Award by the Lambda Literary Foundation. The City of West Hollywood honored him and his longtime partner, Episcopal priest and author Malcolm Boyd, in 2009 with the Rainbow Key Award "for their outstanding contributions to the gay and lesbian community." "A Day and A Night In The Desert," originally appeared in his book *Fellow Travelers: Guides & Tribes* (Fluxion Editions, 2008), a Faerie photo memoir. Thompson's website is www.markthompsongayspirit.com.

Stuart Timmons is an award-winning historian, most recently authoring the Lambda Award-winning *Gay L.A.* with Lillian Faderman. His essay, "The Making of a Tribe," is excerpted from his 1990 biography *The Trouble with Harry Hay: Founder of* *the Modern Gay Movement.* In January 2008, at age 51, Stuart suffered a massive stroke. Comatose for months, he is now showing steady signs of improvement—his mind is sharp and he can speak and move with assistance—and is determined to fully recover with the on-going support of his family and many friends.

Tyler Tone (Stitch) lives in Vancouver, Canada, and was fortunate to have a short story chosen for the anthology *Charmed Lives* (Lethe Press). He successfully edited the first-ever Canadian issue of *RFD*. Tyler counts as his blessings his son Kevin, having his Circle of Faerie Intimates and more recently his partner Ronnie.

Bo Young is publisher and editor of *White Crane* and White Crane Books and founder of White Crane Institute, a nonprofit educational corporation devoted to exploring Gay culture, history and wisdom. He blogs at http://whitecrane. typepad. com/gaywisdom and sends a daily email blast, GayWisdom, a review of gay history from GayWisdom.org and on Facebook at GayWisdom.org. Bo is also a photographer and lives and gardens in Granville, New York, with his spouse, William, and their dog, Brewster, and kitty, Karlyle.

Marissa Zaknich was born in Dubrovnik (formerly Yugoslavia) and now lives and works in Sydney, Australia. She has an MA in Fine Arts and teaches Visual Arts, Photography and Design in a senior secondary college. She is a painter and photographer who loves dancing, staying healthy and talking to all types of people.

Faerie Glossary

A glossary, also known as an *idioticon* (a word we could just not exclude), a *vocabulary*, or *clavis* (i.e. "key"), is an alphabetical list of terms in a particular domain of knowledge with the definitions for those terms. A glossary includes terms within a book which are either newly introduced, uncommon or specialized. Language is the verbal expression of culture.

A culture's language contains everything its speakers can think about and every way they have of thinking about things. For example, the Latin language has no word for the "female friend of a man" (the feminine form of *amicus* is *amica*, which means mistress, not friend) because the Roman culture could not imagine a male and a female being equals, which they considered necessary for friendship. Neither does English.

Assimilation: Cultural assimilation is generally understood as a socio-political response to demographic multi-ethnicity that supports or promotes the assimilation of different ethnicities into the dominant culture. It is opposed to affirmative philosophy (for example, multiculturalism) which recognizes and seeks to maintain differences.

The Faeries are rooted in Harry Hay's definition of gay people as "a separate and oppressed minority" [see "*Radical Faerie*" definition below], which is predicated on extensive historical research and stands in direct opposition to the assertion that gay people "are just like straight people except for what we do in bed." Hay contradicted the latter assertion, maintaining that the bedroom was, perhaps, the only "common ground" gay people shared with non-gay people and that it was in every other aspect of life in which we were different. It was from this difference that our value to the larger society arose.

Call: An announcement of a Gathering or a Circle. A Call may be published or simply circulated by telephone tree. A "Yoo-Hoo" is also a Call to come together, occasionally at larger Gatherings, to assemble smaller, focused events.

Circle of Loving Companions: In 1965 Harry Hay and John Burnside founded a gay and lesbian collective, the *Circle of Loving Companions*, based on "the Whitmanesque ideal of the inclusive love of comrades." The concept grew to become a description of Circles of Faeries who are friends in various cities, "chosen family" as compared to "birth family" and gained greater meaning through the onset of the HIV-AIDS health crisis, when many gay men were abandoned by their birth families and received care and succor through their *Circle of Loving Companions*. It may or may not include former lovers.

In 1999, Harry and John moved to San Francisco from Los Angeles where they had lived together for twenty years. A group of Radical Faeries known as the *Circle of Loving Companions* became caretakers for the two of them. Harry Hay died in 2002 at the age of ninety. Burnside passed away peacefully at the age of ninety-one in their home in September, 2008, surrounded by the *Circle of Loving Companions* who had been caring for him since Harry's passing.

Circle Process/Consensus: Faeries generally use **Circle Process** and **Consensus** decision making as the model of governance and decision-making process.

Circle process is a model based on the ideas presented by Harry Hay and John Burnside, but derived by them from extensive readings and cultural studies. The Circle Process includes the following principles: Speak from the heart, listen from the heart; all voices are important to be heard; what is said in the circle remains in the circle; practice compassionate self-monitoring.

Consensus decision making is a group decision-making process that not only seeks the agreement of most participants, but the resolution or mitigation of minority objections. Consensus is usually defined as meaning both general agreement and the process of getting to such agreement.

Consensus has been used by a wide variety of groups, from the theological, such as the Quakers, to entire nations, such as the Haudensaunee. As a decision-making process, consensus decision-making aims to be Inclusive, Participatory, Cooperative, Egalitarian, Solution-oriented.

Fairie: The term as it was originally published on the Call of the first Spiritual Conference for Radical Fairies in 1979. Derived initially from the word "fairy" a formerly pejorative term for a gay man.

Faerie: The term as it was originally published on the Call of the first Spiritual Conference for Radical Fairies in 1979. Derived initially from the word "fairy" a formerly pejorative term for a gay man. Though the word "faerie" had at first been used experimentally and tentatively, increasing amounts of time were devoured by defining and exploring the term until it became "Faerie" with a capital "F"—and an object of either fast adherence or suspicious rejection. Some gay seekers began to worry that a seeming contradiction loomed: Faerie conformity.

Faerie Name: As opposed to a person's mundane, everyday name, a person's "Faerie name" may be a self-chosen as well as gifted appellation. Occasionally individuals may have more than one Faerie name. They are chosen so as to reflect some essence or facet of the individual's personal nature.

Gathering: A convocation of Faeries, following a Call that is usually timed around various turnings, i.e., solstices or equinoxes. Spring and fall Gatherings are held at various Sanctuaries around the world, occasionally under different names i.e., the Northeast Faeries have The Walt Whitman Gathering in the spring. Gatherings are frequently keyed to pagan festivals. Short Mountain celebrates the Beltane Gathering at the spring equinox; the Northeast Faeries have a midsummer Lammas Gathering.

Heart Circle: A talking circle.

Nomenus Speaks to the IRS: An as-yet-unpublished, bound document (or collection of documents) that tracks the original submission for nonprofit, tax-exempt religious, status on behalf of the Wolf Creek, Nomenus Sanctuary to the Internal Revenue Service from the beginning of the process to the final determination. Originally written by Harry Hay, John Burnside, Will Roscoe and Bradley Rose, it contains:

• The completed IRS Form 1023 application on behalf of Nomenus, dated 6/19/1985, for 501(c)(3) nonprofit status, which includes the explanation of Nomenus as a religious organization. It defines the religious mission of Nomenus, "to live and worship according to the beliefs we share about Balance, Nature, Immanence and subject-SUBJECT Consciousness."

• The initial receipt from the IRS District Director with additional questions regarding the application (dated 9/6/1985).

• The collected responses to those additional questions, signed by Bradley Rose and submitted 9/21/1985.

• A follow-up from the IRS with seven additional questionnaires (designated A/B/C/F/G/H/L) comprised of 41 questions including: A brief history of your organization including your reason for forming. Do you provide ministerial degrees? What are the qualifications, training and/or experience of your leaders? Does your organization require a vow of poverty? Do you have a recognized creed and form of worship? Please describe and explain your creed. Do you have literature of your own? Do you have Sunday schools? If so please describe your services. Do you have ordained ministers? [Not a complete list of the questions.]

• The collected responses to these seven questionnaires, written by the four applicants (Hay/Burnside/Roscoe/Rose), including definitions of "Circle" and a general outline of how to conduct a Circle and "Gathering"; an extensive treatise by Hay on subject-SUBJECT consciousness.

• Collected contemporary papers, ephemera, photos, writings and publications defining and documenting Radical Faerie culture and spiritual wisdom.

• By Laws and Articles of Incorporation for Nomenus.

• An initial ruling denying of 501(c)(3) status (seven pages).

• Nomenus's official protest of that ruling including a Request for Conference and a complete anthropological and archetypal breakdown of the history of same-sex-loving peoples, including Edward Carpenter's "Intermediate Types," "kedeshim," "berdache," "fools" etc., tracking back to the Neolithic period from 9,000—6,000 BCE and through the modern era.

• Two annotated bibliographies.

• More than 100 pages of additional supportive ephemera, poetry, art, songs, chants, Calls, copies of posters and flyers, ritual scripts, Native American and Pagan songs.

• Subsequent follow-up correspondence between the submitters and the IRS acknowledgment, including the final positive determination of tax-exemption on behalf of Nomenus, establishing it as an official Radical Faerie religious organization.

No-Talent Shows: An encouragement to allow people to "get their freak on" and feel the support of the gathered community. No-Talent shows can be readings, musical performances or recitations. It doesn't matter if you're a Tony Award-winner reading *Jabberwocky* (as it has been on occasion) or a wild Faerie clowning as a fundamentalist tent revival for Cheezits ("Help me Cheezits! The Lord of Snack…he does not want you to be hungry!"…and nailing the box of Cheez-Its to the Maypole). All performers are welcome and rewarded with the Faerie "hiss."

Radical [Faerie]: Harry Hay's gay politics represented an alternative to post-modernist Queer theory and dogmatic constructionism. Indeed, Hay was the only contemporary gay thinker who could be said to offer a unified theory of gay-ness—one that begins by defining its subjects in multidimensional terms and then accounts for its individuals and historical origins, its diverse forms and their history, the psycho-social development of gay individuals and the nature and sources of gay oppression. Post modernism offers at best a politics of resignation, one that rejects the possibility of an "outside" to power, of a subject-SUBJECT alternative to subject-OBJECT social relations, and the means of getting there is through a politics that af-firms Queer identities and cultures. Hay was never bothered if his ideas were called "essentialist" or "identity politics" or "constructionist"—he was happy to emphasize his differences with social constructionism and Queer theory—provided that the word *radical* precede these labels. The original meaning of the word, "to the root," serves well to convey the underlying theme of his philosophy and politics.

The key principles of Hay's "Radical" essentialism are summed up as follows in his book of collected writings *Radically Gay*:

It is, first and foremost, gay-centered, reflecting the social standpoint of con-temporary sexual minorities. It is not neutral on the question of Queer well-being.

It posits gay presence rather than absence as the usual state of human society.

It conceives of its subject in multidimensional terms—not merely as a sexual preference but as a difference manifest in gender roles, social identity, economic roles and sometimes religious roles, as well.

It seeks to tell history from "the bottom up," using those documents, records and artifacts that reveal the common experience of the largest number of Faerie folk and not only the discourse of elite heterosexuals and social institutions.

It recognizes various levels of meaning—individual, social, transcultural and spiritual. It does not assume the way an individual describes herself will be identical to the institutional definitions of labels that have been propagated.

It is multi-cultural and comparative. Rather than a unitary instance—"the modern homosexual"—it employs the notion of a family tree (like Wittgenstein's concept of "family resemblance") to conceptualize the relationship between the Queer identities and roles of different cultures and historical periods.

It views history as a process of continuity-within-change rather than as a series of sharply defined periods or ruptures. Concept/labels like "Sodomite" and "Urning," "homosexual" and "gay," have overlapped in their usage. None can be defined without reference to the others.

It focuses on praxis. It seeks to analyze the interactions between individuals and their societies and cultures. It looks for instances of symbols and ideas in action as well as in discourse.[1]

Sanctuary: Land used for retreat by Faeries. Faeries have traditionally placed a priority on reconnecting with nature and sustainable use of land. All current Sanctuaries are located in rural areas, though there has been discussion about how an urban Sanctuary environment might be maintained. The land may be owned or rented. Sanctuaries may or may not have year-round residents or caretakers (titles vary from Sanctuary to Sanctuary.) The idea of having a place where gay men could gather to spend time away from the dominant culture with a specific purpose of self-exploration and development of our own norms and ideas arose from early theorizing about Faeries. It has developed further with each early Gathering and Heart Circle where the need for such a place has been expressed and defined. All Sanctuaries are welcoming places for all people and upon arrival it is traditional to greet new arrivals with "Welcome home." Some Sanctuaries initially allowed for individuals to request "Fag Only Space" in which case, all non-gay-identified males or females were politely asked to vacate the property for the duration of the requested time.

SexMagick: Also called "Daisy Chain Workshops," "SexMagick" was Harry Hay's term for the training workshops he and John Burnside led for many summers at the Nomenus/Wolf Creek Sanctuary. It was always Harry and John's stated intention that those who were invited to partake in these workshops were, in fact, being trained to lead them later. This has been accomplished with various combinations of alumni of these SexMagic Workshops leading other workshops in various Sanctuaries.

Sssss-ing ("hissing"): There are a number of derivations for this response of approval from an individual or a Circle for a Faerie's comments or sharing or a performance; it is akin to applause. At the first great Circle of the Denver Gathering it was proposed that since snakes were sacred to the ancient Earth goddess, the hiss should be a sign of approval. There is a related tale of it arising from the myth of St. Patrick "chasing the snakes out of ancient Ireland," interpreted as a connection with "the Burning Times" the chasing out of the "Olde Religion" by the patriarchal religions and its connections with snake energies, witch hunts and a genocide of same-sex loving men and women, Faeries "hiss" to reconnect and reclaim this history.

subject-SUBJECT/subject-OBJECT: subject-SUBJECT is an essential doctrine of Radical Faerie culture. In Harry Hay's theory, the gay monogamous relationship is one in which the participants, through non-competitive instinctual inclinations *and contrary to cultural inheritances*, perceive each other as Equals and learn, usually through deeply painful trial and error, to experience each other, to continuously grow and to develop *with* each other, in "analog consciousness"—as subject-SUBJECT.[2]

In *"Nomenus Speaks to the IRS"* subject-SUBJECT is discussed: "We must expand our experience from subjects thinking objectively to thinking and acting subject to Subject, equal to equal. ...Living subject to Subject deeply affects our love relationships. A couple coming together subject to Subject are not two complementary halves forming a whole; instead, each supplements the other. Living subject to Subject in our daily lives means eschewing attempts to manipulate others for our own narrow gain. To manipulate another in furtherance of one's personal profit is to deny that other his or her right to develop according to the inner voice. To deny another this right to develop is contrary to our moral code.[3]

Yoo-Hoo: 1. A Call to assemble for meals, for smaller events at a Gathering, or for a Circle. 2. A term of endearment used as a greeting at Faerie Gatherings. There is some evidence that it was first encountered at performances of the San Francisco genderfuck theater group The Cockettes (as seen in the opening of David Weissman and Bill Weber's 2002 film *The Cockettes*). ProtoFaeries would certainly have been in attendance.

---

[1] *Radically Gay: Gay Liberation in the Words of its founder* by Harry Hay, Will Roscoe, editor, Beacon Press © 1996. Used by permission.

[2] Ibid.

[3] *Nomenus Speaks to the IRS*, [1985] printed and bound by donation of Studio 403, publisher of *Sign of the Times—A Chronicle of Decadence in the Atomic Age,* P.O. Box 706672, Seattle, WA 98107. Copies available at various Sanctuaries and the White Crane Institute.

Radical Faerie Resource Directory

The GOAL OF THIS DIRECTORY is to provide descriptions and contact information for Sanctuaries, organizations, Gatherings and resources relevant to the Radical Faerie world. However this world is highly fluid and amorphous, so any such guide will necessarily be incomplete and to some extent arbitrary. What follows is simply a list of some key nodes of the network. Readers are urged to pursue their own research and find the connections that are relevant to their own needs.

This directory contains no separate section for **Radical Faerie Gatherings**. Gatherings are the archetypal crucibles of Radical Faerie culture and most of the Sanctuaries and organizations listed below were created, at least in part, to be able to sponsor them. In this guide, regularly scheduled Gatherings will be noted under the entries for the places and groups that host them, rather than in a category of their own.

Radical Faerie Sanctuaries are rural properties dedicated to nurturing Radical Faerie values and culture. Most are owned collectively by the groups that steward them, but this list also includes a couple of private properties with a long-established history of Faerie use and access.

Most Sanctuaries welcome guests not only for Gatherings, but for individual visits and retreats as well. Readers should contact potential destinations for further information, both about attending gatherings and about visiting at other times.

Central to the character of Radical Faerie Sanctuaries and gatherings is the principle of **Openness.** While visitors are urged to help maintain Faerie space financially as well as in other ways, contributions are on a voluntary basis, and no one is turned away for lack of funds (NOTAFLOF). Similarly, although pre-registration for Gatherings is encouraged to help organizers make food purchases and other arrangements, people come and go as they choose during Gathering times, and Gatherings themselves are typically self-organizing rather than planned in advance.

Under **Organizations** are listed groups which either do not own land, or do not conform to the Radical Faerie Sanctuary model in some other respect, but which are motivated by a kindred vision. More information about these and other related vectors of queer-spirit consciousness can be found through the listings for

Media Resources, which offer gateways to further exploration of a boundless and
ever-changing world.

1. Sanctuaries

Short Mountain Sanctuary, (SMS) near Nashville in middle Tennessee, is
the "mothership" of Radical Queer Sanctuaries, having offered safe space to Queer
folk continuously since 1981. Over the years, thousands of Faeries and their friends
have passed through and many have settled in the region, either at SMS itself, or in-
dependently in the surrounding countryside, or in one of the kindred communities
that have sprung up nearby. It is the hub of an extended family of like-minded folks,
who share resources, play and party together, and support each other in a variety of
ways.

The Sanctuary consists of 365 acres of mostly steep and forested land, owned by
a non-profit educational corporation with a mission of environmental and community stewardship. A collective of residents numbering from twelve to twenty at any
given time welcomes visitors of all genders throughout the year. At the heart of the
Sanctuary is an antebellum log cabin that serves as kitchen, dining room, library and
common space. Residents live in a variety of homebuilt one- to five-person dwellings, and decision making is by consensus. The community lives lightly on the land,
drinking spring water, growing vegetables and dazzling flowers, tending milk goats
and chickens, using outhouses, and heating with wood. The only available electricity
is collected from the sun.

The community hosts two Gatherings annually: one for Beltane at the beginning of May, the other in mid-October. Beltane generally draws several hundred
people to the Sanctuary, making it the largest regular assemblage of the Faerie tribe.
Short Mountain has become a nursery and magnet for radical queer culture, and
has spawned five new intentional communities nearby: IDA, Creek View, Pumpkin
Hollow, Sassafras and Little Short Mountain Farm.

Mail: Short Mountain Sanctuary, 247 Sanctuary Lane, Liberty, TN 37095
Phone: 615-563-4397
Email: none
Website: none

Wolf Creek Sanctuary, "Nomenus," is located on eighty acres of meadow
and woodland in the mountains of southern Oregon and continues the lineage

begun by Harry Hay and his associates when they organized the first "Spiritual Conference for Radical Fairies" at a rented Arizona ashram in 1979. The property at Wolf Creek answers their vision of a West Coast Sanctuary for the Radical Faerie tribe. Wolf Creek, which has a history of queer-spirit activity dating back to the mid-1970s, was purchased in 1987 by Nomenus, a non-profit religious organization established to create, preserve and manage places of Sanctuary for Radical Faeries and their friends. [Editors' Note: See *Nomenus Speaks to the IRS* in Glossary]

In addition to serving as a site for Gatherings, Wolf Creek is home to a small intentional community of caretakers and longterm visitors who live in a variety of rustic dwellings scattered around the land. Communal buildings include the Barn, which houses cooking and serving facilities for Gatherings, and Garden House, the common space of the residential community. There are vegetable and flower gardens, a creek and altars that honor the spirits of the land and the dead.

Nomenus currently sponsors three Gatherings annually at Wolf Creek: the Spiritual Gathering of Radical Faeries in July/August, the Beltane Gathering during the week including May 1 and the Samhain Gathering during the week around October 31. The summer Gathering is a men's Gathering, while the Beltane and Samhain Gatherings are for Faeries of all genders. The Sanctuary also makes space available for personal retreats and activities organized by Radical Faeries and kindred groups, for example SexMagick workshops and the Naraya Dance of All Peoples.

Mail: Wolf Creek Sanctuary, Box 312, Wolf Creek, OR 97497

Phone: 541-866-2678

Email: nomenus@hughes.net

Website: www.nomenus.org

Faerie Camp Destiny is located in southern Vermont. Emerging out of a collective household that lost its rental home, Destiny incorporated as a non-profit educational organization to buy property for a Faerie Sanctuary and acquired 166 acres of undeveloped woodland in 1997. A permanent kitchen/bathhouse was recently constructed and plans are in the works for a handful of small cabins.

Currently there are no permanent residents, but the Sanctuary is open from late April until mid-October with at least one person generally on the land during that time. The year's first big event, the Walt Whitman Gathering, is held over the Memorial Day weekend, followed by Gatherings centered on Independence Day and Lammas in August. In addition, there is usually a small Gathering over Columbus Day, as well as work weeks and weekends that take place throughout the season. Destiny is a pan-gendered community and all are welcome, though queer-male-only space is created for specific events such as SexMagick workshops. An ad-hoc committee, "the Welcome Mats," reviews requests of those wishing to stay more than two weeks.

Mail: Faerie Camp Destiny, P.O. Box 517, Chester, VT 05143

Phone: 413-570-0369

Email: via website

Website: www.Faeriecampdestiny.org

Zuni Mountain Sanctuary sits at an altitude of 7200 feet in the high desert of northwestern New Mexico surrounded by the Zuni Mountains. Established in 1996, the 312-acre land trust features dramatic vistas and an expansive sense of serenity and space. A small number of resident stewards care for the land and strive to create a safe and respectful environment for all who visit. Along with the Common House and two small residential spaces, there is a community studio (the Aakaash, or "place of all beginnings") and a new bathhouse. In August the Sanctuary sponsors an annual Queer Shamans Gathering and various seasonal holidays are also celebrated. In addition, the Sanctuary hosts community potlucks and monthly weekend events dedicated to wellness and the arts. Visitors are welcome at any time, but weather conditions can be hazardous during the colder months, so caution is advised.

Mail: Zuni Mountain Sanctuary, P.O. Box 636, Ramah, NM 87321

Phone: 505-783-4002

Email: zunimtn@wildblue.net

Website: www.zms.org

Blue Heron Farm is a privately-owned property of over 200 acres in the St. Lawrence River valley of upper New York State. The farm hosts a Faerie Gathering over the week leading up to Labor Day, with a set-up weekend immediately beforehand. The drug- and alcohol-free Gathering has been held continuously since 1979 and is open to all gender identities. There is lots of room for camping on the property, along with very limited indoor space for guests with special needs. Vegetarian meals are prepared cooperatively in the Gathering kitchen and all participants are encouraged to share their skills and talents in Circles. Blue Heron also holds an annual Maple Sugaring "Gatherette" in March and Faeries are welcome to visit throughout the year with prior notice.

Mail: Blue Heron Farm, 68 Streeter Road, De Kalb Junction, NY 13630

Phone: 315-347-2178

Email: thompsbs@tds.net

Website: none

Starland sits on a ten-acre bluff overlooking a canyon in California's Mojave Desert, thirty-five miles north of Palm Springs. Founded in 1997 by three gay men—who are still its current owners—it is not a Faerie Sanctuary *per se*, but a spiritually-oriented retreat center where Faeries and their friends are welcome. Visitors become members on their first visit and have visiting privileges thereafter. As a non-profit organization, Starland relies on membership dues, fees and donations for support. Those wishing to participate in one of the retreat center's monthly work-play weekends are invited to come and become members without charge. In addition to several indoor spaces, there is plenty of room for camping or sleeping under the stars. Visitors are asked to bring food; meals are individual or communal.

In addition to the monthly work-play weekends, Starland typically hosts a Faerie Gathering starting on December 26 and lasting until just after New Year's. Starland also welcomes inquiries from potential year-round or seasonal new residents.

Mail: Starland Community, Yucca Valley, CA 92284

Phone: 760-364-2069

Email: via website

Website: www.starlandcommunity.org

Kawashaway is remote, even by the standards of the other Sanctuaries. Established in 1990, the Sanctuary is situated on a sacred lake, deep in the northwoods, twenty miles from nearest town of Finland, Minnesota, and approximately a six-hour drive from Minneapolis. Kawashaway has no permanent residents. There are a handful of structures on the land, but the flavor is deeply rustic. The Northwoods Tribe of Radical Faeries, based in Minneapolis, stewards the land and hosts two Gatherings each year: the Faerie Spirit Gathering, July 1-6, designated as chemical free, and Lammas, which lasts for ten days starting on the first Friday in August. There are also "Gatherettes" over the Memorial Day, Labor Day and Columbus Day weekends. Drug and alcohol use is discouraged and visitors should be accompanied by a tribe member when coming to the Sanctuary for the first time. The community is in the process of purchasing an adjoining parcel of land, which will expand the Sanctuary and improve accessibility, especially for winter use.

Mail: Kawashaway Sanctuary, PO Box 581194, Minneapolis, MN 55458

Phone: 612-237-3096

Email: twobearsrf@hotmail.com

Website: www.kawashaway.org

IDA is a residential community in middle Tennessee, located not far from Short Mountain (see above). The community's focus is on providing a safe space for Queer and trans folk, on fostering rural living skills and nurturing the arts, especially music and theater. Every June, IDA hosts the IDApalooza Fruit Jam, a week-long festival of Queer and trans music, performance and country fun. There are also occasional gardening workshops and other events. IDA has a stronger transgender flavor than many sanctuaries, but Radical Faeries of all genders will feel welcome there.

Phone: 615-597-4409

Email: idapalooza@gmail.com

Website: www.planetida.com

Amber Fox is a secluded private property encompassing eighty acres of rolling hills, fields and forests in the Canadian province of Ontario about sixty miles from Ottawa. The owners are the only residents, but visitors are encouraged to come for four all-male Faerie Gatherings annually: Victoria Day weekend, one week before U.S. Memorial Day; the week including Canada Day, July 1; High Summer Gathering, for the week ending on the first Monday in August; and Canadian Thanksgiving weekend (which is Columbus Day in the U.S.). Common spaces include a kitchen building, lounge, and wood-fired sauna, and there are indoor accommodations for twelve to fifteen, with ample additional space for camping. Amber Fox is off the grid and relies on solar power.

Mail: Amber Fox, Box 65, McDonalds Corners, Ontario K0G1M0 Canada

Phone: 819-770-0920

Email: chiplandia@sympatico.ca

Website: www.akaamberfox.blogspot.com

Australia's **Faeryland** is the first Radical Faerie Sanctuary to have been established outside of North America and dates from 2002. It consists of 134 rolling acres of subtropical rainforest and open land outside of Nimbin in northeast New South Wales. Faeryland does not host regularly scheduled Gatherings, functioning instead as a residential community and Sanctuary for individuals wishing to visit for short or extended stays. There are several rustic cabins that serve as residents' homes, along with a main house, but indoor space is limited and visitors are asked to camp on the land whenever possible. A land-use plan is being developed in accordance with permaculture principles; fruit and nut trees augment produce from the vegetable garden and native tree seedlings are propagated for ongoing rainforest regeneration.

Mail: Faeryland, P.O. Box 495, Nimbin, NSW, 2480, Australia

Phone: 02-6689-7070
Email: ozFaeries@yahoo.com
Website: www.ozFaeries.com

Folleterre ("Land of the Queers") is the Sanctuary of the EuroFaeries, located in the Vosges region in eastern France. The property was acquired in 2005, ten years after the first EuroFaerie gathering on the Dutch island of Terschelling. Folleterre features a farmhouse, a barn, and camping areas, as well as mountains, forests, streams, meadows and fruit trees. A few Faeries are now living on the land during the summer months and the community hosts several Gatherings over the course of the year, including one at Beltane and another in midsummer. There are also work weeks and "Gatherettes" focused on skill sharing, forestry and other themes. There is off-the-grid solar power and plans are in the works for small-scale hydro, which will enable a year-round residential community to establish itself on the land. The EuroFaeries also sponsor Gatherings at locations other than at Folleterre (see listing under Organizations).

Email: info@folleterre.org
Website: www.folleterre.org

2. Organizations

Gay Spirit Visions (GSV) is an Atlanta-based organization dedicated to nurturing heart-centered connection and spirituality among gay and bisexual men. Emerging out of Gatherings held at Running Water Farm, an early Radical Faerie Sanctuary in North Carolina, GSV hosted its first event in 1990, and was incorporated as a non-profit in 1996. The centerpiece of GSV's activities is its Fall Conference, which has been held annually at The Mountain, a retreat center located in Highlands, North Carolina, since 1990. More structured than a Faerie Gathering, the fall conference features guest speakers and small support groups as well as Heart Circles, ritual and play. Scholarships are available, but there is a conventional fee structure and registration is required. GSV also sponsors more informal fall and winter retreats, as well as monthly potlucks in the Atlanta area, online forums and publications. All events are drug and alcohol free.

Mail: Gay Spirit Visions, Box 339, Decatur, GA 30031
Email: info@gayspiritvisions.org
Website: www.gayspiritvisions.org

Cascadia Radical Faerie Resource is a non-profit corporation set up to sponsor Radical Faerie Gatherings at **Breitenbush Hot Springs** that have been taking place since 1982. Breitenbush is a queer-friendly, worker-owned retreat center surrounded by old-growth forest in the mountains of central Oregon's Cascade Range. It offers geothermal sauna, hot tubs and meadow pools, as well as cabins, a lodge and assorted other buildings, all geo-thermally heated, making it one of the most luxurious of Faerie Gathering places. Additionally, food is provided by the Breitenbush collective, so less volunteer energy is needed than at most Gatherings. However this also means that costs are relatively high and while the tradition of NOTAFLOF ("no one turned away for lack of funds") is honored, advance registration is required and participants needing financial help must apply for Faerie Fee Funds to cover expenses. Breitenbush Gatherings are male-only space and happen twice a year, over the long weekend including Presidents' Day in February and in the latter part of August.

Mail/phone/email: those of the Queen Registrar for each Gathering, see Website: www.radfae.org/breitenbush/thecall.htm; also www.radfae.org/cascadia

The Billys (formerly the Billy Club) began life in the early 1980s as a social network for gay men living rurally in Northern California. Although not a Radical Faerie group, The Billys have many similar traditions and goals, notably a focus on heart space. The Billys host six Gatherings a year: New Year's, Midwinter, May Day, Independence Day, Labor Day and Halloween. Billy Gatherings are held at various rented facilities in Northern California and are drug and alcohol free. Three of the Gatherings are for gay, bi and Queer men only, while the others are open to all. Billy Gatherings have a sliding-scale fee structure and scholarships are available. They are held under the auspices of the non-profit Billy Foundation, which also administers The Billy Emergency Support Fund, a resource for Billys and others living with HIV-AIDS in Mendocino, Lake and southern Humboldt counties.

Mail: The Billys, P.O. Box 12205, Santa Rosa, CA 95406
Phone: 707-545-1044
Email: office@billyclub.org
Website: www.billyclub.org

The Edward Carpenter Community of Gay Men is Britain's closest equivalent to a Radical Faerie group. While distinctly less anarchic in terms of organization, the community espouses many of the same values as the Faerie tribe. Named after the pioneering early twentieth-century English reformer and sexual liberationist Edward Carpenter, the community has sponsored gay men's weeks at

Laurieston Hall in southwest Scotland since 1985 and hosts week-long as well as shorter events at other venues as well. The community also produces a quarterly journal and sponsors Heart Circles and other activities in London and elsewhere.

Mail: BM ECC, London WC1N 3XX, England

Phone: (UK only) 080703 21 51 21; (non-UK) +44 8703 21 51 21

Email: contact_ecc@edwardcarpentercommunity.org.uk

Website: www.edwardcarpentercommunity.org.uk

The EuroFaeries not only steward the Sanctuary at Folleterre (see above), but also host Gatherings at other locations across Europe and sponsor an Asian Radical Faerie Gathering which takes place in southern **Thailand** every year in late winter. This Gathering attracts participants from around the world, with special outreach to Faeries from the developing nations of Southeast Asia.

Websites: www.euroFaerie.eu; www.asianFaeries.com

The SexMagick Workshops were developed by Harry Hay to provide space for a more concentrated exploration of intimacy and sexuality than free-form Gatherings could provide and to train a new generation of SexMagick Workshop facilitators. Prospective participants are expected to commit to the full week of each workshop and need to talk with one of the facilitator-gatekeepers before being allowed to participate. The actual process is considered confidential and proprietary, but the form involves intensive Circle work. While the investigation of sexual energies is central to the process, the realization of any actual sexual activity depends on the dynamic of the group. Above all, the workshops give Queer men the opportunity to investigate their deep feelings around sex and intimacy and to connect more fully as a result.

Website: www.Faeriesexmagick.org

The Body Electric School offers classes designed to increase body awareness and acceptance on many levels, including the erotic. Body Electric's programs were originally developed by Joseph Kramer by and for gay men and that focus remains central to its mission, though the school now offers workshops for women and couples as well. Areas of attention include erotic massage, yoga, meditation and tantric practice, and classes are offered on a variety of levels throughout the year at many locations in the United States and elsewhere.

Website: bodyelectric.org or www.thebodyelectricschool.com

Black Leather Wings is a group of Queer-spirit folk interested in exploring BDSM and related activities with the freedom, imagination and heart-centeredness of Radical Faerie events. The group hosts Gatherings and retreats and offers a place where leather Faeries can safely connect and share their diverse experiences.

Website: www.blackleatherwings.org

Comfort & Joy is a Queer community-based collective dedicated to creating special events, art installations and networks of support. Active year round in the San Francisco Bay Area, Comfort & Joy also hosts the main Queer camp at Burning Man, an annual festival and utopian art project held in the Nevada desert. Although Comfort & Joy does not identify as a Radical Faerie group, there is a considerable crossover between the two communities, both in vision and in membership.

Website: www.playajoy.org

There are various **Retreat Centers** which, while organized more like conventional businesses than like Faerie sanctuaries, nonetheless offer workshops and programs designed to nurture radical Queer spirituality and culture. Among them are **Easton Mountain** in upstate New York (www.eastonmountain.com), which also has a small residential community on the land; **Wildwood** (www.wildwoodretreat. com), in the hills above the Russian River in Northern California; and, on Hawaii's Big Island, **Kalani Ocean Retreat** (www.kalani.com), with a particular focus on yoga and the healing arts.

3. Print and Electronic Resources

RFD has been the publication of record of the Radical Faerie movement since before there *was* a Radical Faerie movement, having been founded in 1974 as "A Country Journal for Gay Men Everywhere." Published quarterly, the magazine promotes community building, environmental awareness, Queer sexuality and Radical Faerie consciousness in its varied forms. As an all-volunteer effort, *RFD* relies on reader submissions for its content and on community support, especially through subscriptions, for its financial existence. Issues are often focused on a specific theme, announced two issues in advance. The magazine is produced by a volunteer collective, currently based in New England.

Website: www.rfdmag.org

White Crane is a quarterly magazine dedicated to exploring gay wisdom and culture. Originated in San Francisco by Bob Barzan in 1989 as a newsletter for a local circle of gay men who met regularly to discuss gay spirituality, it is now published by the **White Crane Institute** (WCI), a 501(c)(3) educational corporation, and distributed in twenty-three countries. WCI also publishes White Crane Books and provides fiscal sponsorship to mission-friendly initiatives including touring gay cultural content, creative writing and film projects. In addition to hardcopy print media, White Crane maintains an active Web presence, offering Daily GayWisdom. org, a daily gay history and cultural email blast, and an active Facebook presence. Central to its mission is community building based on the historical underpinnings of same-sex love and GLBT culture.

Website: www.gaywisdom.org

Radfae.org is the Internet's most inclusive portal for information about the Radical Faerie tribe and its activities. Links for almost all of the groups and places listed in this directory can be found on the site, along with contacts for local Faerie Circles, individuals and a wide range of other resources.

Website: www.radfae.org

Queer in Community is a website sponsored by the Fellowship for Intentional Community. It provides a directory of residential communities either created by and for queer folk, or actively welcoming of Queer participation. Some of the projects listed are far removed in vision from the Radical Faerie ethos, but others are quite similar in flavor and intention, making this site a useful resource for Faerie folk looking to live in intentional community with others of like spirit.

Website: www.ic.org/qic/

—based on initial research compiled by Scotty Dog

The text of *The Fire in Moonlight* is in Bembo Standard.
The cover title is in Moonglow.
The cover image is courtesy of Joel Singer.
Cover design by Dan Vera.
Book layout by Toby Johnson.

www.gaywisdom.org

Printed in the USA
CPSIA information can be obtained
at www.ICGtesting.com
CBHW030922070724
11193CB00008B/101

9 781938 246043